READING BAYLE

Pierre Bayle (1647–1706) has been described by Richard Popkin as the key intellectual figure at the outset of the eighteenth century. Examinations of libraries from the period show him to have been by far the most successful author of the century, and his *Historical and Critical Dictionary* is in fact the philosophy best-seller of all time. The concepts, distinctions, and arguments found in his work were so widely adopted by later authors that Bayle came to be known as the 'Arsenal of the Enlightenment.' Despite his universally acknowledged importance, however, there has been from his own time to the present much disagreement about how Bayle is to be interpreted.

The title of this work is deliberately ambiguous, reflecting the multiple levels on which its argument is conducted. One aim is to indicate how a reading of Bayle might be made possible – how the initial impenetrability of his writings and their world might be overcome. On another level, the book offers an interpretation of Bayle's writings. Finally, it is a record of the author's own thoughts upon reading Bayle – what he finds himself thinking about as he looks at Bayle and his world

This work is a critical but sympathetic treatment of this neglected thinker. It will engage anyone interested in the history of modern philosophy, the history of ideas, literary criticism, and the history of seventeenth-century French culture.

(Toronto Studies in Philosophy)

THOMAS M. LENNON is Professor of Philosophy at the University of Western Ontario.

THOMAS M. LENNON

Reading Bayle

UNIVERSITY OF TORONTO PRESS
Toronto Buffalo London

ISBN 0-8020-4488-3 (cloth)
ISBN 0-8020-8266-1 (paper)

Printed on acid-free paper

Toronto Studies in Philosophy
Editors: James R. Brown and Calvin Normore

Canadian Cataloguing in Publication Data

Lennon, Thomas M. (Thomas Michael), 1942–
    Reading Bayle

    (Toronto studies in philosophy)
    Includes bibliographical references and index.
    ISBN 0-8020-4483-3 (bound)   ISBN 0-8020-8266-1 (pbk.)

    1. Bayle, Pierre, 1647–1706.   I. Title.   II. Series.

    B1825.Z7L46 1999   194   C99-930197-7

University of Toronto Press acknowledges the financial assistance to its publishing program of the Canada Council for the Arts and the Ontario Arts Council.

This book has been published with the help of a grant from the Humanities and Social Sciences Federation of Canada, using funds provided by the Social Sciences and Humanities Research Council of Canada.

Contents

vi   Contents

Preface

The title of this book is multiply ambiguous, reflecting the multiple levels on which its argument is conducted. One of its aims is to indicate *how anyone* might read Bayle, overcoming the initial impenetrability of his writings and their world. Popkin has called Bayle the key intellectual figure at the turn of the eighteenth century, but he is none the less an elusive figure, who nowadays needs an introduction. 'Introduction' might, in fact, have been the title, except that some might have been misled thereby into thinking that this is an elementary text, designed to give the gist of Bayle in order to cram for an exam, for instance. Although anyone with any interest at all in the issues of the book should be comfortable here, it is also my aim to extend the borders of research on those issues. *What Bayle read* is also a part of this story, but an inconclusive part, since Bayle seems to have read everything.

On another level, the book obviously offers *a reading* of Bayle, though if the argument is successful, it will be only one of very many possible readings of him. For, on still another level, the book ruminates *on reading* any author of a certain important sort. The result is that this is not really a book about Bayle, at least not in the usual sense of one that aims to give a complete and definitive account of his thought, or even a part of it. The argument, or at least its drift, is that no such account can be given of anyone like Bayle.

Finally, the book is a record of thoughts *upon reading* Bayle, in the sense, for example, of Keats on first looking into Chapman's Homer – of what I found myself thinking about on looking into Bayle. In this sense it is a book about intellectual and political authority, the toleration of dissenting views, idolatry and the presence of God, Providence and the problem of evil. The key for me has been the notion of integrity

in the Ciceronian sense of uncurtailed power of judgment (*integra ...
iudicandi potestas*) that Maia Neto has recently explored as the basis of
Bayle's scepticism. Often the idiom of this record is, like Bayle's own,
theological; but it is often readily translatable into more familiar, secular terms. For example, the debate over toleration is focused on the toleration of putative religious heresy, but it can be extended to the
toleration of any kind of dissenting belief. The same is true even of a
recherché topic such as idolatry, which relates to the intentionality of
thought. Perhaps, then, on a final level, we have discovered a new
idiom for doing philosophy, or have recovered an old one – something
in any case that philosophy seems badly to need. That would indeed be
a view from Darien.

This book has been for me a uniquely intense personal experience.
Much of my previous work has led to it – as is indicated by the otherwise embarrassing number of times my name appears in the bibliography, exceeded only by the volcano known as Pierre Jurieu. Moreover,
reading Bayle has engaged me in issues that I am still sorting out. As
Bayle was led to two radical conversions, so have I been. Confession
apart, one issue reflects back on the book; as Bayle showed integrity in
dealing with others, so have I tried to do the same in dealing with him.
His standard may have been impossibly high.

In arriving at this book I have also accumulated a number of debts,
which I am happy to acknowledge. Harry M. Bracken, Phillip Cummins, Richard H. Popkin, and Ruth Whelan, in their work, in correspondence, and in conversation, convinced me of the historical importance
of Bayle. Many discussions with José Maia Neto, often on the steps of
the Bibliothèque Nationale, focused me on the notion of integrity. With
copies of the Garland reprint edition of the *Dictionary* piled literally
halfway to the ceiling, my 1993 Bayle seminar was a seminal experience
for me. Christine Fauré, like Bayle a scholar from the south of France,
was a daily model of scholarship hardly less inspiring than his own. It is
difficult to imagine a departmental chair more ideal than my own during this period, Kathleen Okruhlik. Catherine Wilson and another,
anonymous referee for my *Battle of the Gods and Giants* convinced me,
with identical arguments, that my chapter on Bayle should be excised in
favour of a book-length treatment – a good thing, too, for as I came to
see it was a terrible chapter. John Kilcullen in his book showed how
amenable Bayle is to the most exacting analytic treatment, and then, as
it turns out, provided very useful criticisms as a referee, as did Fred

Wilson in the same capacity. The Faculty of Arts at the University of Western Ontario helped financially with the final typescript production, expertly executed by Melinda Ellison, Kent Hogarth, and Andrea Purvis.

THOMAS M. LENNON

Bibliographical Note

Bayle's *Dictionary* is standardly, and easily, referred to, across editions, by article (art.) and remark (rem.). The translation used here is the colourful effort of Desmaizeaux (1734–8), checked, and occasionally modified, against the French edition of Amsterdam, 1730.

The standard edition of the rest of Bayle's works is the *Oeuvres diverses* (1727–31, 2nd ed. 1737), now with supplementary volumes (Hildesheim: Olms, 1964–). References are by volume (roman numeral) and page number (arabic numeral). Unless otherwise indicated, translation of this and all other material is original.

Titles of works that have not yet been translated pose something of a problem. Sometimes it is preferable that the title be understood as an indication of the contents of the work; in this case, the title has been translated. Other times it may be preferable that the title serve as a mere label for the work in order that it be readily identified for purposes of consultation, for example; in this case, the title has been left untranslated. In either case, there should be no great problem moving from one to the other.

In references, short titles are generally used that are just sufficient for anyone who is familiar with the work or who consults the bibliography. The following abbreviations have been used for works of Bayle:

CPD   *Continuation des pensées diverses*
Dict.   *Dictionary Historical and Critical (Dictionnaire historique et critique)*
EMT   *Entretiens de Maxime et de Thémiste*
NRL   *Nouvelles de la République des Lettres*
OD   *Oeuvres diverses*
PDC   *Pensées diverses sur la comète*
RQP   *Réponse aux questions d'un provincial*

READING BAYLE

1

Introduction

1: Bayle: His Life and Works

More than for most authors, something of Bayle's biography and of the nature of his works is needed to understand what he wrote. Many have read Descartes's celebrated *Discourse*, for example, without attending to the circumstances of why the method it contains was excogitated in a stove-heated room somewhere in Germany.[1] This is not how Bayle would have read Descartes or anyone else. Moreover, Bayle has theoretical reasons for attending to such external circumstances. Roughly, he believes that belief is formed by grace or, in naturalistic terms, education; it is, to use the language of Hume, for whom Bayle was a source for this theory, a matter of 'taste and sentiment,' a matter of external circumstances generally.[2] Quite apart from the general applicability of this theory, Bayle's own work happens to be a confirming instance of it.[3]

---

1 Or, one *has*, typically, read this and other works of Descartes in such fashion. But Descartes supplies some circumstances in the work itself, including the fact that he was shut up there alone, which is important to any reading of Descartes's method. Moreover, there is the question of Descartes's relation to Rosicrucianism, which partially hangs on this episode, and, in any case, the current spate of Descartes biography, and of philosophical biography generally, indicates a growing belief that context may be more important than previously thought, even for the philosopher thought to have written 'according to the order of reasons.' *Discourse on Method* II; *CSM*, 116. F. Yates, *The Rosicrucian Enlightenment*, chap. 8; Shea, chap. 5; Gaukroger, 101–3.

2 See Lennon, 'Taste and Sentiment.'

3 For Bayle's biography, three works should be consulted, each by an author exceedingly favourable to Bayle's cause, however. Desmaizeaux's *Life*, to be found at the outset of the *Dictionary*, and Labrousse's *Pierre Bayle: Du pays de Foix à la cité d'Erasme*, and *Bayle*. The latter, a model of its kind, is especially useful.

Pierre Bayle was born, no less intellectually and confessionally than geographically, on the periphery of French civilization. Le Carla, now Carla-Bayle, is in fact about as far as one can get in France from Paris. He was born there on 18 November 1647, a Protestant, the son of a minister, and thus he belonged to a religious minority of less than five per cent of the population, a minority that was suffering persecution at the hands of the Catholic majority.

He was able to attend a local elementary school, but such were the straitened financial circumstances of his father that only one younger Bayle at a time was able to move directly to the Protestant school at Puylaurens. While Pierre awaited the completion of his elder brother's training there, his only education was via his father's library, where he read widely but unsystematically, a kind of reading Bayle was later to impose on most of his readers, especially those of his most famous work.

When, at age twenty-one, Bayle had his turn at Puylaurens, there occurred the single most important episode in his life. For he stayed at the Protestant school but three months and then left to study with the Jesuits in Toulouse. He soon renounced his Protestantism, or 'abjured' as one said, and converted to Catholicism. The conversion was short-lived. Immediately upon defending his master's thesis, Bayle left and returned to Protestantism, thereby enormously complicating his situation. It was one thing to be regarded as a heretic; it was quite another to be regarded as a relapsed heretic, the description under which Joan of Arc had been burned two centuries earlier. In the event, Bayle fled France for Protestant Geneva, arriving there in September 1670, never again to see his native region or any of his family except, briefly, his younger brother.

What is to be made of this episode? Although Bayle's material situation was dramatically improved as a result of his conversion at Toulouse, there is no question of his sincerity, for the reconversion entirely negated his gains and irreparably worsened his situation. Labrousse points, instead, to Bayle's previous isolation and his lack of firsthand knowledge of the arguments of his Catholic opponents. In particular, he was naïve with respect to their strategy of minimizing the number and significance of the points in dispute (we shall see an important instance of this below in the work of Bossuet) and then of arguing their case as the logical consequence of a few fundamental points. Labrousse cites the language of Isaac Papin, who described his own abjuration in 1690 as a matter of logic, and of Bayle himself, who alludes to his conversion in the same terms.[4] She says, 'It was as if a mathematician were to correct an error of computation.'[5] But this cannot be the whole story. Certainly, it is one that is at odds with Bayle's own theory of why we believe as we do. More important, in any case, is what the episode means, and here Labrousse seems exactly right. 'His experience taught him a lesson that was lost on the majority of his contemporaries, namely that it was possible to persist in an "erroneous" belief and still be sincere and disinterested.'[6] As we shall see below, this possibility is a key premise in Bayle's theory of toleration.

Bayle's exile may be divided into the Rotterdam period of publishing and the pre-Rotterdam period of teaching. First in Geneva and then clandestinely in Rouen and Paris, he had time- and energy-consuming positions as a tutor, arriving finally as a professor at the Protestant Academy at Sedan until its suppression by the government in 1681. These were especially difficult times for Bayle, for even at Sedan he was kept from the full pursuit of his scholarly interests. Soon thereafter his life was improved in many respects, however, when he obtained a position at the Ecole Illustre in Rotterdam, a school supported for the refugee community there of French Protestants, a community whose numbers were swelled by the Revocation of the Edict of Nantes in 1685. This key event revoked virtually all the rights guaranteed to Protestants by Henri IV in 1598 and made their situation near-impossible in myriad ways. More precisely, it confirmed what had long been a deterioration of those rights.

It was at Sedan that Bayle met and befriended Pierre Jurieu (1637–1713), who later would become his bitterest opponent. Bayle helped bring him to the Ecole Illustre, where they became known respectively as the Philosopher of Rotterdam and the Theologian of Rotterdam. Jurieu was an exceedingly irascible character, given to exaggeration and histrionics. He prophesied the demise of Catholicism for 1689, and then, unfazed by the actually unexceptional vintage of that year, focused on 1715 as the date of the Second Coming and thus the even more definitive defeat of this whore of Babylon. His real métier was polemic, in which he engaged not only Catholics (Arnauld, Maimbourg, Bossuet, et al.) but also his co-religionists (Pajou, Leclerc, Jaquelot, and most notably, Bayle). The temptation is great to make Jurieu the villain of his dis-

---

4 *Pierre Bayle* I, 72.
5 *Bayle*, 17.
6 Ibid, 18.

pute with Bayle, but the issue between them is difficult to sort out and will not be entirely resolved below.[7]

Bayle's publishing may be divided into three periods: that of the *Dictionnaire* and those before and after it. His *Pensées diverses sur la comète* (1682, second edition 1683 under a revised title) was nominally about the comet of 1680 and why, for reasons of both physics and theology, it should not be regarded as portending evil. In fact, it had not been so regarded, and the real topic was what he saw as the idolatry and superstition of Catholicism. The *Critique générale de l'Histoire du Calvinism de M. Maimbourg* (1682) was Bayle's defence of his religion against the attacks of this ex-Jesuit, a defence continued in the *Nouvelles lettres de l'auteur de la critique générale* (1685). The following year saw *Ce que c'est que la France toute catholique*, which continues the general theme in this four-year period of the relation between the two Christian sects, a relation that in the end is far from obvious.

Despite his great output, Bayle was able in 1684 to assume editorship of the *Nouvelles de la République des Lettres*, one of the first of the learned journals, which gave him access to enormous intellectual resources, both literary and personal. But there was a price to be paid, for at the same time Bayle was suffering great personal loss. In the same year Bayle's younger brother died, to be followed in the next, the year of the Revocation, both by his father and, horribly, by his elder brother, who perished in the French jail where he had been placed because of Bayle's *Critique de Maimbourg*. With his mother already dead, Bayle was alone, in exile. In February 1687 he had something of a breakdown.

Production was therefore interrupted, though but briefly, of Bayle's full statement of his theory of toleration. This was the *Commentaire Philosophique [on the Words of Our Lord, Compel them to enter]* (parts 1 and 2, 1686; part 3, 1687; supplement, 1688). The aim was to refute the interpretation of Luke 14: 23, proposed by Augustine among others, according to which force may be used to bring about conversion to the true religion. It was this work that set off Bayle's debate with Jurieu, as a result of which Jurieu lost his credibility and Bayle his job at the Ecole Illustre. Fortunately for Bayle, if not for his former friend, the publisher Leers undertook to support him with an eye to the eventual publication of the *Dictionnaire*.

The first two volumes of the *Dictionnaire historique et critique* went on sale in October 1696, and so immediate was its success that the second

7 For more on Jurieu, see Knetsch.

edition of 1702, 'revised, corrected and augmented,' was assured. In fact, it was to become the philosophical blockbuster of all time. Despite its relative neglect for more than a century now, the work has reached a greater portion of its potential audience than any other, not excepting the works of Plato himself. Shelf counts of private libraries from the eighteenth century show the *Dictionnaire* overwhelming anything from the distant competition of Locke, Newton, Voltaire, and Rousseau.

Its structure and motivation hardly account for its success. Allegedly designed to correct the mistakes of a previous such work by Moréri, the *Dictionnaire* obviously extends far beyond any such purpose. On the other hand, there is no obvious principle of inclusion for its articles. Moreover, the footnotes to the text – 'remarks,' as they are called – are many tens of times longer than the text itself. It is in these remarks that the real action takes place, almost always digressing widely from the nominal topic of the article (thus occasioning another set of notes, in the margin). What is to be said of this gigantic work, whose influence and importance have hardly been appreciated? Here is what Popkin says:

Pierre Bayle, working in Rotterdam in the 1690's, was able to wander hither and yonder through the world of man's intellectual and moral thought, from the beginning of written history to yesterday's newspapers and café gossip, and could portray enough of it from A to Z to encompass all that his age had to offer, and to reveal so many of its failings in such sharp relief. One man's portrayal of the ancient sages, the Biblical heroes and heroines, the kings and queens, the courtiers and the courtesans, the theologians, the philosophers, the crackpots of all times, could fascinate such men as Leibniz, Voltaire, Bishop Berkeley, David Hume, Thomas Jefferson, and Herman Melville. Bayle had roamed from seductions to perversions to murders to massacres to visions to paradoxes, in dazzling fashion, as he marched from 'Aaron' to 'Zuylichem.' He had provided a wondrous suite of themes and variations, on such problems as those of cuckoldry, and castration fears, and religious intolerance, and historical accuracy, and of finding certitude in philosophy, science, and religion.[8]

Obviously, a great read.

Obviously, not all who read the work were happy with it, however. Unhappy on the right were Jurieu and the Consistory of the Walloon Church of Rotterdam, who thought that Bayle had, among other offences, made faith suffer at the hands of reason; unhappy on the left

8 *Dictionary*, trans. Popkin, intro., xi.

were such people as Leclerc, Jaquelot, and Bernard, who thought that Bayle had done just the opposite. This was not the last time that Bayle was to be interpreted from diametrically opposite perspectives. At any rate, Bayle largely devoted the last of his publications to defending himself against the left: the *Continuation* (of his first work on the comet, 1704), the *Réponse aux questions d'un provincial* (1703–7), and the unfinished *Entretiens de Maxime et de Thémiste* (1707).

Bayle died on 28 December 1706, probably of a heart attack precipitated by tuberculosis. His was not a joyful life, but it was an admirable one. Both by temperament, it seems, and by conviction, Bayle was committed to a life of scholarship. While in Rotterdam, he turned down attractive offers of marriage and a university chair because they would interfere with his work, which he pursued to the exclusion of all else.

2: God and Man[9]

The Bible relates that immediately upon creating Adam and placing him in the garden of Eden, God speaks to the first man, giving him this command: 'Of every tree of the garden thou mayest freely eat; But of the tree of the knowledge of good and evil, thou shalt not eat of it: for in the day that thou eatest thereof thou shalt surely die' (Genesis 2: 16–17). This is, to say the least, a remarkable text. For, however unlikely it may seem now, God is said to speak, indeed to speak to man, and moreover, in such a way as to set out expectations (which, in the event, were famously dashed). Each of these aspects of the garden of Eden story indicates a context for Bayle's work.[10]

First, the important conditions required such that God might speak, or communicate at all, are discussed in chapter 3 below; the discussion is part of the larger issue of authority, not the least part of which for Bayle is the Church's claim to infallibility in matters of faith and morals. Second, that God should speak with man in the way that He does with Adam, Abraham, and Moses, is for Bayle utterly at odds with the Catholic conception of God reflected in the doctrine of Transubstantiation.

9 The topic of Bayle's fascinating relations with women will be addressed on another occasion. Meanwhile, it is difficult in a largely historical work such as this to avoid certain traditional conventions.
10 What would have been a typically offbeat connection that one might have expected is not to be found, for Bayle seems not to have taken notice of Huet's 1691 attempt to geographically locate the garden of Eden. Had he still been editing the *NRL*, one feels certain that he would have had some interesting things to say about this book.

According to Rome, Christ's words at the Last Supper, 'For this is my body,' are to be taken literally such that their repetition in the ritual of the Eucharist results in the real presence of Christ on the altar. The defining text for sixteenth- and seventeenth-century debates of the doctrine came from the Council of Trent (1545–63), according to which Christ is 'truly, really and substantially' present in the Eucharist.[11] The accidents of the bread and wine remain after consecration, but their substance is converted into that of Christ.[12] Bayle rejects this doctrine of the Real Presence – it is one of two main differences between his Calvinism and Catholicism. For him, Christ is only symbolically present in the Eucharist, and those who worship the consecrated bread are guilty of idolatry, the topic of chapter 5 below.

Although Bayle's God of Adam, Abraham, and Moses is the sort of God who not only has speech, but also uses it to express anger, negotiate, change his mind, and otherwise enter feedback relationships with man, He is nonetheless a transcendent God, utterly other than His creation. In fact, transcendence will be seen to be a condition for that sort of relationship. It is the violation of this transcendence that explains Bayle's unrelenting animus toward Spinoza. He respects the integrity of Spinoza, but in terms that are harsh even for such a polemicist Bayle condemns the view he holds as 'the most absurd and monstrous hypothesis that can be imagined.'[13] This is the view that there is but one substance and that one substance is God. With such radical immanentism, there is no otherness from creation – indeed, there is no creation at all.[14] Worse still for Catholicism, its ontology of transubstantiation is supported by this 'monstrous hypothesis.'[15]

The third aspect of the garden of Eden story is the most obvious one, for it raises the problem of evil. It is a problem that plagues Bayle,

11 Denzinger, 385.

12 The nature of this conversion is an exceedingly subtle question among those who profess nominally the same doctrine. See Armogathe, sec. 1.

13 Art. Spinoza, rem. N.

14 In a very perceptive article, Klajnman begins with the premise that Spinoza's conception of God as the immanent and non-transitive cause of all things (*Ethics* I, xviii) subverts the essentially *transcendent* dimension of the traditional theologico-political order. What emerges instead, although not identified in these terms (Bayle in fact is not mentioned), is a view based on the *common good* as an immanent value that nearly point-by-point inverts Bayle's conservatism, which, for example, even during the worst days of persecution saw him support the French monarchy. In this sense, Spinoza far more than Bayle was the 'Arsenal of the Enlightenment.'

15 Art. Spinoza, rem. CC. For the argument, see Lennon, 'Bayle's Anticipation of Popper.'

appearing with greater frequency than any other in his work. The problem in its classical form derives from Epicurus.[16] If God is good, He should be willing to prevent evil, and if He is almighty, He should be able to prevent evil; but there is evil; therefore, God is either unable or unwilling to prevent evil, He is either not almighty or not good. By contrast to Descartes, who emphasizes God's omnipotence, and Leibniz, who emphasizes His wisdom, the fundamental divine attribute for Bayle is goodness. It is unthinkable that God not be good. That is, we *ought* not to think that God is anything but good. In another sense of the term, however, it is only too thinkable for Bayle that God is not good, and hence Bayle's near-obsession with the problem. But short of that nightmare, which is the source of the pessimism that pervades his work, Bayle is very concerned with Manicheism and other forms of such dualism that accept that God is good but, in positing a coequal principle of evil, deny that He is almighty.

The problem of evil is connected with another aspect of Bayle's work that has drawn attention disproportionate to its actual treatment there, that is, scepticism. From the most recent commentators,[17] back to the Consistory of the Walloon Church of Rotterdam, which found the *Dictionnaire*'s article on Pyrrho to be 'scandalous and blameworthy,' and called upon Bayle to reform it, taking care 'not to injure our mysteries,'[18] no other topic has drawn more attention. What few have realized, however, is that Bayle's sceptical arguments are directed not just against reason, or even against reason on behalf of faith, but in particular against reason's ability to solve the problem of evil.[19] Thus, in a passage that is a favourite among readers of Bayle, he tells us that 'reason is like a runner who does not know when to stop, or like another Penelope constantly undoing what it creates ... It is better suited to pulling things down than to building them up, and better at discovering what things are not, than what they are.'[20] The context for this delightful piece of figuration is Bayle's late debate with his rationalist colleague Isaac Jaquelot, in partic-

16 See art. Paulicians, rem. E.
17 See works by Popkin, Bracken, Kenshur, et al. O'Cathasaigh gives a very nuanced argument that faith allows certainty in moral questions. He connects this view with toleration and the related duty to seek the truth as best one can. Bayle's approach is thus less sceptical than 'critical.'
18 *Dict.* I, cxxiii, cxxvii. Scepticism was one of four topics from the *Dictionnaire* on which Bayle was led to write an 'Explanation.' *Dict.* V, 830.
19 Paganini is an exception to this general neglect. See 135–60.
20 *RQP* II, cxxxvii; *OD* III, 778.

ular as it concerned reason's impotence in resolving the Manichean challenge. Even more notably, in the article Pyrrho, the crescendo of sceptical argument of the famous remark B climaxes with the problem of evil. It is not scepticism merely as means to fideism, still less scepticism as such, that interests Bayle. His scepticism is about Leibniz's sort of theodicy, about rational penetration of Providence, which for him, though far from incoherent, is from a rational point of view rather a lottery. This is the topic of chapter 6 below.

Providence is an important topic, for it involves the other of the two main differences between Catholicism and Calvinism – the doctrine of grace. The issue is the respective roles of God and man in salvation. Both sides agree that God's role through Christ's Redemption is necessary, that is, that no one saves himself, the assertion of which would be the Pelagian heresy. According to the Calvinists, it would seem, God's freely distributed grace of salvation is also sufficient, and thus man has none but a role of passive cooperation. In these terms, the problem of evil is that not everyone is given grace, the distribution of which is limited and, at least from man's perspective, arbitrary. (Once again, Spinoza finds himself a *bête noire* of the piece. His atheism, or pantheism, is attributed by Bayle to his inability rationally to solve the problem of evil.[21]) Bayle's God is not only transcendent but inscrutable.

21 Art. Spinoza, rem. O.

2

Integrity

3: The Death of Molière

Molière died during the evening of 17 February 1673 at the age of 53.
Although gravely suffering from the tuberculosis that had long plagued
him, he that afternoon had played in, of all things, *Le malade imaginaire*,
so that his troupe would not be deprived of their livelihood.[1] He had a
slight convulsion during the play, and was carried to his room after-
wards, where, refusing his wife's soup with a joke, he had a bit of
Parmesan cheese instead. Choking on blood, he died – as it happened, in
the arms of two nuns he was temporarily housing, to whom he evidenced 'all the sentiments of a good Christian and all the resignation
owed to the Lord's will.' He was buried at St Joseph's, but only after 'the
difficulties that everyone knows about' were overcome, which they
were only because of 'his merit and the correctness of his sentiments.'[2]
What were the 'difficulties' to which this earliest biographer of Molière
alludes?

Surprisingly, Bayle takes no notice of them in his article on Molière
(Poquelin). Voltaire's brief explanation of them was twofold. First, 'the
bad luck Molière had not to die with the help of religion' – presumably,
because no priest was present; but this cannot be the whole explanation,
for then all sudden death would have been problematic. Second, 'the
prejudice against theatre led Harley de Champvallon, archbishop of

---

1 In art. Poquelin, rem. A, Bayle corrects the false belief then current that Molière died
during the play itself.
2 Grimarest, 158, 160.

Paris, well-known for his gallant intrigues, to refuse burial to Molière.'[3] Only intervention by the king himself assured Molière a Christian burial, although even then, the pastor of St Eustache, Molière's parish, refused to comply. Now, theatre people have always been regarded, it seems, as of dubious moral standing because of their transient, unfixed way of life, and for other reasons as well. Molière was not the only one to suffer from the 'prejudice against theatre,' and his case is highlighted here only to dramatize a situation, applying particularly to someone of whom Bayle was clearly fond. Still, the plight of Molière might serve as a concrete image for important metaphysical issues at stake at the time of his death that are of importance in understanding Bayle.

Frances Yates argues that the supreme achievement of the English Renaissance, its theatre, was influenced, through the work of John Dee and Robert Fludd, by a Neoplatonist revival of Vitruvianism. This revival was embodied in the actual construction of the theatres, including most notably the Globe, whose very name indicates Yates's thesis. The theatre was designed to represent the cosmos and to provide a stage for the human drama: 'All the world's a stage. The words [she says] are in a real sense the clue to The Globe Theatre.'[4] Later, Molière's context was somewhat different. The period in France was no longer the Renaissance with all its esotericism, and even if classical, theatre was not, at least not indisputably, the supreme achievement. But in both contexts, theatre represents a threat, for drama is a creation that rivals God's own creation. This is a thesis that might guide research in the sociology of early modern theatre; here it is the abstract version of the image above.[5]

Applied to Bayle, the thesis is that he stands to the authors he engages as God Himself does to Adam, Abraham, or Moses. To begin to understand that relation is to begin to understand not only the threat that Bayle seems always to have posed, the distrust and suspicion that have always attended his work, but perhaps even Bayle himself.

More precisely, we may to begin to understand what Bayle *said*. For in the end, Bayle, like any person, is not to be understood, and in this too the analogy with God is exact. According to Descartes, for example, who was expressing a fairly orthodox distinction, God can be known

---

3 Voltaire, *Oeuvres* XXIII, 96.
4 Yates, *Theatre of the World*, 189.
5 For a bit of structuralist rumination on the connection Bayle suggests in the preface to the *Dictionnaire* between that work as a theatre of mistakes and a book dealing with the theatre of human life, see Weibel, 26.

[intelligere] without being fully grasped [comprehendere].[6] Roughly, we are acquainted with God, but do not fully have His essence as we do that of a triangle, for example. Now, Bayle is hardly a Cartesian, but a way of expressing the Baylean argument of the sections immediately below is as follows. Although there may be other kinds of knowledge, a condition for understanding what a person says, and in that sense for knowing that person, is that we *not* grasp some essence of that person. (There may be no such essence to be grasped; part of what it is to be a person may be just not to have an essence that allows the deduction of properties the way a triangle's essence does.) The authors with whom Bayle creates a conversation in his work are thus allowed to preserve their autonomy no less than do Adam, Abraham, and Moses in conversation with their Creator.[7] In his satisfying this condition lies the integrity of Bayle, who not only 'possesses [his] power of judgment uncurtailed,'[8] but leaves it uncurtailed in others as well.

4: The Bayle Enigma

The literature on Bayle, from his time to the present, universally acknowledges a special difficulty in the interpretation of his work.[9] The problem is not just that there is disagreement, often radical, over the significance of his work, for to take a particularly relevant example, radical disagreement no less obviously characterizes research on Descartes's work. This first great rationalist has recently been interpreted as a sceptic in spite of himself, as a subverter of reason whose rationalist arguments are nothing but parodies, as an empiricist because of his doctrine of the created eternal truths, etc. – not to mention the debates whether he subscribed to (or was at least committed to) dualism, materialism, or idealism. Still, the interpretation of Descartes is governed by agreement over a fundamental structure to his thought, and it seems as if the disagreements, however radical they may be, result from emphasizing cer-

---

6 Descartes, *CSM* II, 81–2. For more on this distinction, see Ariew.
7 For a different perspective on at least one important text, see Kenshur (44), who thinks that Bayle speaks through the voices of Craige and Browne in the Third Clarification.
8 Cicero, *Academica* II, iii, 8. For more on the importance of this notion of integrity in the history of early modern scepticism, see Maia Neto.
9 See, for example, Whelan, *The Anatomy of Superstition*, 9: 'Pierre Bayle ... is surely the most misunderstood writer of his age. Both contemporary and later readers have widely diverged as to his real intentions.' See also ibid, 11, n. 10.

tain aspects of this structure at the expense of others. In the case of Bayle, however, there seems to be no such framework in which even to express the disagreements, which multiply with each new commentator. More often than not, commentators are aware of this proliferation of interpretation; the typical reaction is to acknowledge the problem, express ignorance of the real or essential Bayle, then go on to add to the proliferation. What is needed is not just one more interpretation, but one that will also explain why Bayle is so elusive and hard to interpret.

To take just the twentieth-century literature, the suggestions are that Bayle was fundamentally a positivist, an atheist, a deist, a sceptic, a fideist, a Socinian, a liberal Calvinist, a conservative Calvinist, a libertine, a Judaizing Christian, a Judaeo-Christian, or even a secret Jew, a Manichean, an existentialist ... to the point that it is tempting to conclude that these commentators cannot have been talking about the same author, or at least that they have not used the same texts.[10] There can be overlap among these classifications, so that not all of the interpretations entirely exclude one another. Implausible as it may seem, moreover, all of these suggestions have at least some plausibility. As an introduction to Bayle generally (to give the flavour of his work, as it were, and some of its substance), to document the Bayle enigma, and to indicate the attitude to it that will be proposed here and then illustrated at length, a brief rehearsal of some of the literature will be useful.

Publishing at the beginning of this century, Delvolvé makes Bayle out as a philosopher for the Third Republic, a positivist *avant la lettre*. 'The great originality and main interest of Bayle's work lies in the method according to which it was constructed.'[11] What Delvolvé calls Bayle's method, however, seems to be a commitment he sees in Bayle to the view that empirically verifiable facts are the only basis for knowledge in any domain. On the basis of this view or method, Bayle is supposed to deliver a destructive critique of religion and metaphysics: revelation is contradicted by the facts and reason contradicts itself when it goes beyond experience. Instead, 'for theological and metaphysical dogmas on the nature of being and the origin of the universe, Bayle substitutes simple hypotheses that are admissible on the basis of their agreement with the observable laws of phenomena.'[12] This 'original method,'

10 See Sandberg, viii; Popkin, *Dictionary*, xiii–xix and below.
11 Delvolvé, 425.
12 Ibid, 426.

although never formulated by Bayle as such, was 'constantly and consciously' applied by him.

Against the Christian doctrine of creation, for example, Delvolvé cites from the article Epicurus to the effect that creation *ex nihilo* is rationally inexplicable and from the article Zabarella that a world with a beginning poses problems of an insoluble sort. 'The transition from the One, the Infinite, the Eternal to the multiple, the finite, the successive is no better explained in the Christian system than in the Spinozist – neither one nor the other was able to advance by a single step the metaphysics of old Parmenides.'[13] The upshot is either (a) Bayle constantly dissimulates in his theological work – here, for example, Bayle closes the Zabarella argument with a courteous concession to Christianity by proposing that God from an indivisible duration chooses a point from divisible duration at which to create the world, 'his habitual precaution not to finish an article with a passage that might disturb the faith';[14] or (b) Delvolvé knows better than Bayle himself what he is about, for there is no espousal whatever in Bayle of the positivist method. There is certainly no objection in principle to this approach – on the contrary, when successful its contribution is greater than that of any other (see next section). But the success of this approach is measured by how interesting a reading it yields, and the discussion below may be taken as an extended argument that Bayle's theological positions are far more interesting when read closer to their face value. Delvolvé's thesis is plausible for some few articles of the *Dictionnaire*, but for the overwhelming rest of Bayle's work interpretation seems constrained by Rex's later thesis that although there is much to be said for the eighteenth-century reading of Bayle as a sceptic and libertine, the tradition that dominates Bayle's work before 1687 and at least the article David in the *Dictionnaire* is Calvinism. It is a tradition that Bayle never really relinquishes. His interest is firmly and primarily rooted in the seventeenth-century concerns of his church. Even so, Delvolvé is able to apply his reading to many topics in Bayle – for example, Providence and the problem of evil, morality, free will, atheism, etc. – in what is the most impressively sympathetic and extensive account of his work until Labrousse's monumental contribution.

The positivist reading is given some support by Lacoste, who was interested primarily in Bayle's literary views. According to him, 'Bayle

13 Ibid, 281.
14 Ibid.

never considered literature for its own sake, with no regard for anything but beauty, as a pleasant chimera, or a skill for speaking without saying anything.'[15] Instead, Bayle scoured literary works, in the positivist way he did all other texts, in search of hard information. The key, for Lacoste, is Bayle's temperament as an information-scavenger, or mole who dug up everything,[16] driven by a passion of curiosity, who was unmethodical, disorderly, and self-indulgent in his publications. To be sure, Bayle himself acknowledged these characteristics of his work, but to read Bayle solely in these terms is to leave Bayle himself a mere curio and his work a collection of curiosities.

Recently, these same characteristics have been taken as the primary datum, but with an anti-positivist result. According to Weibel, the *Dictionnaire* must be given a structuralist reading, dictated by 'the impossibility of producing a classical reading of this work without beginning or end, the impossibility of producing a linear, serious reading that leads to the establishment of irrefutable facts.' The order of the *Dictionnaire*, he points out, is not conceptual but, obviously and literally, alphabetical; the entries are largely mere labels, usually with no relation to what is most of interest in the remarks. The upshot is that the only natural reading is 'a discontinuous, drifting, irresponsible, forgetful reading.'[17] Weibel's structuralist approach offers many useful insights into Bayle and for the first time gives a principled, and interesting, account of why a 'totalized' reading of Bayle cannot be given.[18] But it also devalues the more standardly interpretable content of the *Dictionnaire*, and either ignores or fits less well with the rest of Bayle's work.

Weibel's structuralist approach is attacked by Jossua at its foundation in so far as it eliminates the I, especially from the *Dictionnaire*, which Jossua regards as closer to Montaigne's *Essays* than to the *Grand Larousse* that it superficially resembles.[19] The thesis of Jossua's book is well-expressed by its title, *Pierre Bayle, or the Obsession with Evil*. Bayle is 'like a new Job, never yielding on the well-foundedness of his cause, relying on God right to the end of his impassioned polemic, without admitting what his honor as a man and his sense of justice prohibit him from conceding.'[20] After the usual review of the literature and expression of puz-

---

15 Lacoste, 239.
16 'Il est le nouvelliste qui épluche, le fureteur qui interroge' (ibid, 6).
17 Weibel, 12, 20.
18 Ibid, 47.
19 Jossua, 16–17.
20 Ibid, 12. He cites Job 7: 11; 10; 18: 7; 23: 3–4.

zlement over the 'Bayle enigma,' Jossua insists that despite the contextual work of Rex and even of Labrousse, the interpretive enigma remains. He distinguishes the work from Bayle himself, in whom he sees much evolution, although increasingly pessimistic emphasis seems to be the relevant concept rather than any real change of view. In the end, he hesitatingly and hypothetically opts for a fideist interpretation of the man, but the faith involved is 'impoverished, empty of religious or Christian substance, stretched to the breaking point.'[21] With respect to the work, he accepts Labrousse's view that 'the existence of God determines the structure of his vision of the world.'[22]

Undoubtedly, Jossua's optic through the problem of evil clarified a great deal in Bayle, but the framework for dealing with the interpretive enigma is problematic. For one thing, the theocentric perspective does not distinguish Bayle from Descartes, Malebranche, or even Spinoza. And what there is of Bayle apart from or unrelated to his texts is, on good grounds (some of which Bayle himself recognizes), either unknowable (except perhaps to God) or irrelevant. Bayle is indeed present in his texts, but in a special way that distinguishes him from, not just the Cartesians, but virtually all other philosophers. He is there as God is in the Bible, both as author and as character.

Since the Dibon volume (1959), the thrust of the mainline Bayle scholarship has largely been an effort at contextualization of one sort or other, and the principal context has been theological, specifically as relevant to Bayle's own religious beliefs (and thus the Bayle problem).[23] Admitting the importance of the theological context does not guarantee purchase on the Bayle problem, however. Sandberg, for example, argues that since Bayle was free from political or religious censorship,[24] there is no reason to believe that Bayle dissimulated and therefore we can take the *Dictionnaire* at face value, where Bayle was giving 'free and authentic [if also polemical] expression to conclusions grounded in his religions and intellectual formation and molded by his participation in the

---

21 Ibid, 159.

22 Labrousse, *Pierre Bayle* II, 608.

23 Most notably, see Rex.

24 This premise is exceedingly problematic. While Bayle geographically freed himself in person from the yoke of French censorship, its effect on his books was not without effect on him. After all, his elder brother died in a French prison because of Bayle's literary activities. See Labrousse, *Bayle*, 29–31. Nor was even the Dutch scene without its pressures. Bayle was constrained to offer elucidations of four aspects of his *Dictionnaire* found objectionable by the Consistory of the Walloon Church, and a significant part of the article David was suppressed in the second edition.

Catholic-Protestant controversies of 1682–87.' Alas, too often these putative conclusions are unclear, inconsistent, or otherwise problematic for
this approach to yield the essential Bayle it seeks.[25] The most important
contribution to the literature to date sets itself the same goal and looks
for its satisfaction in similar terms. Labrousse begins her monumental
work by observing Bayle's importance for understanding the Enlightenment, Voltaire in particular, yet she warns us that 'an author never exercises the influence that he would have wished and, as to readers, they
are not passive mirrors but react to texts and sort them out according to
their preconceptions.' 'Nevertheless,' she continues, 'we prohibit ourselves from *comprehending Bayle taken in himself* if we underestimate the
capital role played not only by his Calvinist education and milieu, but
by his education and culture as a theologian.'[26]

The most important work on Bayle in English comes, of course, from
Popkin. He too thinks that there is a real Bayle, his 'heart and soul'
whose 'reading has intrigued and baffled many'; he allows that he himself has 'found the attempt to define the actual beliefs and the actual
religion of Bayle quite baffling,' and says that he would be foolish if he
pretended to be 'ready with *the* answer.' Even so, he attempts to place
Bayle in the tradition of Christian scepticism. Roughly, the idea is that
sceptical arguments undo the claims of reason, with the result that faith
is the only basis for accepting fundamental truths. In particular, according to Popkin, the *Dictionnaire* is 'really a *summa sceptica* that deftly
undermined all the foundations of the seventeenth-century intellectual
world.' But as Popkin realizes, Bayle refused to be classified as a sceptic,
claiming that he knew too much to be a sceptic and too little to be a dog-
matist.[27] Still worse, in one of his most important texts dealing with
scepticism, Bayle argues that one cannot even be a consistent sceptic.[28]

---

25 Sandberg, 15. This is not to say, however, that Sandberg is unaware of the Bayle
     enigma. See viii and chapter 2, which provide a useful survey of the literature for any-
     one looking for an introduction to it.
26 Labrousse, *Pierre Bayle* II, ix. Emphasis added.
27 Popkin, *Bayle's Dictionary*, introduction. Kenshur is another who seeks the essential
     Bayle, attempting here to identify 'Bayle's true attitude toward skepticism and faith,'
     'Bayle's true position' (37, 39, 40). See also the articles by James and Bracken, who
     debated whether Bayle was a sceptic. Heyd in this context calls attention to the Bayle
     enigma in so many words: 'A disguised atheist or a sincere Christian? The enigma of
     Pierre Bayle.'
28 Art. Pyrrho, rem. C. 'The passage is patterned after one of the most passionate and ter-
     rifying in Pascal [*viz.* Brunschvig 434]. Popkin, 'Bayle and Hume,' in *High Road*, 154.
     We return to this passage below.

Once again, Bayle seems to elude the effort to pin down what he is essentially all about.

5: The Leibnizian Fallacy

There are a number of explanations that might be given of the difficulty in interpreting Bayle. It might be that he just changed his mind, often and on many issues. Curiously, with the possible exception of Russell, it is hard to find examples of anyone else, among philosophers at least, of whom this would be true. Among seventeenth-century philosophers, Gueroult has distinguished Descartes, whose thought unfolds according to what Gueroult calls an order of reasons, a single logic that determines the apparently most diverse elements of his system, from Malebranche, who, starting from Cartesian premises, ends with 'an annihilation of the true philosophy of clear and distinct ideas in favour of a vast mystical intuition.'[29] Despite his great admiration for Malebranche, there is no question of explaining Bayle by treating him simply, like The Oratorian, as doing philosophy other than according to the order of reasons. For in the case of Malebranche there is a progression, or perhaps regression, from his Cartesian principles to his mysticism – whereas for Bayle the apparent resistance to sytematization is synchronic. To be sure, Bayle changes his views and is candid about the changes. For example, he came eventually to agree with Locke's rejection of innate ideas; but this was a fairly transparent, acknowledged change over time, whereas the Bayle enigma is to be found at every period of his career, with respect to virtually every topic he discussed. It is of a different order.

Another possibility is that Bayle was unclear in his own mind as to what he held. He may have been just sloppy, or inconsistent, or even mad. Thus we might with Popkin say, 'he left us in the dark,' and we might say so because he was in the dark himself. Let us consider the most extreme version of this possiblity, that Bayle was mad. Consider the frequent migraines that he sought to cure by fasting for thirty or forty hours, his self-acknowledged melancholy, his maniacal devotion to a scholarly life that precluded even the possibility of marriage, his reclusiveness that kept him living, unknown to his neighbours, for more than two decades in Holland without learning Dutch.[30] Once again, however, other applications of what is an a priori plausible sort of expla-

29 *Malebranche* I, 327.
30 Labrousse, *Pierre Bayle* I, 35–8.

nation are hard to find. Indeed, even the great madmen of the later *belle époque* of madness do not offer special problems of interpretation. Conversely, it does not seem to help in understanding the work of Schumann, Nietzsche, or Van Gogh, for example, to point out that they were mad.

A less extreme, and perhaps more promising, version of this attempt at explaining Bayle would be to suggest that his *expression* of his views was unclear or incomplete. More generally, the premise is that from our perspective we might express better than the author himself what he meant because we know better what he meant. So, for example, we might better understand and express Locke's own position than did Locke himself.[31] Or recall Delvolvé's positivist reading of Bayle. But this premise is true of *all* authors worth writing about (which is why the claim about Locke is, far from shocking, trivially true). For otherwise we would have nothing to say about them. But, once again, there is a special problem with Bayle. Perhaps another way to indicate this expressive elusiveness on Bayle's part is as follows. To call Descartes a rationalist or Locke an empiricist may be a useful, shorthand way to mobilize certain intuitions that clarify the greater part of their views. But it may also blind us to some few other aspects of them – to the role of experience in Descartes, for example, or the ambiguous status of innateness in Locke. In the case of Bayle, the blinding effect is massive with respect to every classification. Moreover, to classify Bayle at all in such terms is, as will be argued, to miss what makes reading him most worthwhile. How so?

Consider another possibility. Perhaps the reason that we cannot find the real Bayle is that we are mistaken in thinking that he held any views at all on the topics on which people have tried to interpret him. There might be two sorts of reason for this mistake. One is simple anachronism. We, with our concepts, problems, and distractions, look back for what just is not there. Perhaps this has been true of views of Bayle, but there seems no reason why it should be so massively and uniquely true of him. Another reason might be that he was merely the reporter of others' views, a proleptic Copleston, as it were, so that the conceptual failure of fit in the work of Bayle is to be attributed, not to Bayle himself, but, without problem, to those about whom he writes. But in this sense not even the neo-Thomist Frederick Copleston is a Copleston. He talks about the people he does because he has a putatively coherent and more

---

31 For some ruminations on this very case, see Lennon, *Battle of the Gods and Giants,* chap. 8.

or less obvious thesis to demonstrate in his *History of Philosophy*, whereas Bayle's thesis seems to elude us. In addition, when Bayle himself offers disclaimers in precisely these terms, they are exceedingly problematic. Thus, when the Consistory of the Walloon Church of Rotterdam complained of the 'obscenity' in the first edition of the *Dictionnaire* and asked him to suppress 'impure expressions, citations, questions, and reflexions' in the second, he replied, in part, by saying that he was only reporting what others had said.[32]

There is something in all of these views, but as explanations of the difficulty in interpreting Bayle they all involve what might be called the *monologic fallacy of essentialist reification*. It is a fallacy, not in reasoning, but in the sense that G.E. Moore's Naturalistic Fallacy is a fallacy, or perhaps better, a fallacy in the sense of Gilbert Ryle's category mistake. The mistake is to treat people, by explaining them for example, as if they were things having fixed essences.[33] In the recent literature the most notable attack on essentialism comes, of course, from Karl Popper, who regarded it as the predilection of historicists, of those who saw the aim of the social sciences as prediction based on laws underlying the evolution of human history. Essentialism is for him the view that universal terms attach to single things, universals for example (as opposed to members of classes of single things, which is the view of nominalism). Methodologically, essentialism is the view that 'a necessary prerequisite of scientific research, if not its main task,' is the definition of universal terms, which reveals 'the true nature of the essences denoted by them' (as opposed to methodological nominalism, according to which words are merely 'useful instruments of description').

---

32 *Dictionnaire* I, cxxvii; V, 837–58.

33 Although the principal concern here is with explanation, specifically of what people say in print, there is a much broader ethical dimension to this fallacy that will reappear below. Thus Sartre distinguished people from things on the basis that their existence precedes their essence, a formula with which he famously defined his version of existentialism. The thesis that Bayle is one, perhaps the only, philosopher who avoids the fallacy is anticipated by Robinet, who in a very perceptive and illuminating article in 1959 points to what is most idiosyncratic about Bayle's interests and style of writing – his penchant for journalism, for digression, for obscurity, etc. – and likens it to the then-fashionable existentialism. For Robinet, however, this classification is not to recommend Bayle, whose existentialism amounts, essentially, only to a needless rejection of philosophical systems based on a stultifying scepticism. Although Bayle secures toleration as a value, he says, both Malebranche and Leibniz do not allow their philosophical architectonic to impede their liberal rejection of totalitarianism. See especially Robinet, 61. Of this, too, more below.

Methodological essentialism is seen by Popper as putatively support-ing two theses of historicism. First, social occurrences, which are non-quantitative and therefore cannot be explained in the naturalistic fashion of physics, must be understood in a qualitative, intuitive way. (The thesis immediately below will be that reading Bayle suggests a kind of non-naturalistic understanding that notably avoids essential-ism.) Second, since social occurrences perforce involve change, and since change, as has been known since Parmenides, cannot be under-stood as such, there must be unchanging essences that underlie social occurrences. (Here, reading Bayle suggests that understanding is pre-cluded rather than grounded by what is fixed and unchanging.)[34]

Given his interests in the political aspects of historicism, Popper talks only about abstract terms like 'the state,' 'credit,' or 'churchman' – Leib-nizian *incomplete* concepts. But there is another version or application of essentialism, one which invokes Leibnizian *complete* concepts applying to *individual essences*, individual essences of particular things and, most importantly, particular people. That is, most philosophers have recog-nized an essence or nature in some fashion or other had by all human individuals. Leibniz himself proposed essences that are unique to those individuals; more compendiously, then, and less pretentiously, the alleged fallacy of treating people as if they were things having fixed essences might be called the Leibnizian fallacy. This designation ignores Leibniz's attempt to distinguish between essential and accidental prop-erties, the putative result of which is that we as a matter of fact are never in a position to know individual concepts. But these concepts are cer-tainly known to God, and, moreover, the designation does have the his-torical justification that Bayle himself attacked the notion when he attacked metaphysical mechanism.[35] Roughly, the idea is that according to Leibniz everything true of me, including what I say, in principle (that is, by God) can be cranked out from my individual concept; but from Bayle's point of view, this cancels the fundamentally undetermined nature of my speech, especially in conversation. The implications are general, but the dialogue of importance to Bayle is between God and us in Scripture. More immediately, the relevance of the concept of individ-

---

34 Popper, *The Poverty of Historicism*, 3, 29, 31–5. For more on the Bayle-Popper connec-tion, see Lennon, 'Bayle's Anticipation of Popper.'
35 See Lennon, 'Mechanism as a Silly Mouse.' For his part, Leibniz evidently appreciated the depth of his differences from Bayle and, moreover, was able to respect him, 'one of the most gifted men of our time, whose eloquence was as great as his acumen and who gave great proofs of his vast erudition' (*Theodicy*, preface, 6).

ual essence here is that it metaphysically underwrites the attempt to find the 'real' or 'essential' Bayle and what he 'really' or 'essentially' held. To deal with the Bayle enigma, or at least to explain why it has arisen, the metaphysics of individual essences must be rejected, and the key to this approach to Bayle is Bayle's own approach to other authors: he lets them speak *dialogically*.

6: History, Narrative, and Fiction

This concept of dialogic speech comes from the Russian literary critic Mikhail Bakhtin (1895–1975), who attributes it, fully for the first time, to the work of Dostoevsky: the characters in his works speak dialogically. To put it dramatically, the thesis here will be that we may substitute, for Dostoevsky and the characters he creates, Bayle and the philosophers he writes about, and all that Bakhtin says remains true and illuminating. In fact, whether it is true of Dostoevsky or not, it is true of Bayle.[36] Before turning to the Bakhtin thesis, it will be useful to set out a number of connected assumptions that will serve as informal premises, or perhaps background ruminations, for the argument to follow.

First, for Bayle, explanation is largely narrational. The importance of narrative to Bayle is clear at the outset of the preface to the first edition of the *Dictionnaire*. His point there is to apologize for the insignificance of the errors in previous such works that his work was initially designed to relate and correct. 'The fate of mankind does not depend upon them. A narrative abounding with the grossest ignorance is as proper to move

---

36 Bayle and Dostoevsky were both political exiles, both suffered chronic health problems, both were news scavengers who devoured newspapers, on both gambling exercised more than a fascination. Bakhtin himself makes it something of a trio; the chronic bone disease that eventually cost him a leg was the typically Dostoevskian reason he was spared a death camp and was instead sent into exile in Kazakhstan (1929), probably for his activity in the underground church (Bakhtin, *Problems*, editors' preface, xxix).

Although Bayle stands to be enormously elucidated by Dostoevsky and his commentator, more so than can be shown here, the connection is virtually ignored in the literature. Jossua allusively ties Bayle to Dostoevsky with respect to the problem of evil. Concerning Bayle's consideration of the possibility that it would be better for the damned never to have been, he remarks that *The Brothers Karamazov* is not far away. See *RQP*, 2, 78; *OD* III, 657. Weibel makes a connection between Bayle and Bakhtin, 127–30, but restricts it to Bakhtin's work on Rabelais, which allows Bayle to be placed in the Menippean tradition, of which more below. But Weibel ignores Bakhtin's far more relevant work on Dostoevsky.

the passions, as historical exactness. Let ten thousand ignorant people hear you preach that Cariolanus's mother obtained from him what "he refused the Sacred College of Cardinals and the Pope himself, who went to meet him," [and] you will give them the same idea of the power of the holy Virgin, as if this was no blunder.'[37] That is, Bayle concedes the premise that the errors he corrects, even in his redesigned work, are by themselves largely insignificant. What will attract readers, and thereby reward his publisher, is the interest of his stories, which have their effect whether they are true or false.

Although narrative mobilizes the passions, which for Bayle, as later for his reader Hume, are the principal engine of belief,[38] there is more to the story. Bayle is a moralist in the older, broader sense of the term that also applies to Hume, covering interests in history, epistemology, literature and essays, as well as ethics in the narrower sense that would cover his work on toleration, for example. An obviously relevant model is the Gospel, much of whose doctrine is set out in parables. The parable of Christ's that most concerned Bayle was the parable of the man whose supper invitations were refused (Luke 14), which, as will be seen at length, is crucial for the question of toleration. The question raised by this and other parables is the same question raised in so many words by Alyosha, interrupting Ivan's parable of the Grand Inquisitor: what does it mean? (The *indeterminacy* of the parable of the Grand Inquisitor is closely, if less dramatically, mirrored by Bayle's parable of the two abbots on the topic of scepticism in art. Pyrrho, rem. B.) The point is that there is a kind of explanation or understanding that is best conveyed, perhaps uniquely conveyed, through narration.

Second, for Bayle, philosophy is continuous with, if not identical to, the history of philosophy. In this, his work is very much of a piece with that of Gassendi, for whom history, philosophy, and science were a seamless whole.[39] Only his tie to the Enlightenment, in fact, keeps Bayle from being the last pre-modern philosopher rather than Gassendi. For both of them, philosophy is contextual, and, more than this – after all, even G.E. Moore once said that but for reading philosophy he would never have thought of a philosophical problem – both seem consciously to invoke a kind of intertextuality. In the case of Bayle, his correction of error in previous texts, whether they be historical, mythological, or

37 Bayle cites a Dutch edition of a *Receuil de bons contes*.
38 See Lennon, 'Taste and Sentiment.'
39 See Lynn S. Joy, *Gassendi the Atomist*, esp. chap. 10. Also, Lennon, 'Deux acolytes.'

Scriptural, is on the same basis: other texts. Although only intertextual, the truth is in principle achievable with respect to these three kinds of text that were most of interest to Bayle; 'the clouds begin to disappear, and day breaks in upon us.'[40] The relevant contrast to both Bayle and Gassendi is Descartes and his followers, who consciously eschew history and minimize its significance in a way that continues largely to characterize modern philosophy. For them, history is a deposit of error best swept away, as with the method of doubt, in favour of a fresh beginning by each individual philosopher.

Third, Bayle does philosophy, Dostoevsky does fiction. But if philosophy is its history and history is narrative, then the techniques of both will be similar.[41] In fact, it is not obvious how they essentially differ. They do *not* in principle differ with respect to truth, nor even with authorial intention to express the truth, although how we take a work and thus the standards we invoke to evaluate it may well depend on the author's intentions. (If an author intends his account of some battle to be fictional then it will not do as criticism to cite some newspaper account of it.[42] But criticism of the participants' behaviour on the basis of what we know about human psychology is quite acceptable.) Generally speaking, the primacy of narrative does not mean that the facts do not matter. Both in history and in fiction it is important to get the story straight, and different (putative) facts ground, if they do not fully determine, different stories. Some stories have false morals, as in Bayle's narration of the Cariolanus story, which was used to convey the special power of the Blessed Virgin, which Bayle does not accept for a minute.

Once again, the relevant contrast is with the Cartesian position, which rejects fiction even more clearly and with less sympathy than it does history. Fiction is by definition false, and its only value a far from harmless amusement. When Descartes engages in what he calls a fable, he narrates no story but instead *describes* how the world might have assumed the shape it has. This 'fable' occurs in his treatise *The World*,

---

40 Art. Adonis, rem. L. Using the term, but once, when it still had to be enclosed in quotation marks, Weibel draws attention to the intertextuality at least of Bayle's historical work (132). Says Bayle, 'I almost never read historians with the aim of learning about things from the past, but only to know what has been said in each nation and in each group about things from the past' *Crit. Gen.*, cited by Weibel, 36. Weibel goes on to claim that Bayle's originality is to have extended the techniques of the establishment, authentication, and documentation of texts to history (51).

41 See Hayden White, *Tropics of Discourse*.

42 But what to do with Hugo's account of Waterloo in *Les Misérables*?

where, according to not a few commentators, Descartes traces what he takes to have been the actual differentiation of the present world from a primordial homogeneous matter. This is a 'story' only in a very figurative sense.

Fourth, for Bayle, philosophy is conducted through dialogue. There is much external evidence for this claim – his voluminous correspondence, for example, in which with his correspondents he seeks and shares illumination on everything under the sun. Or his work as editor of the *Nouvelles de la République des Lettres*, where he reviewed or noted an enormous number of publications, sometimes extending the discussion in debate with their authors, as with Arnauld in a case to be discussed below.[43] Bayle's attitude in this material is notably different from Descartes's (and from that of his followers, particularly Arnauld and Malebranche), whose correspondence is typically an occasion to repeat and insist upon his own views, and who consciously disdains the work of others (even if he is carefully aware of that work in order to get the better of it rhetorically).

The more important evidence, however, is an internalist account of Bayle in terms of the conversations that Rorty advises us to imagine between ourselves and 'the mighty dead.' Here the dialogical dimension is extended historically in a view of our race as involved in 'a long conversational exchange.'[44] While Bayle's motivation may be rather different from Rorty's,[45] the technique is fundamentally the same. The technique is one whose history begins with the Socratic dialogues, even and especially beyond Plato's use of it, and that is most evident

43 The case is Malebranche's theory of pleasure. See chap. 3. The case of Bayle's nasty relations in print with Jurieu is a special one, however, deserving more special treatment than can be given here. Knetsch reports that according to Schlossberg's *Pierre Bayle and the Politics of the Huguenot Diaspora*, Jurieu treats Bayle better than he was treated in turn.

44 Rorty, *Philosophy in History*, 51.

45 For Rorty, we engage in the great conversation in order to ensure that there is rational progress – 'that we differ from our ancestors on grounds which our ancestors could be led to accept ... We need to think that in philosophy, as in science, the mighty mistaken dead look down from heaven at our recent successes, and are happy to find that their mistakes have been corrected' (ibid). For Bayle, the only errors that ever get corrected are factual, or textual, errors; the theoretical issues of the sort that Rorty would correct (the existence of real essences, or of God) remain unresolved. What is achieved through conversation, we might suppose for Bayle, is an enlightenment or understanding that can only be achieved through conversation. Otherwise, why *converse* with the mighty dead rather than just reveal to them our truths and the arguments for them?

in the genre called the dialogue of the dead, which was in something of a zenith in Bayle's time, as in the work of Fénelon or Fontenelle, for example.[46] What is most notable in these dialogues is that the participants speak for themselves; the dialogues exhibit what Bakhtin calls *polyphony*.

7: Polyphony

Even in a period when determining authorship was often less than straightforward – consider Locke, for example, who never acknowledged his *Epistola de tolerantia* – the relation between Bayle and his work was exceedingly problematic. The *Dictionnaire* is the only work Bayle ever published under his own name, and it appeared there, it seems, only because his publisher, Leers, wanted a *privilège* in France, which required it.[47] Like much of the work to follow (and like many philosophical works in the period – see the exchange between Malebranche and Arnauld, for example), Bayle's first publication, the *Pensées diverses*, took the form of a letter; the work was originally intended for publication in the *Mercure Gallant*, which required Bayle to affect the perspective of a Catholic. When his efforts came to naught – the work was too long – he had it published by Leers in Holland, but still preserved his anonymity. The authorship of the *Critique générale de ... Maimbourg* was so well disguised that initially, at least, not even Bayle's friends recognized it. It takes the form of a series of letters – as the preface to the first edition, supposedly from the bookseller, explains – from an unknown author to a gentleman of the province of Maine. The preface to the second edition is from the author of the letters and expresses surprise at their having being published. The *Nouvelles lettres de l'auteur de la Critique générale* are just that. *La France toute catholique* consists of three letters, supposedly from a Catholic and two Protestants of different temper. The *Commentaire philosophique* is supposedly the translated work of an Englishman urged to write by a Huguenot refugee living in England.[48] The authorship of the *Avis aux réfugiez* was never acknowledged by Bayle.[49] And so on.

46 See Bakhtin, 143.
47 Cf. Weibel, 36.
48 For an explication of the title-page shenanigans of this work, see the commentary of J.-M. Gros in the Agora edition, 43–4.
49 Bayle's exact relation to the work is not perfectly certain. See Briggs.

There are several explanations of this anonymity, not to say misdirection and dissimulation. One is the political situation. The *Critique générale*, after all, was burned in the Place des Grèves, the traditional site for dealing with work judged politically incendiary, and as soon as the author's identity was learned, Bayle's brother was sent to the prison he never left.[50] This explanation offers rather more cogent motivation than does Lacoste's suggestion; he asks whether Bayle's preference for anonymity is not explained simply by modesty and a taste for obscurity.[51] Still, there is a point to Lacoste's soft explanation, one that is connected with the Bayle enigma itself. For Bayle's penchant for anonymity reflects his overriding concern with impartiality and, especially in the *Dictionnaire*, with the accurate and thorough representation, or rather presentation, of others' views. This is a concern that appears to make Bayle himself disappear entirely from his own text.[52]

Texts that exhibit this characteristic of allowing others to speak autonomously, rather than as vehicles for the views of the author, are described by Bakhtin as *polyphonic*. Although this characteristic is anticipated and to some extent exemplified by the genres of the whole serio-comic tradition, in particular by the Socratic dialogue and Menippean satire, it is fully exemplified, according to Bakhtin, for the first time in the work of Dostoevsky. The upshot is that one finds here an exact analogue to both the Bayle enigma and the reactions to it in the Bayle literature. 'Any acquaintance with the voluminous literature on Dostoevsky leaves the impression that one is dealing not with a *single* author-artist who wrote novels and stories, but with a number of philosophical statements by *several* author-thinkers – Raskolnikov, Myshkin, Stavrogin, Ivan Karamazov, the Grand Inquisitor, and others.'[53] The critical reaction has been to identify Dostoevsky with one of these characters and to

---

50 For Weibel (36–7), Bayle's anonymity has not just political but also structuralistic significance. Maimbourg's declared identity, with his refusal to deal with anonymous criticism, is tied to the reigning political power, to the point that the 'I' no longer speaks for Bayle.

51 Lacoste, 32, n. 6.

52 Late in his life, 'Bayle was under attack simultaneously from Jurieu on the right and the rationalists (principally Bernard, Jaquelot, and Leclerc) on the left. He seemed like a lone figure whom it was impossible to classify, like his own *Dictionnaire*, which the French accused of being anti-Catholic, while Jurieu found it scandalously pro-Roman – a conflict of opinion that Bayle himself no doubt saw as proof of his having achieved the impartiality he had been aiming at.' Labrousse, *Pierre Bayle* II, 44.

53 Bakhtin, 5.

interpret or reinterpret all the rest in light of that perspective, or to regard *all* of these characters as somehow expressing Dostoevsky's view, however inconsistent it must therefore be, or to conclude that Dostoevsky has no view at all, that whatever may have motivated him to write in the first place (both he and Bayle wrote for their living, as we would put it), his 'voice is simply drowned out' by the voices of his own characters. The bafflement is exactly parallel in the two cases.

According to Bakhtin, Dostoevsky's characters not only speak just for themselves, but, with their autonomy, they sometimes speak against Dostoevsky himself, even to his surprise and dismay. This notion of autonomy may be elucidated with an analogy that will be of use for several reasons in understanding Bayle. Bakhtin's view seems to be that Dostoevsky stands to the people he creates as the biblical God stands to the people He creates, with whom He disagrees, negotiates, is appalled, etc. When Christ appears in the parable of the Grand Inquisitor, it is Christ Himself who appears, both in Ivan's putative historical account and in Dostoevsky's incorporation of that account in his novel, and not some representation that conveys Dostoevsky's view on evil. Unless it is Christ, in fact, the story makes no sense as a story. Nor is there any reason why Dostoevsky himself cannot appear in his own story, just as God appears in his own story, both of them as voices independent of those they create.

The parallel is very close. All the meaning to be found in *The Brothers Karamazov* is due ultimately to Dostoevsky as its creator; but the same sort of relation (perhaps exactly the same relation) is to be found between God as creator and the Providence He exhibits in creating. Nor does plot or Providence upset the freedom of those participating in it. Just as Christian apologists have insisted with respect to Providence, Bakhtin insists that there is no contradiction between the 'independence of a character' and 'the fact that he exists, entirely and solely, as an aspect of a work of art, and consequently is wholly created from beginning to end by the author.'[54] Perhaps surprisingly, he describes the situation in which the author creates in rather Leibnizian terms: the creator chooses from among objective possibilities. 'To create does not mean to invent. Every creative act is bound by its own special laws, as well as by the laws of the material with which it works. Every creative act is determined by its object and by the structure of its object and therefore per-

54 Ibid, 64.

mits no arbitrariness; in essence it invents nothing, but only reveals what is already present in the object itself.'[55]

Etymologically, there are problems here. The notion that Bakhtin seems concerned to reject is creation utterly *ex nihilo* – creation of the sort exercised by Descartes's omnipotent deity, for example – whereas 'invent,' after all, means *to come upon*. In any event, the Leibnizian twist extends the parallel to Bayle, who, even if he is doing history, must create in Bakhtin's sense in so far as he selects what he chooses to relate and criticize. He is thus in fact much closer to the etymological meaning of fiction, which is not something made (factum) but something shaped (fictum), and which is very close to at least one important sense of the earliest Hebrew term for biblical creation, that is, to hew. Most important, there is even less obstacle for Bayle to speak with autonomous authors in his work.

8: Dialogue and Monologue

Polyphonic thinking is exhibited in the creation of *dialogue* in a fairly constrained sense that may be summarized as displaying three related and overlapping characteristics: i) independence of voice, ii) personalized consciousness, and iii) open-endedness. To engage the substantive issues discussed in chapters below, it will be useful not only to flesh out these characteristics but also to draw the contrasting notions of *monologue*. The positions that Bayle takes on these substantive issues may be understood as required by the possibility of dialogue in the sense to be explicated here. Correspondingly, the positions he rejects will be connected in various ways with monologue, which will therefore be briefly introduced here by way of contrast to the characteristics of Bayle's work.

Independence of Voice

Independence of voice is the notion that characters speak for themselves, not as authorial mouthpieces. Not very successfully perhaps, Bakhtin attempts to elucidate the notion by saying that 'the consciousness of a character is given as *someone else's* consciousness, yet at the same time it is not turned into an object, is not closed, does not become a simple object of the author's consciousness.'[56] For Bayle, or for anyone

55 Ibid, 65.
56 Ibid, 7.

in writing a non-fictional work, to obviously do otherwise with the authors they write about would be hard to imagine. Still, there is a philosophically important point here. Dostoevsky's are characters with whom one could have (a most interesting) conversation – unlike those of Dickens or Hugo, for example. For reasons that will become clearer below, the people Bayle wrote about are endlessly fascinating. But no one would want to enter a conversation with Aristes, the scholastic participant in Malebranche's dialogues, or with Hylas, who represents Locke in Berkeley's dialogues (except, perhaps, to ask them how they could have been so stupid and unimaginative). Nor would Theodore or Philonous have anything to say to us that could not be gotten from the non-dialogical works, the *Search* and the *Principles*. The 'dialogues' of Malebranche and Berkeley have only one voice and it stands outside the work.

Such monologic works as those of Malebranche and Berkeley are *static* and *eternal*. A particularly relevant example for Bayle of this sort of thinking is to be found at the end of his life when he was attacked by the deistic left wing of Protestantism. His rationalist opponent Jaquelot will not allow any status for the temporal, dialogical order of history apart from the eternal order of reason. 'Revelation merely elaborates in story form truths which are available to reason,' as it is put by Ruth Whelan, who quotes Jaquelot: 'The Christian religion is almost nothing other than the proper opinion [*sentiment*] of right reason, enlightened and supported by the authority of God.'[57]

Monologic works are also *objective* and *literal*, with a positive disdain for figurative language. This is not to say that they also achieve moral objectivity, however. Bayle's rationalist, even if irrational, opponent Jurieu relied constantly on ridicule with a direct denunciatory style, constantly employed in the service of his own cause. Bayle was fiercely scrupulous about the facts, and when he resorted to exaggeration, it was only to engage in irony, which, as Labrousse puts it, 'instead of dumping emphatic assertions on the reader, discreetly leaves to him the need to draw [his own] conclusion. By feigning to yield candidly to prejudices, the ironist offers the person harbouring them an occasion to perceive them as such; for the person employing it, irony attests to the intelligence and good faith of the interlocutor, which is the prior condition, although rarely satisfied, of all honest discussion.'[58] This moral

57 'Reason and Belief,' 189.
58 Labrousse, *Pierre Bayle* I, 208–9.

dimension to Bayle's work will be treated at length below under the rubric of toleration. The connection is that Bayle accords to those whose views he discusses the same intellectual toleration and autonomy that he advocates in the political-moral sphere.

Monologic works are also *fixed* and *closed*. Thus Robinet, drawing on the contrast of Malebranche and Leibniz to Bayle, complains that 'his dialectic is incomplete; it remains binary; his antithesis never sees synthesis, nor his aporism system.' Robinet correctly identifies Bayle's work as a dialogue of the dead,[59] but misses precisely what is most attractive about it. It is not itself a dead structure that 'cripples' the *Dictionnaire*, but an invitation to join an ongoing process. Not incidentally, this kind of engagement begins to shed some light on the often-noted *sic et non* character of Bayle's work. His aim is not to produce the Pyrrhonian suspension of belief, which ends philosophical activity, but to generate options that keep it going.

Finally, monologic works are *impersonal* and make claims, even if only implicitly, to *achieving their goal of truth*. Thus objections to Cartesian views, for example, are solicited and expressed only to refute them in order to show that the original views are true because unassailable. (The well-known case is, of course, Descartes's *Meditations*, but there is also the case of Malebranche's *Search*, which was buttressed by *Elucidations* in reply to solicited objections.) To put the matter in these terms may be controversial, but the fact is that neither Descartes nor Malebranche changed a single view of theirs as a result of these objections.

With Bayle, error (objection before the fact) plays a very curious role. Its correction is the main cognitive goal of the *Dictionnaire*. However, error is not just eliminated, but, as Weibel observes, 'exposed, criticized, condemned, at such length and so completely that it assumes enormous importance and actually occupies three-quarters of the text,' with the 'truth of the matter' being stated often enough in a single sentence.[60] One explanation might be bad faith, a deliberate effort on Bayle's part to establish the views he claimed to be refuting. (Recall Delvolvé's positivist reading of Bayle on Christianity.) But it might also be an effort on Bayle's part to generate dialogue. Solipsistically, to say what is false and then what is true is easy and uninteresting. But to be at all genuine, the correction of error requires two people, one who commits the error and one who corrects it, and this duality is the model even for the correction

59 Robinet, 49–50.
60 Weibel, 17.

of one's own errors. The requirement is for two people and not just for pretexts for irrevocable assertion of truth of the sort one finds in Cartesian replies to objections, or even in Malebranche's dialogues.

Despite his anonymity, his refusal to say who he is, Bayle himself is present in his work as an individual in a way that few other authors are. No question here of a Descartes's 'I,' which on his own grounds is replaceable by everyone else's. Even so, Bayle's relation to his work is complicated by what seems to be a surprising number there of Bayle surrogates. A good example that bears obviously on the Bayle enigma is his interest in those who, like him, underwent religious conversion, for instance Uriel Acosta (1600?–46?). Other than this analogy, there is no reason why Bayle's *Dictionnaire* should have an article on this Portuguese Christian who, because of his studies, converts to Judaism and moves to Amsterdam, where his continued studies lead to two excommunications, terrible persecution, and as it happened, his becoming an attempted murderer and finally a suicide. After his second excommunication, however, Acosta continued his studies and decided that the law of Moses was only of human invention; but rather than concluding that he should remain outside Judaism, says Bayle, he instead asked why he should continue to suffer, especially since he was in a strange country whose language he was ignorant of. 'Will it not be better to play the ape among apes?'[61] Part of the Bayle enigma is whether Bayle played the ape among the Protestant refugees, and if so, why.[62]

To summarize, monologic works are static and eternal, objective and literal, fixed and closed, impersonal and advanced as true. These of course are the characteristics of what Gueroult called the Cartesian

61 See art. Acosta. For another example of this sort, see the article on Acidalius, 'one of the ablest critics of the latter ages,' who settled in Breslau, where, finding no employment, he turned Catholic and was made rector at a school there. Bayle's use of *alter egos* is noticed by Kenshur, who discusses a particularly pertinent example, J. Bredenbourg, who professed belief in free will despite rational proofs to the contrary ('Sincérité oblique chez Bayle,' 44–5). Bredenbourg is discussed in the article Spinoza, whose main subject is another Bayle surrogate to conjure with.

62 Weibel (114) carries the question to a higher level than those, for example, who would merely deny Bayle's sincerity and explain his pretence in terms of material gain. For him, Bayle saw that to assert atheism is to speak as if to understand a language that refers to a transcendent God, but that in fact is self-contained and is a condition for society or community. The structuralist reading is not without insight, but the failure to recognize a transcendent God is, Bayle insists, the great mistake of Spinozism, the most mistaken philosophy of all because it precludes the most important dialogue of all. Why, then, the surrogates?

order of reasons. It reaches an epitome as a genre in our own century with the early Wittgenstein. Consider his *Tractatus*:

1.1 The world is the totality of facts, not of things.

1.11 The world is determined by the facts, and by their being all the facts. And so on. At 2.0120 we encounter the first-person singular pronoun, but its referent is not Wittgenstein, but anyone: 'If I can imagine objects combined in states of affairs, I cannot imagine them excluded from the possibility of such combinations.'[63] No wonder that solipsism was such a plague to him at this point.

Personalized Consciousness

A second characteristic of dialogue in Bakhtin's sense of the term is personalized consciousness. Not only is the text intrinsically the product of a person, but the world conveyed by the text is personal. 'Dostoevsky's world is profoundly personalized. He perceives and represents every thought as the position of a personality.'[64] What this means is that the Dostoevskian character, particularly but not only the heroes, are not sets of traits, individual concepts, but, to use another piece of Leibnizian language, 'particular points of view on the world and on oneself.' The character emerges not from antecedent features either of his situation or of himself, but from the '*significance* of these features for the *hero himself*, for his self-consciousness.'[65] The characterization of characters in this way explains why scandal, outrageous acts, and crime figure so prominently in the work of Dostoevsky – they bring personalities into collision with the environment, personalities that thus reveal and further create themselves.

Bayle's work too exhibits personalized consciousness. In an obvious and trivial sense, the *Dictionnaire* deals with people and their thoughts. Noteworthy is the article dealing only with a river, for example, that does not flow into discussion of such favourite topics as idolatry or sexual high jinks.[66] Less trivially, Bayle's concern with documentation may be less a matter of obsession with detail, or even of scholarly apparatus, than an effort at personalization of the views he presents, at least to the extent of

---

63 The rejection of monologue, or at least an aversion to it, is another part of Bayle's distaste for the author of an earlier *Tractatus*, Spinoza, who also cast his philosophy *more logico*.

64 Bakhtin, 9.

65 Bakhtin, 48. This line of argument was very much in the direction of the existentialist position alluded to above. Consider *The Underground Man* as quoted by Bakhtin, 50.

66 Or both. See art. Scamander.

what was said by whom. (Again, there is an obvious contrast with Descartes, who works atemporally with abstract positions that no one need
ever have held.) Perhaps most striking is the possibility of explaining in
those terms one of the more unusual aspects of Bayle's work, its obscenity
– to use the term of the Consistory that condemned him for it.

In other, less charged times our word for this aspect of Bayle's work
would be pornography. The Consistory's word, in terms of which Bayle
replied, seems too strong. 'Ribaldry' captures the flavour. Often it seems
gratuitous, contrived, confected for its own sake.[67] In the *Projet*, for
example, Bayle wants to make the point that only those who themselves
write should criticize the writings of others and perhaps the more general point that only practitioners of an activity should criticize the practices of others. But how closely does this relate to the 'Italian story' that
Bayle cites? 'Once upon a time a Peasant, who, as you may easily judge
by his request, was a very knowing man, came to the Pope, and begged
his holiness would suffer the priests to marry, that we laymen, said he,
may caress their wives, as well as they caress ours.'[68] Trivial explanations
would either seek an extrinsic justification for it (Bayle wanted to make
money),[69] or discount its significance as far as Bayle himself is concerned.[70] In this, as in so much, however, Bayle's work is of a piece with
that of Rabelais and Montaigne, and if it is read in that serio-comic tradition, it will be much easier to understand and credit Bayle's own explanation that he was only flavouring the work, and that, in any case, he
was only reporting what *others* had said.[71]

67 See the article on the Mamallarians, for example, which does not much advance the
   history of heresy.
68 *Dictionnaire* V, 791, rem. C.
69 In the preface to the *Dictionnaire*, Bayle shows notable concern with the saleability of
   his work. 'I was made sensible, that a work which is bought only by the learned, sel-
   dom pays the printer, and that if any profit is to be made by an impression, 'tis when a
   book can equally please the learned, and those that have no learning; that it was therefore necessary for the sake of my bookseller ...' (7). Lacoste (39–40) points out that ribaldry is rare in Bayle's correspondence, and rather rare in works other than the
   Dictionnaire, and he takes at face value Bayle's own explanation that 'such a work
   needed some spicing up.'
70 Making the point that an author cannot always be known from his works, the editors
   of the OD assure us that 'certain places in [Bayle's] *Dictionnaire* will lead one to suspect
   that he liked sex, from which he always had great detachment' (OD IV, 2).
71 Bayle's claim is supported by Weibel's reading. Because Bayle himself is not in the text,
   having been *eliminated* from it on structuralist grounds, there is no pornography in it
   either, since in his view pornography is an invitation to imitate the author (Weibel,
   138–9).

But just the representation of consciousness, however, or even of personality, is not sufficient for polyphony. The representation could be no more than empirical psychology, which is objective, mechanically caused, and closed, and against which Dostoevsky constantly rebelled.[72] What is needed is the affirmation *thou art*. 'For the author, the hero [and not just the hero] is not "he" and not "I" but a fully valid "thou," that is, another and autonomous "I" ("Thou art") ... In Dostoevsky's novels, the author's discourse about a character is organized as discourse about *someone actually present*, someone who hears him (the author) and is *capable of answering him*.'[73] This requirement introduces the ethical dimension alluded to above in terms of the existentialist reading of Bayle and can be seen here as an adumbration of Kant. The second formulation of the categorical imperative reads: 'Act so that you treat humanity, whether in your own person or in that of another, always as an end and never as a means only.'[74] Presumably, this means that one cannot use others merely as a means to express one's own views. Kant talks about humanity; if Raskolnikov is an instance of humanity, then in some sense even in fiction there may be a moral imperative. It certainly applies to the treatment of other authors and respect for their autonomy. Pointedly, Kant also extends the application of humanity to the agent – 'whether in your own person or in that of another.' One's self must always be open to reinterpretation by oneself. A monological treatment or representation of oneself might therefore be morally problematic; that Bayle himself satisfied the imperative on both counts, in the presentation of his own and others' views, shows his integrity and gives rare ground for esteem among authors.

Open-endedness

Finally, polyphonic thinking is open-ended – always open to resumption and revision in the way that dialogue is. Completion is always a temporal, contingent notion, having to do with publishers' deadlines, for example. Bakhtin draws attention to the critic Shklovsky, who relates that Dostoevsky 'loved to jot down plans for things; he loved even more to develop, mull over, and complicate his plans; he did not like to finish up a manuscript ... But Dostoevsky's plans contain by their

---

72 Bakhtin, 40.
73 Ibid, 63.
74 *Foundations of the Metaphysics of Morals*, 47.

very nature an open-endedness which refutes them as plans ... *As long as a work remained multi-levelled and multi-voiced, as long as the people in it were still arguing, then despair over the absence of a solution would not set in. The end of a novel signified for Dostoevsky the fall of a new Tower of [Babel].*[75] This is a psychological profile that would make possible the sort of work that went into the *Dictionnaire*, always incomplete and ready to go into another edition as still more information was gathered and processed. But there is another part to this story, which concerns the Leibnizian Fallacy and the conversational model of philosophizing. As Bakhtin continues: 'dialogic relationships are a much broader phenomenon than mere rejoinders in a dialogue, laid out compositionally in the text: they are an almost universal phenomenon, permeating all human speech and relationships and manifestations of human life – in general, everything that has meaning and significance. Dostoevsky could hear dialogic relationships everywhere, in all manifestations of conscious and intelligent human life; where consciousness began, there dialogue began as well. Only purely mechanistic relationships are not dialogic, and Dostoevsky categorically denied their importance for understanding and interpreting life and the acts of man (his struggle against mechanistic materialism, fashionable 'physiologism,' Claude Bernard, the theory of environmental causality, etc.). Thus all relationships among external and internal parts and elements of his novel are dialogic in character, and he structured the novel as a whole as a *'great dialogue.'*[76]

Even if dialogue as a genre does not guarantee dialogic relationships or polyphonic thinking, it still seems to be the most natural vehicle here. A problem for the interpretation of Bayle in these terms is to explain why he used it so little in his work, why when he did use it it was so ineffectual, and why even outside his work Bayle seemed not much given to dialogue. The *Dictionnaire*, most obviously, however open-ended it may be like a dialogue, has none but an alphabetical structure, and his other works can be read in parcels, almost regardless of the order. How does the structure of his work reflect the direction and order

75 Bakhtin, 39.
76 Ibid, 40. 'The major emotional thrust of all Dostoevsky's work, in its form as well as its *content*, is the struggle against a *reification* of man ... nowhere as far as we know, did he use the actual term "reification," but it is this term precisely that best expresses the deeper sense of his struggle on behalf of man. With great insight Dostoevsky was able to see how this *reifying devaluation* of man had permeated into all the pores of contemporary life, and even into the foundations of human thinking' (ibid, 62).

of narrative – of the fundamental fact of human history for him that Christ comes after Adam? Moreover, even the few conversations that it contains, such as that between the two abbots, are not very good stories. The account of Uriel Acosta is a rare instance of a long and continuous narrative. Bayle's last work, the so-called *Entretiens de Maxime et de Thémiste*, was, appropriately, left incomplete, but even the editors of the *OD* were chagrined by Bayle's combative style in the work. 'Despite his love for tolerance and moderation, he perhaps took the freedom to defend oneself a bit too far.'[77] In his life apart from his work, Bayle was a recluse who never learned the language of the country in which he spent more than the last half of his adult life.

Nor is the problem of finding the occurrence of actual dialogue only a late one. One of Bayle's earliest manuscripts reads as the very antithesis of dialogue in Bakhtin's sense. This is the draft of a letter, written in 1674 and intended for his friend Minutoli.[78] It reports three imagined conversations; in none of them is there any change of position, nor much more than a single declaration, which, since he is a participant in all of them, is Bayle's own position, expressed at length and with flowers. Most disturbing is the third conversation, on the topic of the disproportion between merit and material compensation. Bayle reports that he 'scurried' from it, 'cursing in [his] heart every opinionated individual who is willing to go to a third or fourth reply.' Alas, his interlocutor wrote down and sent him his next reply – as Bayle saw it because 'people think it a matter of honour to carry the day in every sort of dispute. This is not one of my faults; I was once made a bit of a martyr by my judgment, but no longer, so for the sake of peace I readily concede others to be more right than I.'[79]

In part, this failure as a dramatic narrator is a matter of nothing more than temperament on Bayle's part, or of lack of ability. One does not become a Molière just as a result of some moral volition to do justice to people's speech. But there is more to the objection than can be met by pointing to Bayle's lack of skill as a dramatist. For the fact remains that his most important work, the *Dictionnaire*, has none but an alphabetical order and that his other work can largely be read in parcels almost

77 *OD* IV, 2.

78 Gigas, 11–74. Labrousse thinks that the format allows Bayle simultaneously to maintain two different points of view (*Pierre Bayle* I, 122, n. 102), but this is the respect in which the text most disappoints.

79 Gigas, 62. This is a particularly disturbing text in light of the ape-among-apes issue discussed above.

regardless of their order. How then can there be in these works any narrative or dramatic structure? How can Bayle's work itself reflect the importance of whether Christ came before or after Adam other than by boldly and objectively, that is, monologically, stating this fact once and for all? This sort of question, however, belies what happens in the real-life situations whose integrity polyphonic writing is supposed to reflect. Here there is no script, so that until they actually occur, episodes are indeed reversible. It is only after the fact that, with a permanent order, they assume dramatic significance. This open-endedness with respect to the future is precisely what characterizes human conversation as well as the conversational style that Bayle wryly acknowledges as his own. It is not lack of focus or coherence that leads Bayle early on to observe that 'I never know when I begin a composition what I will say in the second sentence.' Or, still earlier, 'I find myself on a daily basis falling into Montaigne's weakness, which is to know sometimes what I have said, but never what I am going to say.'[80] This is not to say whatever comes into one's head, but to 'follow the argument, wherever it may lead' without knowing in advance, as perhaps Plato disingenuously did know, the path of the argument.

If this conception of narrative is at all plausible and at all plausibly applicable to the work of Bayle, then we can understand both why he is so liable to digression and why he almost takes pride in it. For it is the way we speak, at least when we engage in polyphonic dialogue. Says Bayle of the author of his first major work, 'all the digressions of this author are instructive, interesting and amusing.'[81] That author himself says that 'I do not know what it is to meditate steadily on one thing; I am easily given to change; I often wander from my subject; I leap into areas where it is hard to make one's way, and I am impatient with the doctor who seeks method and regularity everywhere ... [A plan for a book] is fine for professional writers who need well-defined and settled perspectives. They do well first to make an outline, divided into books and chapters, and to form a general idea of each chapter which they stick to. As for me, I make no claim to the status of writer and do not subject myself to that sort of slavery.'[82] Bayle is a conversationalist, not a writer.

Bayle's work is very much in contrast with Descartes's *Meditations*,

---

80 26 December 1678. 31 January 1673; *OD* IV, 1737.
81 *PDC*, preface; *OD* III, 4.
82 *PDC*, i; *OD* III, 9.

for example, which despite its title is a fixed piece with a final outcome. It is thus utterly foreign to Bayle's way of thinking that there ever should be an unconditional, definitive demonstration of the existence of God and of the existence and nature of both the world and the human soul. And here we have something of an answer to the apparent failure of narrative to be more prominent in Bayle's work. It is that the relevant concept of narrative itself is unfixed and open-ended. What counts as an appropriate vehicle for exercising and acknowledging personal auton- omy cannot be set out in advance. There is no formula for it, no mecha- nism that guarantees its production. (For one thing, such formula or guarantee would be open to exploitation. It would be like saying, 'It is true that ...' as a formula or guarantee of the truth of what follows.) How, then, do we know when conversation occurs? By engaging it. What is offered next is an opportunity to engage Bayle and the issues that he engaged.

3

Authority

Why do we believe what we do? The question is ambiguous. In one sense it asks for the causes of our beliefs. This question will be investigated in chapter 6 below, on Bayle's views concerning grace and Providence. Another sense of the question asks for the justification of our beliefs. Here we are asking about the authority for our beliefs.

The question to be investigated in this chapter concerns authority over what ought to be believed. From what source ought our beliefs to come? Specifically, the question concerns the *recognition* of authority in two closely related senses. First is the recognition of authority in the sense of determining where the authority lies. Second is the recognition of that authority in the sense of accepting it for what it is. In the religious sphere, the question is nothing less than that of the Reformation itself. Apart from direct communications of the Mosaic sort, how is it that God communicates with us? Given that His communication is now contained in the Scripture that Moses wrote, is it the Church or the individual conscience that determines what Scripture means and all that is thereby implied? But the question will be seen to extend, beyond the religious sphere, to the possibility of any communication and to even more extensive concerns.

The vehicle for investigating the question of authority, and of much else below, is a distinction drawn by the Jansenists in an effort both to remain in the Church and yet to avoid the Church's apparent condemnation of their views. For they held views that appeared indistinguishable from those condemned as Calvinism. The distinction is between two kinds of question: questions *de fait* and questions *de droit*. (The *de facto – de jure* distinction, of course, transcends this period, beginning in Roman law and extending notably to Kant's *Critique of Pure Reason*. Part of the thesis here is that the distinction was drawn on philosophically contestable grounds. The French terms for the the kinds of question, therefore, will be left untranslated as technical terms, since what was intended by each kind of question was, as will be seen in great detail, very diverse.[1])

Now, the Jansenists were known, and certainly sought to be known, as opponents of the Jesuit practices of casuistry. But from Bayle's perspective, it was they who, in attempting to remain within the Church, were guilty of casuistry with their use of the *fait-droit* distinction. In an effort to preserve what in Bayle's view is a false authority (that of the Church of Rome), the Jansenists make impossible the exercise of the one, true Authority. The short of the story to be told below is that for Bayle the two kinds of question are not independent, as the Jansenists held, but in fact entail each other. The upshot is that for him, as for others, the distinction backfires as the intended strategy and succeeds only in raising sceptical questions about sincerity, honesty, and the possibility of communication.

There is reason to believe that the distinction originated with Pierre Nicole, but in the period, and ever after, it came to be indissolubly associated with the name of his colleague Antoine Arnauld (1612–94). What to say about this prime example of seventeenth-century analytical genius, this unrelenting and penetrating critic of Descartes, Malebranche, and Leibniz among others, including Bayle, this scourge of the Jesuits within the Church and the Calvinists without? His work is better known and more accessible than it once was,[2] and a great deal might be said, but our concern here is, rather, focused on his distinction and what it offers to the reading of Bayle. We begin with a sketch of the multiple relations between Arnauld and Bayle. For Bayle shared the general view at the time of Arnauld as an extraordinary genius of great learning and insight, and expressed that view in so many words.[3]

9: Bayle and Arnauld

On 5 May 1675, while living clandestinely in France, and almost seven years before his first major publication, Bayle wrote to his friend Bas-

1 Even the term 'Jansenist' is not without its problems. It was applied to those seen to defend the views expressed in the *Augustinus* (1640) of Cornelius Jansenius, bishop of Ypres, but in a way that they themselves generally resisted. See Schmaltz.
2 Arnauld's complete works have been available in an excellent edition for more than two centuries, but only now do we have proper translations of his two philosophically most important works. See his *Logic* and *On True and False Ideas*.
3 *Réponse de l'auteur des Nouvelles de la République des Lettres*, OD I, 446.

nage concerning Arnauld. 'No one will be able to persuade me that even those who argue against Arnauld do not admire his eloquence, his ability to think systematically, and especially that astoundingly prodigious reading that he exhibits.'[4] Such praise required great equanimity on Bayle's part, for he goes on in the letter to discuss the difficulties that Arnauld had posed for the Protestant cause. Although Arnauld was intolerant in the extreme – Bayle was later to observe that the publisher Leers was the only Huguenot with whom Arnauld would enter into conversation[5] – Bayle was able to claim that he treated Arnauld with dignity. Indeed, Bayle, who treated everyone with dignity, did so especially in the case of this implacable adversary of Protestantism.

A systematic study needs to be done of the relations between the Calvinist Catholic who was Arnauld and the Catholic Calvinist who was Bayle.[6] Quite apart from the volume and diffuseness of the writings of both, a complication is that on what ought to have been the central issue between them, grace, Arnauld exhibits exceeding discretion, not to say misdirection, while Bayle, though maintaining the expected view, exhibits very little interest or motivation with respect to it. (In Bayle's view, grace is impenetrable. While grace may determine how we behave, it does so inexplicably, such that we cannot know even when it is operative. Its only theoretical significance for him is the disruption and error occasioned by the debates attempting to explain it, a moral he might have drawn from the Jansenist debates.)

Even so, three areas of connection are readily picked out in Bayle's work. One is the question that irreparably divides them, that of the Real Presence, which is treated below under the rubric of idolatry (chap. 5). The second is a topic on which, by Bayle's own testimony, he was influenced by Arnauld. Below, the question of Providence will show Bayle to have been led away from Malebranche's views on this topic by Arnauld's criticisms of them (chap. 6). A third area concerns authority and is controversial, not because of doubt that there is a connection between Arnauld and Bayle, which is clear enough, but about how it is to be interpreted. To understand it, a distinction needs to be drawn, one that was very much controverted in the period, between three concepts: religion, morality, and salvation.

Initially we can say that questions of religion have to do with what is

4 *OD* IV, 597.
5 To Minutoli, 5 December 1690; *OD* IV, 650.
6 For a good start see McKenna, esp. 653–4.

to be believed in a certain domain, those of morality with how we ought to behave, and those of salvation with one's ultimate fate. Many thought the three to be intimately connected: only if one believed in a certain way could one act in a certain way, and only if one acted in that way could one be saved. For many, these connections represented an application in three domains of the same concept.

For various reasons, Bayle wants to distinguish between religion, morality, and salvation such that the domains are conceptually independent of one another. Both in his own practice and in his writings, Bayle tended to treat religion as largely *ceremonial*. Whether such ceremony could ever have supernatural significance for him, it often enough lacked it. In a naturalistic account of religion that would have much appeal to the Enlightenment, Bayle sets it out as a principle among all people of the same religion that religious laws are observed only when it is convenient to do so. The engine of religious observance is the passions, 'which are so ingenious in seeking compensation that they find in the very things designed against them the basis for a great victory.'[7] Feast-days are observed, not only because failure to do so would incur sanctions, but because it is fun to do so. For an hour or two given to God, one enjoys ten or twelve in nice clothes, dancing, drinking, and mixing with the opposite sex. None of this has any necessary connection with morality. If the Jews practice circumcision, they do so at no inconvenience to the parents, who go on 'deceiving, calumniating, making love, and getting drunk as they wish.' Fasts imposed by the Church are more of a burden, but have no more beneficial effect on conduct; some one fasting is still capable of his usual vices.

As opposed to ceremony, morality concerns good works. But for a Calvinist, good works can never produce salvation, which depends entirely on grace. (Insistence on this point – one of two, along with transubstantiation – distinguished Geneva from Rome.) Thus the domains of morality and salvation clearly are conceptually distinct for Bayle. An obvious complication emerges, however, with the connection between this grace and religion. It was argued (especially, but not only, and not always) by Catholics that this grace was given only to those within the Church, where the Church included only a subset of all people. For the Jansenists, this number of saved was very small – as they were supposed to have indicated by the small space their crucifixes depicted

---

7 *PDC*, cxxxvii; *OD* III, 88. While Bayle may offer the practice of Jews and Persians as examples, his principal target here is clearly Catholicism.

between the hands of Christ above his head. For Bayle, not just many, but all are called, even if not everyone is saved, a view that underlined his disdain for religious observance and that resulted in Jurieu's charge against him of 'indifferentism': the view that differences between religions are irrelevant, and that one can be as good as another.[8]

A complication also emerges from the connection between grace and morality. For Bayle, even the performance of good works is accompanied by grace, perhaps the same grace, so that all and only those are saved who incidentally perform good works. This connection can be seen in his response to an objection against his view that atheism is no worse than idolatry. The objection is that atheism is worse than idolatry in so far as Providence permits idolatry in order that fear of false gods should at least regulate passion and maintain civil society among pagans. Bayle's response contests the factual accuracy of the connection between idolatry and the maintenance of order. Not incidentally, his response contains some of his most powerful writing, condemning, without ever mentioning it, what he takes to be an idolatrous and uncivil Catholic France. (The larger context is Bayle's argument that, because of their view on the Real Presence, Catholics are idolatrous, and that, even if the Calvinists are wrong about their views on transubstantiation, they should be tolerated.) He also argues that the objection faces a dilemma. Either the pagans receive grace, contrary to 'good theology,' or they resist by their own effort, which is the Pelagian heresy. If pagans had this capacity, then Christians by their own efforts could pass from 'historical faith' (the dead faith of merely intellectual conviction) to 'justifying faith' (the living faith that yields engagement in a way of life).[9] Significantly, Bayle refers at length to the Jansenist Nicole's *Essais de morale*, 'that excellent treatise ... filled with proofs of this thesis.'

Bayle also drew, in an important way, from Nicole's collaborator Arnauld for the distinction between religion and morality. In a curious blend of testimony from Arnauld and the Jesuit Rapin, Bayle asserts that the true marks of Christianity are practically extinct in morality, the failings of which he eloquently catalogues at some length; yet, according to him, the churches and monasteries are packed and it is standing room only at the communion rails.[10] He also cites Arnauld on behalf of the

---

8 Bayle mockingly reassured Jurieu that in the domain of salvation he would find a gratifyingly large number of those *not* called, that is, who would be damned.

9 *CPD*, cxxxix; *OD* III, 387–9. See also Labrousse, *Pierre Bayle* II, 295.

10 *PDC*, clvii; *OD* III, 101–2.

claim that philosophy was useless to the pagans in supplying the deficiencies of their religion, which was restricted to external worship; among them only a small élite were able to reason to the existence of the one true God. In addition, Arnauld is cited to the effect that according to the pagan philosophers themselves, virtue did not depend on God and hence was independent of religion: 'all men agree that we should ask God only for good luck, and give ourselves wisdom and virtue.'[11]

In all of this, Arnauld draws a distinction between morality and religion only to argue that, properly understood, each depends on the other (as indeed, does salvation on each of them and conversely). But Bayle employs Arnauld's arguments for the distinction itself in an effort to show that morality and religion are independent. This difference between Arnauld and Bayle is reflected in their differing attitudes towards toleration, the question here being whether the actions of atheists and heretics are *eo ipso* wrong. In the case that will concern us for the rest of this chapter, however, the connection between Arnauld and Bayle is exactly reversed. Arnauld draws a distinction between two kinds of question in order to show that they are independent, whereas Bayle exploits what he takes to be a necessary connection between them. Here the difference between Bayle and Arnauld will be reflected in their differing attitude towards questions of authority, the main topic of this chapter.

10: Jansenism and Scepticism

A sceptical outlook was logically, temperamentally, and strategically characteristic of Jansenism: logically in that it followed from Jansenist views on grace, temperamentally in that it sat well with their rejection of speculative theology, and strategically in that it obscured their unorthodox views.[12] As a Cartesian, even as a Cartesian fellow-traveller,

---

11 *PDC*, lii–liv; *OD* III, 259–61. Bayle also cites Arnauld as part of an argument that, contrary to Arnauld's own view, atheists are capable of morality (and thus, once again, that not only is there a difference between religion and morality, but that atheism may be no worse than idolatry). The Jesuit authors of the doctrine of philosophic sin, according to Arnauld, who rejects the doctrine, had distinguished two components in a wrong act: its being contrary to right reason, and its being contrary to the law of God. Arnauld's example none the less makes it clear, according to Bayle, that he thinks that one can have the former kind of quality without the latter. *CPD*, cxliii; *OD* III, 395. For more on the philosophic sin controversy, see Kilcullen, essay 1.

12 See Lennon, 'Jansenism and the *Crise Pyrrhonienne*,' 'Arnauld and Scepticism.'

Arnauld ought to have been the arch-opponent of scepticism; but Arnauld's use of the *fait-droit* distinction committed him *despite himself* to scepticism.[13]

The distinction implies that the Church's infallibility is, at best, hypothetical in the sense that it is infallible with respect to a proposition P if, but only if, in exercising its infallibility it means P, but that we can never be sure that it means P. The result is an open-ended challenge to Church authority. None of the Church's pronouncements need be binding because of open questions about what any of them might mean. For anyone relying on Church infallibility to overcome doubt, scepticism in matters of religion is the result. This result calls into question either Arnauld's sincerity in employing the distinction or what might be called the pragmatic coherence of the distinction itself. Arnauld's situation offers a nice foil to Bayle's views on what is required for human communication generally. But first, some background.

In 1653, the bull *Cum occasione* of Innocent X condemned the famous Five Propositions. They amount to the view that grace is necessary and sufficient for salvation; all and only those whom God freely chooses to save are saved. Everyone took these propositions to be definitive of the Jansenist position on grace. Everyone, that is, but a group from among the Jansenists headed by Arnauld. Faced with the inconsistent triad of papal infallibility, papal condemnation of the propositions, and the Augustinian, hence orthodox, character of the propositions, this group chose to deny that the Pope had condemned the propositions *in the sense in which they accepted them*. Following the suggestion of Nicole, apparently, Arnauld distinguished between questions *de fait*, about which the Church is fallible, in this case the question whether certain propositions are to be found in a certain book, or are held by certain people, and questions *de droit*, about which the Church is infallible, in this case whether certain propositions are heretical. Arnauld claimed to cede on the question *de droit*, but maintained a respectful silence on what he took to be the question *de fait*. The Pope had no doubt condemned something, and correctly, but he did not condemn Jansenism. (That Arnauld never indicated what he thought had been condemned by the Pope raises the vexed question of his motivation in employing the distinction.)

Later in that year, the Jesuits published and defended the thesis *Assertiones Catholicae*, in which they argue that the Pope has the 'same

---

13 That is, Arnauld was a sceptic in the sense in which Descartes was a sceptic, according to Popkin. See *History of Scepticism*, chap. 10.

infallibility' that Christ had, that the Pope is 'an infallible judge of controversies of faith ... as well in questions *de fait* as *de droit*. Therefore, since the Constitutions of Innocent X and Alexander VII, we may believe with a divine faith that the book entitled the Augustinus of Jansenius is heretical, and the five propositions drawn from it, are Jansenius's and in the sense of Jansenius condemned.'[14] Ferrier, for instance, argued that if indeed the Pope had not understood Jansenius in condemning him, he might not have understood Augustine, for example, in approving him.

In reply, Arnauld argued, *ad verecundiam*, citing even people like Bellarmine, that the Pope is not infallible with regard to matters *de fait*, and, *ad absurdum*, that the Jesuits might as well have argued that the Pope is unable to sin as that he is unable to err with respect to matters *de fait* – history shows the one to be about as likely as the other. The Jesuit position amounts to idolatry; it deifies the Pope, endowing him with omniscience. According to Arnauld, the role of the Pope is to *interpret* what has *already* been revealed by God. Nicole replied to Ferrier that the questions he raises must be handled on a case-by-case basis, relying on reason; history shows the Church sometimes to have been right, sometimes in error concerning these questions *de fait*. 'One cannot therefore know in general whether it be lawful or not to affirm that an author has been ill understood by the Church, since it depends on the particular reasons that induce one to say it.'[15]

Bayle indirectly accepted the Jesuits' premise and argued that there is no Church infallibility. For him there is no infallibility *de fait* (as he thought most Catholics other than the Jesuits admitted) and therefore no infallibility at all. However certain we may be about some matter *de fait*, we may always be mistaken. In short, if the *fait-droit* distinction applies to the interpretation and evaluation of Jansenius, it does so no less in the case of Scripture.[16]

Bayle's argument is investigated below. Here it is worth noting that

14 *Assertiones Catholicae de Incarnatione contra saeculorum omnium ab incarnato Verbo praecipuas haereses*. Quoted by Arnauld, *La Nouvelle hérésie des Jésuites ...* (1662) in *Oeuvres de Messire Antoine Arnauld* (hereafter *OA*) 21, 515.
15 *Les Imaginaires, ou Lettres sur l'hérésie imaginaire* (s.l.n.d.) 2nd letter (March 1664), written under the pseudonym of Le Sieur de Damvilliers. The letter was important enough to be translated into English, along with two others by Nicole, Arnauld's *Nouvelle hérésie*, and other documents, by John Evelyn: *Mysterion ... that is, another part of the mystery of Jesuitism ...* (London, 1664) 108.
16 See McKenna, 652–3.

Arnauld's fellow Cartesians would agree with Bayle's premise that there is no infallibility *de fait*. For them, matters *de fait*, at least of the sort relevant here, are not objects of knowledge, but of belief. At the end of the *Principles*, and elsewhere, Descartes seems to distinguish between what we apprehend of individual things in the temporal realm, which is restricted to what he calls phenomena, and which depends on sensation, from our apprehension of their essences, in an eternal realm, via the mind alone. Only in the latter do we have metaphysical certainty, as in the case of mathematical demonstrations. In the former we have at best moral certainty. The example that Descartes gives is of particular relevance. If an initially unintelligible text makes sense when each letter in it is replaced by its alphabetic successor, we can be morally certain that this is the author's sense rather than some other, the possibility of which would be incredible, or, presumably, there being no sense at all.[17] Now, this question of textual meaning is one of Arnauld's questions *de fait*. A mathematical demonstration, on the other hand, would fall into his category of questions *de droit*, and not just by default. With the doctrine of the created eternal verities, Descartes recognizes in God a kind of authority even stronger than the Church's authority over matters of faith. The important contrast is between *fait* and fallibility on the one hand, and *droit* and authoritative certainty on the other. We shall return to this Cartesian position at the outset of section 11.

Whether intended or not, the upshot of Arnauld's use of the distinction, meanwhile, would seem to be not just fallibility, but religious scepticism: we must suspend belief with regard to matters of faith because we literally do not know what to believe. Before we can determine whether a believed proposition is true or false, we must determine what it means, but this is always problematic. No appeal to an external criterion of religious knowledge like the Pope or Church councils could be certain, even if the criterion were certain, because no use of the criterion could guarantee its own relevance to an individual belief. The applicability of the criterion must always be infected with matters *de fait*: interpretation, vagueness, ambiguity, and so on.

Yet Arnauld did accept this external criterion as the only way to reli-

---

17 *Principles* IV, 205. When in the next, and next-to-last, principle, Descartes goes on to assert that there are some things that are not just morally, but absolutely certain, the examples he gives are all of the second category above. He concludes by restricting absolute certainty to the general features of 'the universe and earth' by contrast to the phenomena.

gious knowledge. Thus, the effect of his distinction and the extreme uses to which it was put – it became clear after a while that no matter what the Pope said, it would be met with protests that what was condemned was not what was meant by Jansenius – was really to question the possibility of any kind of religious knowledge, and perhaps of any knowledge at all. One observer remarked that 'the [Jansenists] are come now generally to disavow, not only the *Popes*, but all *human Infallibititie*. This is one of the last refuges they have made use of against their adversaries.'[18] The extreme use of this argument, however, was to be made by others. Popkin points to three works of 1688, 1700, and 1757 where the following argument was employed: 'The Pope and no one else is infallible. But who can tell who is the Pope? The member of the Church has only his fallible lights to judge by. So only the Pope can be sure who is the Pope; the rest of the members have no way of being sure.'[19] Yet even the knowledge by the Pope that he is the Pope is a matter *de fait*. This is no artificial question. Centuries earlier there was the Babylonian Captivity of the papacy, with one and sometimes two antipopes claiming to be Peter's successor. With the Reformation, the more general version of the argument concerned the characteristics of the true church, how they are to be determined and applied, etc. In this dispute, of course, Arnauld and Bayle were as prominent as anyone addressing the issue.

11: The Elusive Distinction between *Fait* and *Droit*

The *fait-droit* distinction is associated with the Jansenist controversies, but it in fact gained currency in a wider circle and was used with a great deal of flexibility. The designation '*de droit*' was generally taken to mean *authoritative*, in a number of senses of this term. Thus, among authors of interest here, La Placette uses the expression in the sense of *authorized*; for him, the *fait-droit* distinction is between fact (whether a certain action was performed) and value (whether an action was right, wrong, or indifferent).[20] The Cartesian Regis uses *de droit* to designate *logically* authoritative truths; thus necessary truths, such as those of geometry, which follow from the essence of things (on which they depend as their

18 Theophilus Gale, 161.
19 *History*, 13.
20 *Traité*, 13. He also introduces a third 'order of question': whether the action is pleasing to God, and the difference this makes. This Protestant author figures prominently below in sec. 15 of this chapter and chap. 6.

formal cause) are truths *de droit*. Contingent truths, for example, that a given triangle has a certain size, which do not follow from the essence of things and thus need an efficient cause, are truths *de fait*. Truths *de droit* are known by reason; truths *de fait* are known only by the senses, in any of three ways: direct experience, the testimony of others, and, most indubitable of the three, divine revelation. Given that God is infinitely wise, powerful, good, and veracious, according to Regis, we must believe all that He reveals to us.[21] An additional reason for accepting Revelation, which Regis does not give, is that the truth that God reveals is His own in that He is its efficient cause. Regis was among the few Cartesians who accepted, and drew many of the implications of, Descartes's doctrine that God is the creator of all truth, including eternal truth. But, as the Malebranchist Henri Lelevel argued, the *fait-droit* distinction thus breaks down.[22]

The use by Regis of the distinction illustrates two related problems in sorting it out in this period. First, the very kind of question that Arnauld tried to isolate as a question *de droit* turns out to be a question *de fait*. For Regis, *all* questions of religion are questions *de fait*. Whether Christ is really present in the Eucharist, for example, does not depend on the nature of the things involved in the way that a theorem in geometry depends on the nature of extension. Reason alone may demonstrate the latter, but the special kind of sense experience called revelation is required to know the former.

Second, the grease for the skids in this shift, as in other instances of it, is the analysability of the relevant terms in terms of each other. Thus, whether a claim is authoritative in the sense of being binding may depend on some fact; for example, Lelevel would hold that a man should be valued more than his dog because it is a matter of fact that a man has more value than a dog. The difference in value is grounded in a relation between ideas in the divine understanding. This is the Male-

---

21 *Système* I, 135–7.

22 Lelevel, *La vraye* , 129–31. A short form of the argument is that for Regis all truth has an efficient cause and thus is *de fait*. (Cartesians committed to this view saw the empiricist implications of it. See François Bayle, *The Cartesian Empiricism of François Bayle*, especially the introduction.) Lelevel's argument is a Malebranchean epistemological argument. Knowledge of all truths is dependent on their exemplary cause; in the case not only of truths *de fait*, e.g. the sun exists, but also of truths *de droit*, e.g. the three angles of a triangle equal a straight angle, the exemplary cause is the same, viz. created matter, which, in Lelevel's (correct) interpretation of Regis, is the doctrine of created eternal truths.

branchean position. But on the voluntarist line espoused by Regis, the order of dependence is the converse. All truth, including morally and logically necessary truth, is grounded in the divine will. A humorous extreme to which this flip-flop was pushed is to be found in Jurieu's last attack on Bayle, where he uses the *fait-droit* language to distinguish what is debatable from what is not. One would have thought that a question *de droit* would be one that is not debatable, but no. His specific thesis is that Bayle destroys Christianity by pushing impiety to the point of atheism. 'It is not a question here of any question *de droit*, in which the author is so skilful in finding detours and false turns. It is a pure and simple question *de fait*, which he will be hard-pressed to elude.'[23]

The flip-flop of the distinction occurred in both directions, for the same sorts of reasons. Whether a certain statement is to found in a given book looks to be a clear question *de fait*. Certainly, Arnauld offered it as such when he restricted the Church's authority to the question *de droit* whether the statement was true. But the Bible contains the statement that there is no God. Of course, the statement is famously qualified by the observation that only the fool makes the statement in his heart. The real question concerns what the statement expresses, or what is meant by it given a certain context. The set of problems thus raised was crucial in a period when what was meant by the Bible in particular meant so much. One way of framing one of the questions was, and is – even if there are no authors, as many now think – to ask about the author's intention: what did he or He mean? To put it another way, what is, or what would be the response of the person responsible for the statement? The very question, then, on which Arnauld based his distinction, turns out to be a question, not *de fait*, as he thought, but *de droit*. What Jansenius said is a question of authority. We shall return to this question in section 13.

The slide between author and authority in the senses connected with the question *de droit* is not just an etymological connection. The historical connection is the one alluded to above; the debate over religious authority, specifically the Catholic claim to infallibility, was a question as to the source of that authority. An indication of this connection is to be found in the use of the distinction by David-Augustin Brueys (of whom, more in chap. 5). An obviously important issue in his response to

---

23 *Le philosophe*, 6. Elsewhere in the same work (42), however, Jurieu has a different understanding of the distinction. Whether God exists is a question *de droit*, and whether an author's meaning has been understood is a question *de fait*.

Bossuet's attempt to reconcile the Reform is the notion of justification: how are people saved? The question *de fait* concerns what Rome holds with respect to justification. And what Rome holds, according to Brueys, appears to be contradictory: both that Christ's death is sufficient and that man's good works play a necessary role. The question *de droit*, it seems, is whether Scripture provides the distinction Bossuet claims it does to resolve this apparent contradiction, namely between two sorts of justification: Christ's remission of sin, whereby justice is imputed to man, and good works resulting from voluntary cooperation with grace, whereby justice is communicated. Brueys thinks that Bossuet has confused justification with sanctification, the result of justification. However that may be, the point of relevance here is that both questions involve meaning, with one of them an *authorized* meaning.[24]

12: Arnauld's Response to Bayle

Arnauld's defence of Port-Royal was not the only instance of his appeal to the *fait-droit* distinction. He also used it against Bayle. The issue to which it was applied, Malebranche's view of sensory pleasure, is of no great interest here. But the discussion this issue mobilizes clearly reveals the most important dialectic to be found anywhere in Bayle. By seeming contrast to Arnauld, Bayle holds that before one can engage the question of *truth*, one must achieve *comprehension*, a condition for which is *sincerity*, which itself is a condition, indeed the only condition, for *morality*. Is pointing to these connections anything more than a trivial observation? Certainly the last connection is more than trivial, as will be seen in the next chapter. As for the others, they might for the moment be taken as injunctions, or reminders, that were too often relevant.

The context was the dispute between Arnauld and Malebranche, one of the longest and most bitter exchanges in the history of philosophy. The dispute has come to be known almost exclusively for the issue that in fact dominates it, namely the nature of ideas. But the initial and fundamentally abiding concern of the dispute was theological rather than philosophical. The dispute was launched in 1683 by Arnauld's criticism of Malebranche's theory of ideas, occasioned by the Oratorian's observation that a proper understanding of that theory was needed to understand his views on grace. Even as the philosophical issue was pursued through lengthy *Letters*, *Replies*, and *Replies to replies*, the theological

24 Brueys, *Réponse*, 91–3.

line was played out in a parallel exchange. Arnauld's *Réflexions philosophiques et théologiques* was his second salvo, two years into this exchange.

Soon after its appearance in 1685, Arnauld's book was reviewed by Bayle in the *Nouvelles de la République des Lettres*.[25] There are a number of points in Bayle's review that bear on the issue of scepticism. For example, he observes, quite apart from Arnauld's attack on Malebranche, that the issue of whether perceived irregularities in the world can be explained by their being required by the uniformity of God's ways cannot be decided, because, for all we know, they may be adornments necessary to the universe and, in any case, because we are ignorant of God's aims. That is, if, as the Cartesians hold, we know and understand the world in terms of laws that describe the uniformity of God's ways, then there may be events that are unknowable and incomprehensible. One reason for this is that the events lie outside that uniformity as 'adornments' of the universe. Secondly, the uniformity itself may depend, as it does according to Malebranche, on divine goals, which, according to Bayle, are unknown.

Another version of this epistemological issue was the debate over particular and general divine volition. The latter was taken to be what was expressed by laws, not only natural but supernatural – what God always and predictably does. But if in addition to, or instead of, general volitions there are particular volitions, with resulting states that are unique and unpredictable, then parts or even the whole of the world fall outside the Cartesian model of explanation. Bayle ended his review by noting Arnauld's discussion of Malebranche's attempt to save general volition by explaining apparent particular volitions, especially in the Old Testament, as occasioned by angelic desires. The extraordinary events that were so much wondered at were actually part of a more comprehensive, supernatural system that made them to be in principle predictable. This was the thrust of Malebranche's position in his *Traité de la grace et de la nature*, and it was debated back and forth between him and Arnauld.[26]

Bayle reviewed all of this material in the same year,[27] and found two

---

25 August 1685, art. iii; *OD* I, 346–9.
26 *Dissertation de M. Arnauld ... sur la maniere dont Dieu a fait les fréquens miracles de l'ancienne Loi* (Cologne, 1685), *Réponse à ... Arnauld* (Rotterdam, 1685), *Réflections philosophiques*.
27 *NRL*, March, art. iv; July, art. viii; August, art. iii.

of Arnauld's objections particularly cogent. First, angels would have to be the real cause of their own desires and volitions, otherwise the problem of particular volitions reappears with respect to them; but this would make angels the true author of all the wonders of the Pentateuch. Secondly, if they have the real power to cause their own desires, then they should be able to move matter, which only God is supposed to be able to do. It appears, then, that Bayle by rejecting occasionalism is on his way to scepticism. But he ends the review with the worry that the line of argument proposed by Arnauld removes from God's control events that depend on free volitions, 'which would ruin practically the whole of Providence.'[28] Bayle's own, non-sceptical account of unique events would be in terms of the narrative model of Providence, which relies on neither occasionalism nor freedom of indifference.

As seems to have been typical of all his reviews, Bayle's account of Arnauld's book was complete, fair, and accurate, but also generally sympathetic. Obviously, it is one thing to intend to be fair and objective (or to announce the intention to be so), and quite another to succeed in being so. Still, in writing to his younger brother about his early involvement with the *Nouvelles de la République des Lettres*, Bayle seems not to have exaggerated his position at all. 'It is necessary to be wise in these sorts of discourses, disinterested and honest. I will speak indifferently of Catholic and Reformed books, and honestly about everybody.'[29] Alas, on one point, and on one point only among many others, Bayle's fairness led him to defend Malebranche, going so far as to accuse Arnauld of quibbling in an effort to taint Malebranche's religious orthodoxy.

Bayle found eminently defensible Malebranche's view that pleasure makes those who enjoy it happy while they enjoy it. The various kinds of pleasure, and their moral status, are distinguished on the basis of their efficient cause, but not their formal cause. There may be no difference in the pleasure itself caused by the sovereign good and by some passion. In addition, the intrinsic distinction Arnauld tries to draw between spiritual and bodily pleasures is not going to be very effective in converting voluptuaries, who are ensconced in their pleasures.[30]

---

28 Bayle's comment is not a criticism directed at Arnauld, for it 'does not regard Arnauld, who believes in neither the *science moyenne* nor in freedom of indifference,' who defended the key premise that only God can move matter only as a 'partisan of Descartes,' and who raised the options only to embarrass his opponent. OD I, 349, 335.
29 17 April 1684.
30 OD I, 348. Here is a rare instance in which Bayle confuses the truth of a view with its usefulness.

Nadler has shown that the difference between Arnauld on the one hand, and Bayle and Malebranche on the other, is the intentionality of sensations, particularly pleasure and pain.[31] For Bayle and Malebranche, pleasure and pain in themselves are non-intentional; that is, unlike ideas, they do not have objects that they are about. For Arnauld, all conscious states are intentional and there is an intrinsic difference between physical and spiritual pleasures that depends on the intentional relation that each bears to its object. (Without this distinction, he thinks, concupiscence would be justified and one of the main proofs of original sin would be upset.)

Arnauld was not long in responding, producing an *Avis*, an anonymous twenty-three-page pamphlet dated 10 October of the same year.[32] It is no quibble, he says, to point out that the term 'happy' in Malebranche's position can be taken in two senses – one popular, according to which those are happy who think themselves happy; the other philosophical, according to which the only happiness is enjoyment of the sovereign good – which is the only sense in which he took the term.[33] He goes on to insist that for the proper evaluation of his arguments, two questions must not be confused. 'One, whether he has understood [*bien pris*] his opponent's sense. The other, whether in the sense he has understood his opponent, he has refuted him.'[34] The first is a question *de fait*, but of the five propositions to which Arnauld had conveniently reduced Malebranche's view on sensory pleasure, three are 'independent of this question *de fait*; that is, concerning them one can not claim that he has not attacked the true position of Malebranche.' Arnauld continues, confusingly, as follows: 'thus, in order for what [Bayle] says about his [Arnauld's] attack to be true, viz. that what the attack says about sensory pleasure is neither evident nor reasonable, his [Bayle's] criticism must extend also to these three propositions.'[35]

The five propositions are as follows:

1   Those who enjoy pleasures of the senses are happy in so far as, and to the extent that, they enjoy them.
2   They none the less do not make us permanently happy.

---

31 Nadler, *Arnauld*, 176–8.
32 *Avis à l'auteur des* Nouvelles de la République des Lettres (Delf [sic], 1685). *OA* XL, 1–9.
33 Ibid, 8. *OA* XL, 3.
34 Ibid, 12. *OA* XL, 4.
35 Ibid, 13. *OA* XL, 5.

3 Although they make us happy, they must be avoided for several reasons.
4 They must not lead us to love bodies, because bodies are not their real, but only occasional cause, God being their real cause.
5 Pleasure is imprinted in the soul in order that it love the cause making it happy, that is, God.

Arnauld says that he finds great difficulties in all these propositions; the second, fourth and fifth are the propositions that are independent of the question *de fait*.

As the anonymous editor of the *Nouvelles de la République des Lettres* Bayle dutifully reviewed this work in the lead article for December 1685. His dispassionate account opined that the engine of Arnauld's response was, not unnaturally, the issue of grace and freedom, and that Arnauld's concern was to distinguish himself from Bayle on this issue, lest the Jesuits profit from any agreement between them. Bayle had seen the *Avis* before its publication, communicated to him by someone instructed by Arnauld to get his reaction to it. (Arnauld was then living clandestinely somewhere in the Netherlands.) Bayle's immediate response was inconsequential, but since Arnauld seemed to have 'a certain philosophical mind, ready to dispute,' Bayle in his review promised a more proper response, to be produced over the Christmas vacation. This appeared the following year, six times as long as Arnauld's pamphlet.[36] The tone of Bayle's response is irenic – whether ironically so is perhaps another question. For after setting out Malebranche's doctrine on pleasure, Bayle observes that it seems so true and morally harmless that opposition to it can be attributed only to misinterpretation or bad faith. 'To suspect that Arnauld has not understood a doctrine that he has examined for the purpose of refuting it does not easily penetrate the mind,' for Arnauld's genius and learning are acknowledged by all. The only conclusion is that he turns things to advantage, especially since 'Arnauld's enemies, and latterly Malebranche, have complained of this against him all over Europe.'[37]

The specific reply to Arnauld's invocation of the *fait-droit* distinction makes a perhaps obvious but important point. On the question *de fait*

36 *Réponse de l'auteur des Nouvelles ...*, Rotterdam, 1685; *OD* I, 444–61.
37 *OD* I, 446. As to the issue of grace and freedom, the short of Bayle's response was that all he did in the review was to make Arnauld out not to be a Molinist. 'I don't think that he should take that for an insult or a heresy.'

whether Arnauld has properly understood Malebranche, Bayle thinks that Malebranche did not mean by happiness what Arnauld meant, and thus that what Arnauld says proves nothing against him. (Whether Arnauld proved something in the sense in which he took the term is restricted by Bayle to the first proposition, the only question he intended to raise in the review, which thus in one way or other occupies him for the rest of the work.) The point of immediate importance here is that Arnauld failed to prove anything against Malebranche because he failed to understand him. Bayle does not develop the point here, and its appreciation will have to await reconstruction below, but the drift is towards saying that the question *de fait* must be presupposed if there is to be refutation or even disputes at all, or perhaps for there to be communication of any sort. (The point becomes even more obvious when put in terms of confirmation and agreement.) However obvious or not, the point comports with and extends Bayle's position that restricting the Church's putative authority to questions *de droit* eliminates its authority altogether. Even if Church pronouncements were infallibly true, we could not be sure of understanding them.

On the other hand, Arnauld himself did not claim scepticism on the question *de fait* concerning the more important set of Jansenius's five propositions, although he was respectfully silent on the matter. On the contrary, he must have believed, or have been committed to believing, that the five propositions condemned by the Pope are *not* to be found in Jansenius – otherwise he would have accepted the condemnations without any *fait-droit* distinction. This is on the assumption, of course, that Arnauld was sincere in his acceptance of church infallibility – an assumption that will be examined below. Meanwhile, the point of relevance with respect to scepticism is that the denial of Church infallibility concerning a question does not mean that it cannot be answered at all. The upshot may be that infallibility takes on a hypothetical character: if the Church says 'P' and means P by 'P,' then P. That the Church saying 'P,' and its meaning P by 'P,' are questions *de fait* does not upset the infallibility of its pronouncement. Still, this concession may mean only that when the Church speaks, what it says is true, not that we are ever in a position to know what is true. Once again, that is, the Church's infallibility is by itself not sufficient to overcome doubt. Arnauld's own responses to the Church's pronouncements on questions of grace showed that an answer to the question *de fait* needed to make infallibility sufficient would never be forthcoming.

The historical denouement of this exchange was in the end disappointing, at least with respect to the *fait-droit* distinction. Arnauld responded to Bayle's *Réponse* with a work of equal length, a *Dissertation sur le prétendu bonheur des plaisirs des sens*, which is of philosophical interest because it sets out in no uncertain terms the intentionality of all mental states, including sensations such as pleasures and pains.[38] But there is no mention of the *fait-droit* distinction. The publication of this work was delayed, as Arnauld explained, in the hope of seeing Malebranche's replies to his first work, the *Dissertation*, that Bayle had said were soon to appear. This occasioned one last gibe from Arnauld, his final statement on the topic. Bayle picked it up again, after Arnauld's death, in remark G of the article Epicurus. He would have replied earlier, he says, but he was sick when Arnauld's *Dissertation* appeared, and when his health would have permitted him to reply, it was too late to do so. The remark criticizes Arnauld for failing to distinguish between ideas, which bear the intrinsic, necessary relation to their objects that Arnauld ascribes to all mental states, and sensations, which have only an extrinsic, accidental connection to what occasions them. But, again, there is no mention of the *fait-droit* distinction.[39] Its explication, and ultimate significance for Bayle, therefore, must come from elsewhere – from reconstruction and from its connection with other issues.

13: A Philosophical Account of the Distinction

One way of expressing Arnauld's response to the Church's attempted condemnation of Jansenius's doctrine was, apart from his respectful silence, as follows: 'I agree that what you say is true, indeed must be true; but I don't agree with what you say you mean.' However much it may question Arnauld's motivation, the literature has been remarkably homogeneous in taking his statement at face value as embodying a transparently valid distinction. Yet, if it is not treated as a throwaway line from Lewis Carroll, the statement ought at least to be examined on its own terms for its philosophical significance.

---

38 Second point, sec. 16, especially 112–13.
39 A natural place to look for the distinction would be the article Arnauld; but only once (remark R) does the distinction appear there, and then only incidentally, obscurely, and with only a tenuous connection to the issue of grace. In Arnauld's debate with the Jesuit Simon over the availability of Scripture in the vernacular, 'what he said with regard to *droit* on this matter is admirable; what he said with regard to *fait*, that is, to show that according to the spirit of the Church the laity are never excluded from reading the word of God in the vulgar tongue, is interesting and sound.'

The attempt to examine it here must be prefaced by two kinds of disclaimer. One is that even in the end, the use of the distinction in the period will have been found unclear and flexible in the ways indicated above, and this for the very good reason that it involves issues still much under debate in the philosophy of language and mind. Reconstructing and tracing the distinction does none the less help to understand Bayle. Second, to engage the distinction at all in the abstract, and often flippant and inconsequential, way that characterized the contemporary debate should not ignore the heartbreaking distress that its use caused at Port-Royal. Consider the plight of the nuns in one of the more dramatic episodes involving the Formulary, the document Catholics were required to sign denouncing Jansenism. Harassed throughout 1661 to sign that 'they condemn the Five Propositions in the sense they have in the book of Jansenius,' many of the nuns finally capitulated on 28 November with a statement reading, in part, 'considering our ignorance of all things above our profession and sex, all we can do is testify to the purity of our faith ...'[40] There is a particular poignancy to this aspect of the story since the distinction and the debate around it came from the Messieurs, as they were called, while it was the nuns who suffered the terrible torment at having to sign, and who were eventually turned out of their convent.

To begin, then, Arnauld's response to Bayle is confusing, for the *fait-droit* distinction ought to apply to all five propositions that Arnauld attributes to Malebranche, and not to just three of them. That is, of *each* of the propositions we should be able to ask whether it is to be found in Malebranche, that is, whether Arnauld and Malebranche meant the same thing by the same words – in short, whether Arnauld has understood Malebranche (question *de fait*); and secondly, we should be able to ask of *each* of the propositions whether in the sense intended by Arnauld it is true (question *de droit*). The only way to separate the second, fourth and fifth propositions as independent of the question *de fait* would be to make their attribution to Malebranche irrelevant. But this would seem paradoxical, since Bayle did not undertake to defend *whatever* Malebranche said; that is, he was not in a position like the Catholic's position *vis-à-vis* the Church of having to defend propositions under the description simply of having been uttered by the Church. Rather, he was defending what he took Malebranche to have meant by the proposition and he did so, not because it came from Malebranche, but because he

40 Quoted by Pascal, *Oeuvres* X, 165; also, Gerberon, *Histoire*, t.3, 2.

thought it was true or at least defensible. In this sense he was defending a proposition that incidentally was held by Malebranche. So perhaps Arnauld's point, the most charitable interpretation of his remark, is that in three of the propositions he was making points independently of what Malebranche may have held. But then charity, not to mention clarity, would obviate mention of poor Malebranche. Moreover, a charitable interpretation of what Arnauld thought he was doing with respect to the other two propositions then becomes problematic. For it seems that he was refuting *whatever* Malebranche said, an impression not without support from elsewhere in his *ad hominem*–infested exchange with the Oratorian.

One thing is clear, and that is that Arnauld's distinction is *not* the distinction between matters of fact (the order of nature), and matters of faith or religious belief (the order of grace). In the seventeenth century it would have been natural to draw the distinction in these terms, and the title to the crucial sixth section of Arnauld's *Seconde Lettre* suggests that this is the distinction: 'the difference between points of faith and doctrine called *de droit*, and points that regard facts and people.'[41] (The title of the work by Malebranche that launched the whole dispute is *Treatise on nature and grace*.) Strategically, of course, such a distinction would neatly isolate Church authority from the question of what is in Jansenius's book; but it does not comport with Arnauld's use of it against Bayle. For whether Arnauld has refuted Malebranche's view understood in this or any other sense (question *de droit*) is not a matter of grace or faith – except in so far as what the view is about is a matter of religious faith. But this subject-matter for it seems incidental to the distinction, for otherwise Arnauld would be claiming for himself a special status with respect to faith. He would be claiming that his refutation of Malebranche was inspired; that is, he would be placing himself on a par with the Church in deciding questions *de droit*.

Now, a perceived challenge to authority was, of course, the engine of the Church's response to Arnauld's distinction, and some important recent literature has thus tended to place Arnauld in the liberal, freethinking tradition in which the larger tradition has tended to place Bayle. Thus, Sedgwick takes the Jansenists to have raised with their distinction 'fundamental questions about the nature of ecclesiastical authority at a time when both Church and state were particularly sensi-

41 *OA* XIX, 455.

tive to these issues.'[42] And Whelan takes Arnauld's isolation of questions *de fait* from the issue of heresy to have been 'tantamount to a defence of the erring conscience: apparent support of a heresy, as in the case of Port-Royal, may only result from a misguided – from the point of view of the accuser – intellectual misapprehension of available data.'[43]

But this startling revision of Arnauld's outlook cannot be correct. For defending the rights of the erring conscience was the precise issue that diametrically opposed Arnauld and Bayle over the issue of philosophic sin.[44] According to Arnauld, the erring conscience by definition has no rights. While all mental states may be intentional, in order to sin I need not know God or even be conscious of anything in particular. In fact, merely not to know God is to sin. Like offending generally, it can be unintentional in the narrow sense of being involuntary. Consider Christ on the cross: 'Father forgive them, for they know not what they do.' His tormentors are doing something, and likely voluntarily, but do not know that what they do is sinful, and in that sense it is not voluntary. Yet they do sin and stand in need of forgiveness. Secondly, the point of the *fait-droit* distinction, if there is a legitimate one, is to isolate, but thereby to establish and protect, Church authority; whereas Bayle's response to the distinction is the *ad hominem* argument that there is no authority except God's.

Now, it might still be asked whether the distinction, despite the Jansenists' conservative outlook and the historical circumstances, might not have contributed to the recognition of individual rights. That is, why were the Jansenists not liberals despite themselves (just as, according to the thesis argued here, they were sceptics despite themselves)? The answer is a historical one, that no such liberalism was ever noticed among the Jansenists; they continued to be perceived as authoritarian into the crucial period of the eighteenth century by Voltaire and others, and in fact played an important role precisely against Voltaire and other freethinkers in the Enlightenment.[45] So although the *fait-droit* distinction may have been intended by Arnauld to make the nature-grace distinction, it itself was not that distinction, not even implicitly or by implication. What, then, was going on?

---

42 *Jansenism in Seventeenth-Century France*, 110.
43 *Anatomy*, 48.
44 See Kilcullen, essays 1 and 2.
45 Thus the R.R. Palmer thesis, *Catholics and Unbelievers in Eighteenth-Century France*. Princeton: Princeton University Press, 1939.

To call the question whether a certain proposition is to be found in a given book a question *de fait* is highly misleading. It might be thought answerable on the basis of whether the proposition is quotable from that book. The question *de fait* concerning Jansenism is not this kind of question, since the *Augustinus* of Jansenius was obviously available to everyone for quotation. In other words, the question was not an editorial one of establishing the authentic text. The real question that Arnauld tried to separate from the faith was what any quoted proposition might *mean*. By contrast, the question *de droit* concerned its truth, to which the Church had infallible access in so far as it concerned faith or morals. But this was not the settled significance of the distinction, which as illustrated in section 11 above tended to be used in a variety of ways, in this case even with just the opposite meaning. In June of 1664, Hardouin Péréfix, the archbishop of Paris, apparently instigated by the Jesuit Annat, issued a no-nonsense order to the members of Port-Royal to sign the Formulary, but gave them several weeks to reflect. The Jansenists used the interval to come up with the following formula: 'je me soumets de coeur et de bouche au constitutions des papes, la soumission de coeur étant pour le droit et celle de bouche pour le fait.'[46] Whether I say something in the sense of pronouncing certain words is a question *de fait*; as we saw in section 11 above, this question is the sort of question of fact that Regis construed as settled on the basis of sense, testimony, or Revelation. But whether I *mean* what I say in the sense of saying it sincerely, is a question *de droit*. This question, as we saw in the same section, is of a piece with the question of responsibility and authorship. In this sense, I exercise authority over what I say, for I am its author.

The tendency, in any case, was to construe the question of meaning as a question *de fait*. A natural explanation of this construal is one that assumes a reference theory of meaning. A proposition means what it is used by someone to refer to, that is, what would make it true. This theory holds for all propositions, both for what the *Port-Royal Logic* calls singular propositions and for all others, including universal and indeterminate particular propositions.[47] Singular propositions intend would-be temporal states of substances, indeterminate particular propositions intend a partial conjunction of such states, and universal proposi-

46 I submit with my heart and my mouth to the papal constitutions, the submission of my heart to *droit*, the submission of my mouth to *fait*. *Histoire des persécutions*, 263; quoted by A. Gazier, *Histoire générale* I, 165.
47 *Logic*, part 2, chap. 1.

tions intend something about essences. That universal propositions refer to essences rather than to a whole conjunction is cued by Descartes's account of how God establishes the truth of the eternal verities, that is, by acting as the efficient cause of what makes them true, which is to say, for the truths of geometry, by creating extension. That Arnauld subscribed to this voluntarist doctrine may be open to question;[48] but that these essences be created is not essential, however, in order for them to answer a question naturally raised by this account, namely, how false propositions might be meaningful.

We know that in his debate with Malebranche over the nature of ideas, Arnauld argued for possibilities as the object of non-veridical perceptions, which here might be read as essences or relations between essences.[49] So, to take the least problematic case, to say of a rectangular object that it is square is to say something about the essence of extension that allows that possibility. This account works with tolerable clarity for propositions about individuals taken both singly and in conjunctions. As to false universal propositions, one position might be that they are contradictory, and do not refer to anything and thus are meaningless. How far beyond the opening moves of this dialectic Arnauld gave any evidence of going is here too complicated and digressive a question.

That possibilities should be the referents of propositions for Arnauld came up historically in a way of more than passing relevance to the larger significance of the *fait-droit* distinction. At one point the Jesuit Annat tried to rebut Arnauld's attempt to exculpate the Jansenists as follows. If the Jansenists did not hold the views condemned by the Church, and if, as may be presumed, no one else did either, then the Church is combatting a phantom and 'does not know what it is doing.' Arnauld's reply was that the Church does not act needlessly in condemning heresies erroneously attributed to people innocent of them, since it must prevent people from falling into heresy, and it must defend 'the honour of the Church ... by showing its enemies that it does not authorize or hide these heresies by not condemning them.'[50] Condemning imaginary heresies, he is saying, is a good thing because it protects and sets a good example. The alleged prophylactic and exemplary power of such real possibilities is an open invitation to witch-hunting, however, and to

48 See Ndiaye, 'The Status of Eternal Truths.'
49 For a case for Arnauld's strongly actualist account of possibilities, see Nelson.
50 *OA* XIX, 439.

witch-hunting in a literal sense. And it would have been perceived as such by Bayle, who found only too much evil in what was already actual.[51] Moreover, such speculation ran contrary to his methodology of historical-critical scholarship.

But quite apart from the offence both to his sense of toleration and to his positivism, Bayle does not accept the reference theory of meaning and truth on which the invitation to witch-hunting is based. Ontology, which purports to establish ultimate reference, is for him relative to a certain domain of enquiry, one that is in the end self-contradictory (such is Bayle's conclusion with respect to the infinite divisibility of matter, the mind-body connection, and other seventeenth-century chestnuts)[52] and anyhow contradicted by what is accepted on the basis of faith.[53] And faith, instead, mobilizes a narrative form of enquiry that would be paralysed by the scepticism entailed by Arnauld's *fait-droit* distinction. Here what is *meant* is far more important than what is *true*, at least in any ultimate sense. The more crucial semantical evaluation is in terms of sincerity, which was also undermined by questions concerning Arnauld's motivation in employing the *fait-droit* distinction. Dialogue obviously breaks down between us if you do not understand the meaning of what I say, or if you doubt my sincerity in speaking it. For Bayle, the crucial dialogue is with God, either directly as with Moses at the burning bush, or indirectly through Scripture. In these terms, the sceptical situation generated by Arnauld's distinction is the equivalent of that generated by Descartes's demon deceiver of *Meditations* II.

This breakdown is another, and not incompatible way of reading Bayle's *ad hominem* that the *fait-droit* distinction undermines ecclesiastical authority. Divine authority is also undermined because it cannot be expressed. The image from the ancient world that best expresses the failure of communication so important to Bayle is the finger-wagging of Cratylus. This follower of Heraclitus believed that since everything was in flux, a speaker's meaning never persisted long enough to be understood by any hearers; and so when spoken to he wagged his finger to indicate that he had heard something, but that any reply would be use-

---

51 For Bayle's sceptical, tolerant attitude towards those accused of witchcraft, see *RQP*; *OD* III, 559–62; trans. Kors and Peters, 360–8.
52 On the former, see art. Zeno of Elea, rems F, H; for the latter, see art. Rorarius, rems B-H.
53 See art. Pyrrho, rem. B.

less. (Not only would the reply be doubly useless as involving two messages, but the signal of its uselessness would be useless.)[54] God's message is thus silenced. He may speak, but amid finger-wagging, or hand-waving, He cannot be understood.

However fuzzy the edges, the centre of the distinction focuses on authority. Perhaps the best translation of 'question *de droit*,' then, is *question of law*, or *of jurisdiction*, or *of authority* in the sense picked up by Regis. Understood in terms of legal positivism, rather than of natural law, this notion would capture the performative aspect of meaning and of alleged Church infallibility. My words mean what they do just because I use them to express that meaning, and the Church cannot err in what it says because its saying so makes it so. The question *de fait* is analogous to the question of the facts of the matter falling under the authority of the law. Not surprisingly, the issue comes down to the source of authority. Both Arnauld and Bayle, both Catholics and Protestants generally, agree that the ultimate authority lies only with God. Whether that authority is exercised through the Church is what obviously separates them, so the debate over the marks of the Church detailed by Rex – its antiquity, etc. – really is the central issue it appeared to be in the period. One result of this analysis of the *fait-droit* distinction is what it should be, for it shows that Arnauld and Bayle each took their respective Catholic and Calvinist positions on the question *de droit*.

14: Nestorianism, Calvinism, and Jansenism

At one point, Arnauld tried in effect to limit the sceptical consequences of his *fait-droit* distinction. He tried to do so by arguing that 'the doctrine of Jansenius,' that is, the description of the doctrine that the Pope had infallibly condemned, had no settled meaning – unlike 'the doctrine of Nestorius' or 'the doctrine of Calvin.' In the latter two cases, everyone knew what was meant, and therefore the Pope's condemnation was clear. In short, respectful silence on the question *de fait* concerning the doctrine of Jansenius did not commit one to silence, respectful or other-

---

54 Bayle does not mention Cratylus, but he does worry about Heraclitus. In art. Euripides, rem. E, Bayle relates that according to Tatian, Heraclitus 'concealed his Writings in the Temple of *Diana*, believing that one day or other they would take them from thence, and publish them as a mysterious Work.' Such mysteriousness is the antithesis of the Bakhtinian openness and access prized by Bayle.

wise, on every such question.[55] That the meaning of 'the doctrine of Jansenius' was not settled was, of course, in no small part due to Arnauld's own efforts. Moreover, it is a good question whether the doctrines of Nestorius and of Calvin were any more settled, as we shall now see.

The latter half of the seventeenth century saw a surprising recrudescence of Nestorianism, or to employ something like the bedeviling *fait-droit* distinction, a recrudescence of charges of this heresy. Although there was little if any discussion whether 'Nestorianism' was a heresy (question *de droit*), there was much discussion whether it was being advocated (question *de fait*). The issue, in short, was whether Mary was the mother of God. This remarkable conundrum had been debated in the fifth century between Nestorius, the patriarch of Constantinople, and Cyril of Alexandria, and had been decided under very complicated circumstances in favour of Cyril by the Council of Ephesus in 431. The issue is a very elusive and abstract one turning on how the divine and human nature(s) of Christ is (are) to be understood. To secure divine impassivity, Nestorius emphasized the distinction between the two natures in the hypostatic union. Cyril meanwhile insisted on the Incarnation as an enfleshment of the Word.[56]

That such an issue should have received the attention it did in the seventeenth century perhaps testifies to the inverse relation between the cognitive and emotive force of charges of heresy in this or any other period. The more threatening the charge, the more difficult it is to define. Socinianism is a good example of this sort of label used to smear everyone by everyone, and Nestorianism may be another, even better example.[57] In his *Dictionnaire* article on its eponymous source, Bayle

---

55 *De la véritable intelligence des mots ... OA* XXXI, 735–50. This argument was likely in response to Pascal, who, although he did as much as anyone to promulgate the *fait-droit* distinction by introducing it at the outset of his first *Provincial Letter*, his *Ecrit sur la signature* (first published in 1912), condemned its use as 'abominable before God and contemptible before men.' *Oeuvres* X, 198–221.

56 For more on this debate, see Whelan, *Anatomy*, appendix 1.

57 The term 'Socinianism' had a wide spectrum of meanings in this period, from a reasonably [sic] well-defined set of views deriving from Socinus (Fausto Sozzini, 1539–1604), to mere abuse for anyone said to hold views described as Socinian, whether in fact the views of Socinus or not. For a dispassionate account of Socinus's views, see Ogonowski. For consistency with most authors of the period, the term and its cognates are used below somewhere in the middle of this spectrum, to indicate a certain outlook or drift of argument. See Jolley (13): '[Socinianism] is certainly a difficult term to define precisely; it is an open-ended concept which covers not just a number of specific doctrines but also a generally rationalistic approach to religion.'

remarked that a rather peculiar thing had been observed in the Netherlands since the year 1690. Almost at the same time that the Jesuits accused the fathers of the Mons Oratory of renewing the heresy of Nestorius, a minister of Rotterdam had brought the same action against a minister of Utrecht. The outcome of the one was like the outcome of the other of these accusations. They came to naught, reports Bayle, 'without the accusers having been censured.'[58]

For Bayle, however, the issue was likely invested with deep philosophical and theological significance. His support for Nestorius's separation of the two natures may have anticipated the deism that came to be associated with Bayle. To the extent that Jesus was only human, a fully naturalistic explanation of the historical facts of his life becomes possible. Certainly, this approach characterized the methodology of Bible criticism employed by Bayle in the *Dictionnaire* and elsewhere.[59] More specifically, the separation of the natures may have been a literal version of his opposition to transubstantiation. Whelan convincingly argues that Bayle's repudiation of the Cyrillian orthodoxy of a fusion of divine and human natures in Christ is paralleled by his rejection of the orthodoxy of transubstantiation, whereby, as Bayle puts it, 'a spiritual, immense, infinite God ... has a body like you and me.'[60] She also argues, hardly less convincingly, that both are supported by Bayle's implicit invocation of Cartesian dualism, which makes the relation between an immaterial God and a material body, either in the Incarnation or in the Eucharist, just as problematic as the relations between an immaterial mind and a material body in humans. Moreover, she notes that all of these issues emerge in the same chapter of the *Critique générale* in which Bayle discusses the distinction between questions *de fait* and questions *de droit*.[61]

---

58 Art. Nestorius. An important question immediately below is whether Bayle's discussion of Nestorianism represents Calvinism and also Jansenism among other persecuted sects. Bayle's comment above occasions the one clear reference to the Jansenists in the whole article. He goes on to say that the charges were better founded against the translator of the homilies of St John Chrysostom, who subsequently apologized, taking full and sole responsibility for the alleged errors. He did so, according to Bayle, because as the former secretary to Sacy and Nicole, he gave opportunity to the Jesuit author of *Le Nestorianisme renaissant* to smear Port-Royal with the charge.
59 For a debate on the significance of Bayle's Bible criticism, see Popkin and Rex in Lennon, Nicholas, and Davis, *Problems of Cartesianism*.
60 *Crit. gen., OD* II, 134; Whelan, *Anatomy* 36.
61 Whelan, *Anatomy*, 36, fn. 19.

Whelan's thesis is that from Bayle's perspective, Nestorius on the nature of Christ, the Jansenists on grace, and the Calvinists on a range of issues have all been unjustly (and probably falsely) condemned because of Church intrusion on matters of fact, with respect to which there should have been toleration. The thesis is irresistibly argued from a close reading of a wealth of textual evidence. Part of this case, however, is the argument that Bayle in his article on Nestorius exploits the Jansenist distinction of questions *de fait* and questions *de droit* as a 'reading grid' for this episode of alleged heresy 'and – by deliberate echo to the polemical literature of the early 1680's – defends the rights of the erring *Protestant* conscience.' If the argument succeeds and we must take Bayle as having made use of the distinction in this fashion, then the approach to Bayle taken here, which views the distinction as inimical to his values of intellectual honesty and sincerity, will have been upset. The argument therefore requires close attention.

The argument is presented in three phases. First is the general identification of Jansenists and Calvinists on issues of free will and predestination. The Jesuit opponents of Jansenism were far from straining credibility when they made this association and wondered why the Jansenists remained in the Church. Bayle had the same wonder. Whelan's account of Bayle's reaction seems rather paradoxical, for she sees him as wondering why, if the Jansenist version of Augustinianism did not yield heresy, the indistinguishable Reformed version did. The fact is, however, that a position that the Church called Jansenist was no less condemned than the positions identified as Calvinist or Nestorian. In any event, Bayle makes no use here of the distinction.

A second phase concerns the crucial issue of transubstantiation. Here Bayle invokes the distinction, according to Whelan, in order to argue that the alleged Church infallibility is in fact based on a question *de fait*, with respect to which it has, and makes claim to have, no authority. The general question that Bayle raises is the possibility of ever interpreting the meaning of an another, which is contrary enough to Bayle's outlook. And the specific question is the interpretation of Scripture, in particular the words of the Last Supper. Are Christ's words 'For this is my body,' to be taken literally, as the Church contends, or only figuratively, as the Calvinists contend? If the Church claims no infallibility in interpreting the question *de fait* as to what Jansenius meant, Bayle argues, it should make no such claim in interpreting what Christ meant. But the Church's claim to infallibility is restricted to matters of faith (and morals), which is to say, what ought to be believed (and done). Since faith in this sense derives, as both parties agreed, from Scripture, the Church's claim to infallibility is restricted to interpretation of it, and not of every text. Bayle's application of the *fait-droit* distinction was bound to be even less convincing, therefore, than the attempt to exculpate the Jansenists, which raises the question of his motivation. Why should he have mounted such an obviously ineffectual argument based on the *fait-droit* distinction? In the larger context to be developed in the next section below, Bayle will be seen to employ the distinction only to subvert it.

The third phase that Whelan sees is in the remarks to the article on Nestorius. Here, expropriating recent efforts to rehabilitate Nestorius, particularly by the Catholic historian L.-E. Du Pin, Bayle turns the epi-sode to the advantage of Calvinism. 'The reformed/Jansenist distinction between *fait* and *droit* transmutes the heresiarch into an early supporter of a figurative interpretation of the Christian mysteries. The allusion to the Council of Trent elevates the entry into a typology of the creation of schism, not by the dissenters, innocent of heresy, but by a numerically and politically superior group, mistakenly convinced of its own ortho-doxy.'[62] Whelan's reading of Bayle's motivation in rehabilitating Nesto-rius seems, once again, beyond dispute. But the distinction between *questions de fait* and *de droit* seems to have played either no role at all in his strategy, or, at best, one entirely incidental to it. How so?

First, the only point in the article Nestorius, either text or remarks, at which the distinction occurs, at least as such, is remark O. This relatively short note occurred only in the second edition, after the appearance in 1698 of the *Histoire du Nestorianisme* by the Jesuit Louis Doucin, who in a footnote of his own drew attention to Bayle's article, in particular to remark A in which Bayle had made use of Du Pin's rehabilitation of Nestorius.[63] What this means is that Bayle's argument was already in place before the *fait-droit* distinction ever came up, and, moreover, it was not Bayle but Doucin who drew it.

Second, there is an oblique reference to Arnauld in remark A, but it does not involve the distinction. In a passage that Doucin quotes, Bayle argues that the dispute between Cyril and Nestorius is only verbal, and concludes by saying that he remembers a chapter from Arnauld's *Logic or the Art of Thinking*, 'where it is shown that a thousand disputes would end provided the disputants took the trouble to say what they meant by

62 Ibid, 50.
63 Doucin, 551–2.

the terms they employed.'[64] That some disputes are only verbal, and thus perhaps questions *de fait*, does not mean that other disputes are questions *de droit*.

Third, Doucin in a footnote[65] quotes part of Bayle's account of the dispute between Cyril and Nestorius, and then observes, correctly, that while Bayle relies on Du Pin, he fails to notice that Du Pin later condemned 'these things' (presumably his account of the Nestorian heresy in the sense of Nestorius) 'and retracted them himself.' The point of Bayle's remark O is an evaluation of Du Pin's retraction. On this estimate Whelan seems absolutely and importantly correct in her comprehensive account. Bayle's refusal to accept Du Pin's retraction is of a piece with his conviction of Nestorius's innocence; both are matters of the pressure of ecclesiastical politics, and both relate to the use of history as a tool of oppression and homogenization, which is a major concern of the *Dictionnaire* as a whole. Indeed, this is the major thesis of Whelan's chapter. However, Bayle's argument for discounting the retraction and accepting the original account of Nestorius is a fifth-century account, quoted by Doucin himself, that makes, not the *fait-droit* distinction, but the claim simply that Nestorius was misunderstood and misrepresented. The best reason for insisting on the original account, according to Bayle, is given by Doucin himself, incidentally, in his account of how the *fait-droit* distinction has been used to defend Nestorius. According to Doucin, it arms all heretics against the Church. For, not only might the Nestorians 'refuse to subscribe to the anathema of the three articles [by which Nestorianism has been defined by the Church] in the sense of Nestorius, but Nestorius himself could have properly refused to accept the condemnation of [his doctrines] ... Now which heresiarch will not be able to say the same thing, especially in such delicate matters?'[66] The original defenders of Nestorius tried this tack, and contemporary writers, namely Bayle, make out the dispute between Cyril and Nestorius to be a matter of words. Even more than this, says Doucin, the original defenders complained of misrepresentation, and here Doucin refers to the complaints catalogued at the time. Doucin takes the list to be evidence of the

---

64 Rem. A, ref. to *Logic* chap. 12, actually chap. 10, where the point is that for failure to define their terms, many philosophers get into 'disputes that are only verbal,' which is the expression used by Bayle to begin his argument.

65 Doucin, 551.

66 Ibid, 551, 553.

exploitation of an invidious distinction. Bayle in remark O quotes the passage to justify accepting Du Pin's original account, or rather not rejecting it, but the distinction itself plays no role in his arguments, for the charges of misrepresentation can be, and are, made, independently of the distinction.

Fourth, Whelan believes that the distinction covers Bayle against charges of Socinianism and Nestorianism,[67] in just the way the Jansenists sought to cover themselves by it. Yet at only one point anywhere in the whole article does Bayle so much as address it himself. It remains to be determined, he says in remark O, whether Du Pin's change was a matter of honest reconsideration, or whether he came to see that 'since Nestorius was condemned by an ecumenical council it is the duty of a good Roman Catholic to acquiesce in that condemnation, without introducing any unfortunate and very dangerous distinctions between *fait* and *droit*.' The comment is incidental, likely ironic and condescending, and, as far as the distinction is concerned, of unclear intent. As has been seen and as will be further argued below, Bayle more literally takes the distinction to undermine papal authority, not to protect the faith and isolate himself against charges of Nestorianism, Socinianism, or anything else. For Bayle, after all, was, unlike the Jansenists, outside the Church and both content with that situation and aware of its permanence. In fact, there is a nice irony in Bayle's use of the Jansenist dispute itself to argue against Roman infallibility. He assumes that Scripture does not ground such infallibility and that it must therefore be based in reason. But reason's only plausible argument would be that infallibility is needed for the proper functioning of the Church as a society, an argument that is belied by the history of schism, heresy, and disorder generally, including the Jansenist *imbroglio*.[68]

Finally, fifth, Bayle is non-committal – pointedly, it would seem – about 'the observations that Father Doucin has advanced to refute the distinctions of the Gentlemen of Port-Royal.' It is conceivable that this comment, which concludes remark O, is a confident recognition of the obvious weakness of Doucin's attack on the distinction, to which Bayle thus invites his readers. But, again, this is not an employment of that distinction by Bayle, as may now be seen by putting his treatment of it in a context larger than Nestorianism.

67 Whelan, 45–6.
68 *Crit. gen. OD* II, 141.

15: Rationalism and Irrationalism

The thrust of Bayle's work is to extend toleration almost without limit. He thus obliterates, if not the *fait-droit* distinction itself, then at least its relevance; for the significance of a question *de droit* is precisely to define orthodoxy. Now, even absolute toleration does not *eo ipso* entail that all views are equally orthodox,[69] but it obviously reduces the role to be played by those who define orthodoxy. Bayle's restriction of that role is clear and dramatic, for he limits the Church's authority, *any* church's authority, in questions *de droit* to a single, trivial one that has already been independently decided. The upshot is that Bayle finds himself in a delicately balanced position between outright deism and blind fideism. The subverted use he makes of the Jansenist distinction drives him in the direction of the former, but what he salvages for faith leaves him open to criticism from his liberal Protestant opponents. This complicated, three-cornered contest emerged in a text by LaPlacette, whose discussion closes this section below.

For Bayle, the crucial question on which the Church has pronounced is, of course, the interpretation of Scripture, specifically the words of consecration. The Church's interpretation is rejected,[70] not because of the *droit-fait* distinction, but because there are no questions *de droit* to be decided on authority other than God's, while all else is a fallible matter *de fait*. The following is how Bayle argued in his *Critique générale de l'Histoire du calvinisme de M. Maimbourg*, published in 1682, fourteen years before the *Dictionnaire*. '[The Church] in good faith admits that every question in which it is a matter of the sense of an author is a question *de fait* and that it has not received from God the privilege of infallibility in order to decide whether Jansenius, for example, has said on a given page this or that thing. [The Church] must therefore agree that when it is a matter of determining the sense of a verse of Scripture, it is a question *de fait* for which God has not granted it the grace of being infallible.'[71] Bayle just assumes that the theses maintained at the Jesuit College of Clermont in 1661 'cannot be regarded as the dominant view', and then uses this assumption that the Church is not infallible on questions *de fait* to argue against its infallibility on any sort of question. (This is why the

---

69 See Newman, chap. 3, esp. 87.

70 Or, more precisely, it is not accepted. It is positively *rejected* because it is meaningless.

71 *Crit. gen.* xix; *OD* II, 138. Cited by Whelan, *Anatomy*, 50.

Catholic Du Pin's use of the distinction is 'unfortunate and very dangerous' – from a Catholic point of view.)

The context for Bayle's introduction of the distinction is a long argument against the putative infallibility of the Church, either of the Pope or
Church Councils, or of both together. Given the Jansenist use of the distinction, and the assumed fallibility with respect to questions *de fait*,
Bayle thinks 'it follows that the only deference that the Roman Church
can reasonably demand of us is that we blindly submit to her in questions
de droit. And this we will not refuse her; for what are these questions *de
droit* in our view? I hardly find but one, which is to know whether all that
God has revealed is true; and on that I respond to her in the name of all
Protestants, that provided she decides it in the affirmative, as she does,
we will all subscribe to her decision without examination.'[72]

Hardly one such question, he says; but in fact there is none at all, at least
none that is decided on the Church's authority, because the affirmative
answer that Bayle requires must be validated independently of anything
the Church might say. In submitting to the Church, or conditionally
offering to do so, Bayle is clearly being ironic. Beyond this single, predetermined question, all else is a question *de fait*, not only on the idolatry-
related issues such as feast-days, worship of relics, and so on, that Bayle
constantly harps on, but also on what God has revealed on a given topic.
Once the initial premise of faith only in God has been accepted, then the
entire field is occupied by positive theology – scholarship with respect
to Scripture of the sort that Bayle exhibited in the *Dictionnaire* with
respect to the whole of human knowledge. In sum, Bayle exploits the
alleged concession of fallibility on matters *de fait* with respect to the
interpretation of Jansenius's book to argue the same conclusion with
respect to the whole of Scripture. To put it still another way, he introduces the distinction only to subvert it. Even if the Church were infallible, he argues, each individual would have to be infallible in order to
interpret what the Church has to say. The resulting breakdown of the
distinction is welcomed by Bayle because 'acts of faith must be performed every day, without hesitation or wavering,' which could not be
if so many questions *de fait* had to be decided by the fallible ecclesiastical
bureaucracy.[73]

An important context in which Bayle in effect argues that there are no
questions *de droit* to be decided on authority other than God's occurs in

---

72 *OD* II, 138.
73 *Crit. gen. OD* II, 141.

his response to one of the four charges laid against the *Dictionnaire* by the Walloon Consistory in Rotterdam. Against the charge that what he had said about Pyrrhonism was prejudicial to religion, Bayle first establishes the following 'maxim,' as he calls it: 'That Christianity is of a supernatural order, and centres in the supreme authority of God proposing mysteries to us, not that we may comprehend them, but that we may believe them with all the humility that is due the infinite being, who can neither deceive nor be deceived.' From this it follows, according to Bayle, that there is a radical cleavage between the tribunals of philosophy and of religion, and it looks as if he sees only one question ever coming before the latter tribunal. 'Any dispute concerning question *de droit* or the reasonableness of the thing ought immediately to rejected at the outset [*dès le premier mot*]. No man ought to be admitted to examine whether we ought to believe what God commands to be believed. It ought to be reckoned a first principle in point of religion. It is the part of Metaphysicians to examine, whether there is a God and whether he be infallible; but Christians, as Christians, ought to suppose it as a thing already determined. The question then is only a matter of fact [*question de fait*]; viz. whether God requires our belief in this or that thing. Two sorts of people may doubt of it; they who do not believe the Scripture to be of divine inspiration, and they who do not think the sense of the Revelation to be such as is put upon it by this or that sect. The only dispute that Christians can enter with Philosophers, is on this question *de fait*; Whether the Scripture was written by inspired authors? If the arguments the Christians allege on this subject do not convince the Philosophers, they ought to break off the dispute,' for the rest is irrelevant detail.[74]

Perhaps the most interesting question here is one that has already been seen, that is, whether the *fait-droit* distinction might not be applied to divine infallibility, with the same subversive consequences. The question has great urgency given the biblical conception of God as *hidden* [*Deus absconditus*], and especially for Bayle, who was nearly obsessed with the question of idolatry, which for him was a question *de fait*. When the children of Israel worship the golden calf, they make a *factual*, or *cognitive* error, not a volitional one. The question thus has enormous ramifications, but a short answer to it is as follows.[75] It may be a question *de*

---

74 *Dict.* V, 830.

75 The longer answer is in terms of Bayle's rejection of speculative theology, on which the distinction rests, and his insistence on both positive theology and, especially, dialogue as the only acceptable forms of 'explanation' – in conversation, even problems of meaning can be, if not resolved, at least ameliorated.

fait whether a person with whom one converses, or whose words one reads, is God, or whether His words mean what they appear to do, or whether one understands them at all, etc. But it is a question about which one can achieve moral certainty, that is, the sort of certainty on which one is prepared to risk one's life (or salvation). In any case, the question does not preclude accepting what (we believe) He says because He is (believed to be) God. What distinguishes Bayle from those like Locke, Leclerc, La Placette, and other liberal Protestants who leaned towards deism in looking for philosophical answers to the question *de droit* is that his reliance on God is blind and utterly without rational foundation. However often he may cite God's inability to deceive or be deceived, he does not accept what God says because of divine veracity. Indeed, all the rational evidence – witness the problem of evil – argues against accepting what God says.

La Placette, in particular, saw Bayle as committed to 'the total extinction of reason,' and he devoted a book to combating the Pyrrhonism[76] that he, like the Walloon Consistory, found in Bayle. It is important for the connection between scepticism and Jansenism that in this work La Placette also criticizes the Port-Royal *Logic*.[77] The context is a defence of reason, which in matters of faith cannot be blind as Bayle would have it, for among other difficulties, we would then have no way of arguing the divinity of Scripture from certain marks it bears and no way of interpreting it since rules of interpretation are validated and applied by reason. Here is the text from the Port-Royal *Logic* quoted by La Placette: 'It is certain that divine faith should have more power over the mind than our own reason. This is because reason itself shows us that we must always prefer what is more certain to what is less certain, and that it is more certain that what God says is true than what our reason convinces us of, because God is less capable of misleading us than our reason is capable of being misled.'[78] According to La Placette, nothing is more certain than what God says is true, for even atheists would agree that veracity is contained in the idea of a perfect being. But then, in effect drawing a version of the *fait-droit* distinction, he argues that *every* act of faith depends on a much less certain proposition, namely that something has been said by God, which is very much a matter of dispute, not

---

76 *Réponse*, chap. 2. La Placette takes Pyrrhonism to be an incurable form of negative atheism that does not deny the existence of God so much as refuse to affirm it.
77 Ibid, part 1, chap. 16, 119ff.
78 Part 4, chap. 2. Buroker trans., 262.

only among atheists, but even among Christians. Many other propositions can be known more certainly by reason. (As an example, he actually quotes without acknowledgment the *Logic*'s Cartesian principle that what is manifestly contained in the idea of a thing can be affirmed of that thing.)

The drift of La Placette's criticism is clearly towards deism: 'The grand source of the author's illusion [presumably, Arnauld's] in this passage is that he has regarded the certitude of divine faith and that of reason as two collateral certitudes independent of each other. On this basis he thought we could ask which was greater. He did not observe that the certitude of reason enters that of faith, and that the certitude of faith is based on that of reason, such that if reason had none faith would be absolutely destitute of it.'[79] One wonders here, as in Locke's chapters on faith and reason, which La Placette had probably read since he elsewhere cites the *Essay*, just what role remains for faith. La Placette implicitly invokes Arnauld's own *fait-droit* distinction to show, against Bayle, that faith depends on reason to the point of being in principle dispensable in favour of reason.[80]

The three-cornered opposition between Bayle, Arnauld, and La Placette is further complicated by La Placette's failure to read the *Logic* at all carefully. He correctly addresses Bayle's view with the passage he cites from the *Logic*, but only if – and this is very unlikely – the notion of reason appealed to in the passage is one transcending the Cartesian notion of objectively compelling clear and distinct ideas, which is La Placette's own notion.[81] Moreover, the passage misrepresents, at least at an obvious level, the *Logic* itself, which is very close to La Placette's own position. For in the very passage previous to the one cited by La Placette, Arnauld holds that 'it is certain that faith always presupposes some

79 *Réponse*, 124.

80 A complication is that, as we have seen, Bayle also acknowledged, at least *ad hominem*, the dependence of questions *de droit* on questions *de fait*. Thus, it should not be surprising that Bayle was read by others, later in the Enlightenment, as a deist himself.

81 This claim about La Placette's own notion of reason may be something of a Procrustean bed. He in fact distinguishes three notions of reason: 1) the faculty of conceiving, judging and reasoning, in whatever way it applies itself and whatever light it follows; 2) this faculty restricted to the natural light; 3) the natural light itself, which he takes to involve either innate notions or the evidence of the senses. The first notion is nominally close to the notion that can be attributed to Bayle, and La Placette even explicitly attributes to it the faculty of discoursing (20). But the rationalistic, deistic tone and drift of La Placette's work seems clearly to preclude anything like a Bakhtinian reading of him.

reason.' It is reason that persuades us that some things beyond it ought to be believed, specifically that God ought to be believed and that through miracles He indicates what is to be believed. In fact, according to this text, to believe blindly and unreasonably is the origin of false religions. Arnauld wants a sharp distinction between faith and reason, authority and evidence, belief and knowledge.[82] A great service of Descartes was to make these distinctions, and by securing reason against scepticism, to strengthen faith. 'To ballyhoo scepticism as much as Huet has done in his critique of Descartes is to upset religion, for faith is based on Revelation, about which we must be assured through knowledge of certain facts. If therefore there are no human facts that are not uncertain, there is nothing on which the faith might be based.'[83] Indeed, because of his own confidence in reason, Descartes is accused by Arnauld of having gone too far, of having embraced Pelagianism; 'his letters are full of it,' he says.[84]

Yet for Arnauld there is no incompatibility between the two orders. They are 'autonomous but not independent.'[85] Here, Arnauld's worry is with respect to apologetics. If there were an opposition between faith and reason, the freethinker or the infidel could not be brought to a belief in Scripture that was presented to him as contrary to his reason. Such a mechanical process of conversion would make no more sense to Bayle than the objective conception of reason on which it is based. Both involve an abdication of responsibility, authenticity, humanity.

Moreover, Arnauld's grounding of faith in reason invokes a notion of reason that Bayle rejects. For him, reason is open-ended in a way that it is not for Arnauld. To put it dramatically, for him it is always an open question whether one ought to be reasonable *given any sense of the term 'reasonable'*. The open-endedness of this question is what he argues in a celebrated text concerning the reasonableness of sceptical doubt given certain arguments for it. Here, reason 'confounds itself; for if it were solid, it would prove that it is certain that we must doubt. Therefore there would be some certainty, there would be a certain rule of truth.

---

82 Cf. Ndiaye, *La philosophie d'Antoine Arnauld*, 272–83.
83 *OA* III, 425. Another Cartesian, Malebranche, makes these distinctions, even paradigmatically: 'to be among the faithful, it is necessary to believe blindly, but to be a philosopher, it is necessary to see with evidence.' *OC* I, 425. He winds up in his treatment of the orders of nature and grace making both subject to reason.
84 *OA* I, 671.
85 Ndiaye, *La philosophie*, 281.

That system [of scepticism] would be destroyed by it; but you need not fear that things would come to that: the reasons for doubting are doubtful themselves: one must therefore doubt whether he ought to doubt. What chaos! What torment for the Mind!'[86] The only way out of the rational chaos and torment, which is an otherwise permanent state for the mind, is, as the sequel of the text makes clear, by faith. That faith is the only way out is a key premise in Bayle's argument for toleration. For no appeal can be made to an objective, intersubjectively valid standard of truth as a basis for constraining belief.

86 Art. Pyrrho, rem. C.

4

Toleration

16: Mistaken Identity

Le Carla, where Bayle was born and spent the first two decades of his life, lies in the foothills of the Pyrenees. Not three miles away, up a hill to the south-east, lies Artigat, where, a century before his birth, there took place a series of events that was to be a prime illustration of Bayle's conception of toleration. The events contain the elements of irresistible drama: love, death, longing, war, envy, legal confrontation, and most crucially, mistaken identity. There are other cases that he repeats, but none has these or any other elements to make them so compelling.

Martin de Guerre and Bertrande de Rols were joined as young teen-agers in a marriage that was not consummated until its eighth year, because, it seems, of the husband's lack of vigour and general inability to commit himself or relate to others. The picture of him is one that would not have inspired in Bertrande anything but general regret. A child was finally born of the marriage, but at age twenty-four Martin stole from his father and left Artigat, eventually to serve in the Spanish army in Picardy. There, fighting against the French, he lost a leg and, perhaps, encountered Arnaud de Tilh, who in any case somehow learned enough about Martin's life to impersonate him in Artigat eight years after he had left. Arnaud seems to have been as outgoing, capable, and amiable as Martin was withdrawn, inept, and melancholic. Perhaps in part because of these changes for the better, Arnaud's impersonation was accepted by many in Artigat, including Bertrande. Some did not accept him, however, including Martin's uncle and mother-in-law, who were married, and who stood to lose property because of Martin's reappearance. In 1560, they successfully brought suit in Rieux. They were about to lose against an appeal to the court at Toulouse, however, when Martin himself returned on wooden leg to reclaim his life, including his wife, who could not but recognize him. The impersonator, Arnaud, was executed.[1]

The story of these events has been retold locally in Artigat from the sixteenth century even to the present, so it is likely Bayle first heard it as part of the region's oral history. But the case was far from unknown outside the region. Montaigne, for example, was present in Toulouse for the verdict and discusses the case in his *Essays*. The case was written up by, among others, the prosecutor in Toulouse, Jean de Gras, in what became not only a best-seller, but also a central text for anyone training in jurisprudence.[2] Bayle's interest in the case relates to the morality of Bertrande's life with Arnaud. By submitting to a man she thinks her husband, says Bayle, Bertrande is not only innocent, but performs her duty in what would otherwise be an act of adultery. The self-evidence of the case becomes for Bayle a primary argument by analogy for his view that conscience, whether true or errant, always obliges.

There are remarkably many literary uses in the period of the problems posed by mistaken identity in sexual liaisons. Perhaps most famous, certainly most relevant, is Molière's *Amphitryon*, first performed in 1668. Molière based his play on Plautus's version, as did Dryden, who also drew on Molière, as did Kleist; but the story is transcultural. Voltaire, for example, reports a version of the story among the Brahmins in India.[3] Molière's play is, of course, a comedy, but one through which there runs a poignant ambivalence, specifically with respect to the significance of the deceived wife's behaviour. 'Nature sometimes produces resemblances, of which some impostors have availed themselves to deceive; but it is preposterous that, under such a semblance, a man should pass himself off as a husband; and in such a case there are a thousand differences which a wife can easily detect.'[4] In this case, however, the deception is divine – it is no less than Jupiter himself who deceives Alcmena, wife of Amphitryon – and a major resolution of the play is how the deceived Amphitryon none the less prevails against the god. He is told near the end by Jupiter: 'I see

---

1 For more of the story, see N.Z. Davis, *The Return of Martin Guerre*.

2 Ibid, 115. Gras was a Protestant, and was later lynched after St Bartholomew's Day. Davis speculates about the significance of Gras's Protestantism, 107.

3 Molière, 231–7. Bayle thought Plautus's play to be his best, but Molière's version to be much better. See art. Amphitryon, rem. B.

4 Molière, 284. Did Bertrande detect such differences? For someone who thought so, see Gayot de Pitival, I, chap. 1.

no reason in it that your love [for Alcmena] should murmur, and it is I, god as I am who ... should be jealous.' Even so, Amphitryon's position is unresolved; in his last important statement he says: 'Ah! in the matter in question, a simple error becomes a real crime, and against its will innocence perishes in it. Such errors, look at them in whatever light you will, touch us in the most delicate parts; and reason often pardons them, when honour and love cannot do so.'[5] And the play ends with Sosia, the servant of Amphitryon, originally played by Molière himself, offering this observation: 'It is always best in these matters to say nothing.' Bayle picks up on both the theme of triumph over divine deception and the residual ambivalence.[6] But the latter he attributes to man's irrationality and the corruption of the world, whence spring suspicion, both justified and specious. In moral terms, however, the case is perfectly clear to Bayle.[7]

To highlight Bayle's view, and especially its distinction from Jurieu's, one might begin with a surprising conclusion Bayle draws concerning the impostor's moral position given the deceived wife's position. According to Bayle, the impostor has the right to treat her as his wife because she, thinking he is her husband, has the duty to submit to him. 'It does not follow, however, that he can innocently exercise his rights; for since he has acquired them through an immoral ruse, he cannot enjoy them without being guilty.[8] Sovereigns have the right to inflict injustice on their subjects because it is not permitted to subjects to oppose them, and yet sovereigns cannot exercise this right without culpability before God.'[9] That someone should have a right the exercise of which is wrong seems to be a flat contradiction, however; one may lose

---

5 Molière, 296.

6 He quotes from Jupiter's words of consolation to Amphitryon: 'Jupiter orné de sa gloire immortelle / Par lui-meme n'a pu triompher de sa foi / Et ... ce qu'il a reçu d'elle / N'a pas son coeur ardent été donné qu' à toi' (*Nouvelles lettres* IX, xiii; *OD* II, 225).

7 In art. Alcmena, rem. B, Bayle observes that the author of the *Nouvelles lettres* makes use of the example of Bertrande de Rols to show that ignorance exculpates and that 'a thousand things may be said upon this Subject.' Alas, the great deal he says here is restricted to versions of the story, without commentary on their significance. The same is true of the article Amphitryon. The example, of course, occurs in the *Commentaire philosophique* (II, x; *OD* II, 442).

8 It is an interesting question how this case differs from Kilcullen's case of the illegitimate ruler who according to Bayle's theory is a priori guilty of seizing power, and only on a case by case basis for what he may do with it. Putting oneself in a state of ignorance, like drunkenness, which is the kind of case Kilcullen wants to analyse in terms of Bayle's theory, may be very different from deceiving wives and seizing power where consciousness and conscience persist.

9 *Nouvelles lettres* IX, xiii; *OD* II, 225.

a right to do something the performance of which thus becomes wrong, but that is not to wrongly exercise the right. So what is going on?

Bayle begins with a plausible intuition about the deceived wife's duty but finds that in conjunction with the principle that duties entail rights a problematic conclusion follows: the impostor *ipso facto* has rights. Just to the extent that deception is successful, it generates a right for the impostor. Since this is intuitively implausible, he denies the impostor the exercise of the right; to avoid (or perhaps explain, or mitigate) this outcome, he draws a distinction between two kinds of rights. Against the objection that he contradicts himself by saying that the king may have rights the exercise of which is wrong,[10] Bayle responds that there are two notions of right: immunity from punishment and justice.[11] Kings, who are answerable only to God, always act with a right of the first sort, but not always with the second. This distinction does not help, however, for the impostor husband is not a king and hence has a right of neither sort. And here a dead end is reached. Why has Bayle pointed us down this road in the first place?[12]

He argues in this direction because the wife's duty and hence right to perform what would otherwise be wrong is crucial to his case for toleration. Bona fide heretics, whoever they may be, are in the same situation as the deceived wife; in both cases conscience determines duty, and the individual should be autonomous. Bayle's intolerant critic Jurieu accepts the principle that duties entail rights (and conversely), but denies that one can ever have a duty to do what is forbidden by God. For Bayle, to obey conscience is to obey God, but Jurieu finds it bizarre that God should 'cede His rights and authority to an erring conscience that commands contrary to what God commands.'[13] Jurieu is respond-

---

10 *Crit. gen.* II, x; *OD* II, 94.

11 *Nouvelles lettres* IX, i; *OD* II, 218.

12 Kilcullen tries to avoid the paradox of a right that it would be wrong to exercise as follows. If I mistakenly believe that I have a duty to you, then it would be wrong for me not to do it and for you to *blame* me for doing it, but wrong for you to *call on* me to do it (unless you shared my mistaken belief). Kilcullen, 63–4. But this may be no less paradoxical. If I do what it would be wrong not to do, then presumably you should not only *not blame* me, but even *praise* me for doing it. Kilcullen seems to think that Bayle just ignores this implication (ibid, 71, n. 60). How Bayle can do so is not clear. Perhaps the idea is that, while blame would violate my conscience, and thus be wrong, praise would go too far; for I am still acting on a false belief that it may well be your duty to change, not entrench. So I am allowed to act, but finding no praise I begin to examine the basis for my action.

13 *Le vray système*, 193–4.

ing to another intuition, no less plausible and one that is shared by many from Plato to G.E. Moore, namely, that no one can have a duty to do what is objectively wrong. One might accommodate both intuitions with the distinction between agent and act morality: what the wife does is wrong and should be prevented (act morality), but that she is doing it is none the less praiseworthy (agent morality).[14] But this is to miss what is at issue in the historical case – moral autonomy and toleration. For Bayle, the connection between rights and duties cuts across the act/agent distinction as follows. If the heretic has a duty to act as he believes, then he has a right to do so; but if he has a right to do so, then the magistrate has a duty not to interfere. Because the individual conscience is autonomous, it ought to be tolerated.[15]

17: Context and Kinds of Argument

The debate between Jurieu and Bayle was set in a larger context of previous, and ongoing, debates between, among others, Jurieu and each of Maimbourg, Arnauld, and Nicole, and between the latter two and Jean Claude. Significantly, the saw-off between Bayle and Jurieu was, unlike the others, which posed Catholics against Protestants, wholly within the Protestant camp. A key text, in any case, is Bayle's *Nouvelles lettres de l'auteur de la critique générale de l'Histoire du Calvinisme de M. Maimbourg* (1682), which sets out the version of the doctrine of the erring conscience criticized by Jurieu in his *Le vray système de l'Eglise*. The ninth of Bayle's *Lettres* may indeed be, as it has recently been called, 'decisive.' 'In a few pages, the essence of Bayle's theory of toleration is set out, and, in a sense, the *Commentaire philosophique* was to be only a detailed development of these few key ideas.'[16] Jurieu's criticism occasioned the full-blown version of Bayle's doctrine in the *Commentaire philosophique [on the words of Jesus Christ, 'compel them to enter,' in which it is proved by several demonstrative arguments that there is nothing more abominable than forced conversions and in which all the sophisms of those forcing conversion and the*

14 This standard distinction thus does not assign contrary moral attributes to the same object as does relativism, but to different objects (act and agent).

15 The question becomes more complicated when, as too often happens, the individual conscience calls for persecution. Bayle seems not to have fully thought out this question, certainly not to have expressed a full answer to it. His best answer would seem to be that the conscientious persecutor should be restrained, but in a way that least poses a direct threat of temptation to conscience. See Kilcullen, 97–9.

16 E. Labrousse, 'La tolérance,' 250; *Notes sur Bayle*, 180.

apology of St Augustine for persecution are refuted]. The full title of Bayle's work conveniently and accurately indicates its contents, although it belies the liveliness and accessibility of the work.

Sorting out the precise context of Bayle's work is important, not only for the interpretation of its individual arguments, which obviously depends on the target they are aimed at, but also, as will shortly be argued, for the the characterization of the kind of argument that Bayle is prepared to make in a given work. One account has it, in any case, that Bayle was disturbed by the libelous character of Jurieu's *L'Esprit de M. Arnauld* as a response to the great Jansenist's *Apologie* and wrote the *Nouvelles lettres* as his own response. That is, the attack from Arnauld was too important to be answered only by the 'hodge-podge of actual facts and calumnious gossip' that Jurieu's book was, however 'brilliant' it might also have been. Coming as it does from the most authoritative of our Bayle scholars, the account commands attention.[17]

While not impossible, Labrousse's account is difficult to accept, for three reasons. First, the only evidence cited of Bayle's dissatisfaction with Jurieu's work comes much later, in 1691, by which time global relations between Bayle and Jurieu had soured. At this later date, Bayle is supposed to have delivered a devastating verdict on Jurieu's book, but even at this later date the single relevant sentence from the passage referred to by Labrousse says only, and only incidentally, that Jurieu 'has published many books that serve to confirm the papists in their errors through the dreadful idea that they make for themselves of our Communion by focusing on the tone in which he writes, a style of writing such that if you wanted to depict him, you would give him only claws and teeth and none of the attractive mildness that characterizes the Gospel.'[18]

In 1685 and as yet uncut by Jurieu's teeth and claws, Bayle was supposedly silent about Jurieu's book, according to Labrousse, taking no notice of it in the *Nouvelles de la République des Lettres*, for example. But the reasons for Bayle's failure to review the book are at least a matter of dispute,[19] and in any case Bayle discusses it in his own work. The *Nouvelles lettres* describes Jurieu's *Esprit de M. Arnauld* in unmistakably glowing terms as a book 'capable of delivering a death blow to this hero

---

17 Ibid. The length and detail of the disagreement here with Labrousse's account testifies to her authority.
18 *La Chimère; OD* II, 739.
19 Labrousse, 'La tolérance,' 249–50; *Notes sur Bayle*, 179–80.

of Jansenism, and of simultaneously avenging both the Jesuits and the Huguenots for all the insults they have received from the Messieurs of Port-Royal.' Bayle says that it is an interesting book, full of unusual and amusing information and commentary, with something in it for everybody – subtlety, precision, wit, political commentary, theological and philosophical sophistication, etc. – and that to be attacked by such a book is very damaging indeed. Perhaps most relevantly, 'the style is throughout so full of fire, clarity and charm that it by itself would make the book valuable.'[20] No one with such views as these on Jurieu's book could have been motivated by disappointment in it to write the enormous work that Bayle produced in the *Nouvelles lettres*.

A second reason why Bayle would not have been entering the Arnauld-Jurieu fray is a strategic consideration. Arnauld's *Apologie* was a response to Jurieu's *Politique du clergé*, and no doubt the tone of the exchange did not harmonize with Bayle's tenor, as it were; but the screeching was not limited to Jurieu. On the contrary, Arnauld was no less shrill. How, then, could Bayle have responded to Arnauld out of dissatisfaction with Jurieu? He could not plausibly have thought that the understated, ironical, *Dictionnaire*-adumbrating style of the *Nouvelles lettres* would be an effective reply to the firebrand Arnauld. For one thing, the only real audience for the book was the French Protestant community *outside* France, which apparently was disappointed by Bayle's lack of fire. (Unusually for Bayle, the work was not a great publishing success.[21])

A final reason for reading the *Nouvelles lettres* as other than a response to Arnauld concerns chronology. The twenty-two new letters respond to eighteen objections supposedly raised against the *Critique générale*. The objections do not come from Arnauld, at least not in his *Apologie*. The first volume of that work appeared in 1681, the second in July of 1682; the *Critique générale* had appeared in March of 1682. The chronology makes it barely possible that Arnauld was mounting an attack on Bayle, but it is just not there. Rather, Arnauld has his aim securely fixed on Jurieu, and thus defends Bossuet in his dispute with Jurieu. Bayle would not attack Arnauld by fabricating objections to a work unrelated to these other disputes. Although the *Nouvelles lettres* is a polemical work that deals with nominally the same topic that drives the Arnauld-Jurieu dispute, it cannot plausibly be interpreted as a part of that dispute.

20 *Nouvelles lettres* I, vii; *OD* II, 206.
21 Labrousse, 'La tolérance,' 247–8; *Notes sur Bayle*, 177–8.

What was Bayle up to, then, and why does the question matter? It seems obvious that, as the title suggests, and the preface confirms, the *Nouvelles lettres* is a continuation of the *Critique générale*, and that Maimbourg, not Arnauld, is the target. Quite apart from the specific target, the significance of the question lies in how the *Nouvelles lettres* is to be read. A reading hypothesis would be the following. If Arnauld's *Apologie* contains a fair amount of Church history, its thrust lies in contemporary political, and to some extent, philosophical argument. Like Arnauld's work, Bayle's *Nouvelle lettres* debates the Reformation, but does so, like Maimbourg's work, primarily in historical terms. Bayle takes up the debate in philosophical terms only in the *Commentaire philosophique* and in political terms in *La France toute Catholique*.

For Bayle there is not a single context, but many, and his arguments are always limited to, and by, one of them, even if the distinction between contexts is not always as clear as it seems to be here. He does not attempt to establish the truth, once and for all time, as Arnauld and Jurieu appear to think they can, but instead argues for what he takes to be the truth in a given context.[22] Thus, in the *Dictionnaire* Bayle is concerned to correct what he takes to be mistakes in previous treatments of various kinds of texts: historical, biblical, literary, philosophical, etc. The correction is always in terms of a text of the same kind – a generically restricted intertextuality, as it were. This is an important claim about Bayle's method – one, moreover, that is hard to argue with anything like conclusiveness. Perhaps, instead, it can be taken here as a reading hypothesis. In any case, if it turns out to be false, then a main premise of the argument of the epilogue below is simply false.

18: Jurieu's Condemnation of the Erring Conscience

Although not a part of the Jurieu-Arnauld debate, the *Nouvelles lettres* became part of a debate on their own. For Jurieu, without knowing the author of the work,[23] attacked it in his *Vray système* (1686), which occasioned Bayle's *Commentaire philosophique* of the same year (part 3, 1687) leading to Jurieu's *Des droits des deux souverains en religion* in the following year, which defended the right of the secular arm to extirpate heresy, and finally to Bayle's *Supplément du Commentaire philosophique*. The

---

22 The suggestion is less a double-truth theory than Tarski's 'true-in-L.'
23 Jurieu here refers to this unknown author as 'one of the best writers of our century.' *Le vray système*, 113.

dispute between the two refugees, of course, grew into a much more extensive imbroglio, but the connecting thread of this debate was the topic of toleration.

The earliest occurrence of Bayle's case for toleration was prior to the *Nouvelles lettres*, in the *Critique générale* itself. The thirteenth letter from that work is a historical examination of Maimbourg's thesis that heresy is a cause of disobedience and civil disturbance, and must therefore be extirpated by the king.[24] In additon to his historical counter-examples, Bayle argues that the persecution of perceived heresy is itself a cause for disorder. If the Calvinists and Jansenists can be persecuted in France, then Catholics can be persecuted in England, China, and Japan. Everyone believes himself to be in the true church. If anyone has the right to persecute others because they believe them to be heretical, according to Bayle, then everyone will have that same right.[25] This is Bayle's reciprocity argument.[26]

The twentieth letter from the *Critique générale* draws together the themes of the duties and hence rights of the erring conscience, of idolatry (or at least of how God may be known), and even of transubstantiation.[27] This unlikely constellation of themes will again be encountered, at length, in chapter 5 below. The context in the present case is the broad historical one of the Catholic argument from prescription; according to this *argumentum antiquitatis*, the Catholic Church has greater claim to being the true church than the Reformed Church because it is older.[28]

Bayle's rebuttal of the argument from prescription is that it makes all conversion impossible. Louis may justify his religion as that of Clovis, but Clovis himself, like Constantine, was a convert from a still older religion. On the other hand, to say that by embracing Catholicism Clovis and Constantine converted to the true church but that, by embracing the Reform, Elizabeth of England left the true church is to give up the argument by prescription and to take up precisely the historical question on which Bayle thinks the issue rests. And that question is not to be decided, according to Bayle, by distinguishing, as Maimbourg does, the conversions of Clovis and Constantine from the conversion of Elizabeth on the

24 *OD* II, 54–60.
25 Ibid, 56–7.
26 As Kilcullen calls it. For a discussion of the argument, and a resolution of difficulties in it that depends on making a distinction between act and agent morality in Bayle's theory, see Kilcullen, 89–93.
27 *OD* II, 85–8.
28 See, especially, Rex.

basis of miracles alleged to attend the former but not the latter. For the only result of miracles, visions, special signs, etc. is the production of belief in those who experience them; but belief in those who do not experience them can be just as strong. Moreover, belief without such miracles, visions, and special signs, is worthier, as is evident by the episode of the doubting apostle Thomas, the words of Christ against those who require them for belief, and the Catholic view itself on transubstantiation, which is believed contrary to reason and common sense. The true church, whichever it may be, and its rivals are, all other things being equal, on an equal footing (as far as we can tell) with respect to conversion, appeals to age, and grounds for conviction generally. From all of this Bayle employs the reciprocity argument to draw the conclusion that the true church, 'whichever it may be,' has no more right to use force against others than they have to use force against it. The only basis for such persecution would be the conviction that every other church is a false church, but that conviction is only a conviction, never knowledge, and it is one possessed by every church – by definition, one might add.[29]

A still earlier version of the argument is to be found, surprisingly, in Jurieu's *Politique du clergé de France* (1681), a work that Bayle was familiar with before he wrote the *Critique générale*.[30] Here Jurieu sets out his standard view that the prince should not tolerate religions contrary to the fundamentals of Christianity, at least to the extent of not allowing their introduction into the realm. But he also sets out the following positions (contrary to what he saw in the current practices of Catholic France). In the moral sphere, it is good for the prince to lead his subjects to the true religion, but only by means approved by that religion and not by violence and bad faith. In the political sphere, in any case, it is false that a single religion is necessary for a great, flourishing, and peaceful state. Why? First, because history shows that a multiplicity of sects yields the prince greater authority in dealing with the whole; but also because otherwise the pagan emperors would have been justified in their persecution of the Christians. 'There is no man who is not con-

---

29 *Crit. gén.* xx; *OD* II, 87. See also ibid, xx; *OD* II, 94, where Bayle uses the same argument to attack the literal interpretation of Luke 14: 23.

30 Bayle cites Jurieu's work to counter Maimbourg's parity-of-treatment argument: Louis is justified in persecuting Protestants because Catholics are persecuted in Protestant countries. Not incidentally, Bayle calls Jurieu 'one of our best writers' (*Crit. gén.* xxiii, i; *OD* II, 103–4. This work is not directed any more than the *Nouvelles lettres* against Arnauld, who comes up only incidentally because of the suppression in France of his *Apologie*, 'as angry a book as can be written' (ibid; *OD* II, 154).

vinced that he is in the true religion. The Great Sultan believes himself to be on the road to salvation just as the Christian king does.'[31] This is the reciprocity argument, or at least its most important premise.

Jurieu certainly did not draw out the consequences of this premise as Bayle did. Moreover, he became an unrelenting opponent of toleration, at least in the form that it was being advocated by Bayle. The reasons for the change in Jurieu's attitude are not clear. Bayle himself later regarded Jurieu's reversal on the question of toleration to have been a result of what Jurieu took to be a revelation from on high concerning an impending overthrow of papism.[32] But this psycho-supernatural explanation, however seriously or not it was intended by Bayle, does not take into account Jurieu's arguments. Moreover, it does not address the considerable difficulty even in establishing the differences between the views of Jurieu and Bayle himself.

In his *Vray système* (1686), written principally against Nicole's *Prétendus reformés*, Jurieu preached a doctrine of limited toleration – of what Bayle derisively referred to as semi-toleration.[33] Not all sects, but only those that are both consistent with the foundations of the (Christian) Church and established in the jurisdiction, should be tolerated. Otherwise, although 'death, iron and fire are means whose use is entirely contrary to the spirit of the Gospel and the intentions of God,' they may none the less be used when God, in order to punish His Church, as He often does, allows schisms to develop with such rapidity that violence is the only way to deal with them.[34] Now, according to Jurieu, Calvinists are not schismatics and in France, at least, they do satisfy the two conditions above; hence they should not be persecuted there. As he later puts it, addressing the objection that his position gives no basis for exacting the terms of a contract (the Edict of Nantes is the obvious case), 'it is necessary to distinguish between heretics and heretics';[35] the difference between Catholics and Calvinists is not the difference between them and Socinians or pagans. (Disguise of special pleading, or subtlety of

31 *La politique*, 226–9.
32 The change 'from white to black' on this question of whether the magistrate is right to use his authority in stopping idolatry and preventing the spread of heresy was, according to Bayle, one to which Jurieu succeeded in leading the Synod of Walloon churches of the United Province and one that Augustine had made in response to the Donatist heresy. Art. Augustin, rem. H.
33 *Comm. phil.* II, vii; *OD* II, 421.
34 *Le vray système*, 177.
35 Ibid, 202.

any sort, was not Jurieu's strength – or concern here either, for after all he was soon to be convinced that the Edict of Nantes would be restored, that Louis would convert, and that Calvinism would prevail.) The principle, on which Jurieu repeatedly insists, is that only (an objective) justice and truth yield right. To think (erroneously, of course, but even if correctly) that one is punishing heresy (and therefore doing the right thing) does not give one the right to punish it. If one does have the right to punish heresy, as when the two conditions for toleration noted above are not satisfied, only the fact of the heresy gives this right.

For Bayle, by contrast, the persecution of heresy, if it is ever justified, would be justified by the belief that one has a duty to persecute it. Now, Bayle himself believes that in certain cases heresy should be persecuted. Or at least this is what he claims. Whether on his own principles he should hold that belief is another matter.[36] In the present context, the distinction between what Bayle said and what he ought to have said is irrelevant. For it is also his view that conscience is autonomous in that belief that one has a duty entails that one has that duty. It is important that the example, the persecution of heresy, not mislead us here as to what is at issue, the basis for duty, whether with respect to heresy or anything else. The complication is that according to Bayle's principles, heresy should not be persecuted because the basis for duty is belief.

This view was the main target of Jurieu's attack. Without knowing that Bayle was the author, Jurieu attacks his claims that 'error dressed as truth has all the rights of truth itself,' and that 'the rights of truth depend absolutely on the condition that it be known.'[37] He distinguishes between errors *de fait* and errors *de droit*. The distinction here is between matters of fact, which are knowable with limited certainty, and with respect to which error exculpates, and moral values, which are knowable with full certainty, and with respect to which error inculpates. When a man kills his father innocently mistaking him for an enemy, he is innocent. But the man is guilty who knowingly kills his father thinking that some injustice committed against him by his father justifies the killing.[38] The difference

36 See Lennon, 'Bayle, Locke and the Metaphysics of Toleration.'
37 The term that Bayle had used in the first claim is *revetu*, 'clothed'; the term Jurieu uses, however, is *travesti*, which in the seventeenth century also had the meaning of 'cross-dressed' (*Le vray système*, 183; *Nouvelles lettres* ix; *OD* II, 219, 221). Even so, Bayle later allowed that his language was 'a little too raw and undigested' for a 'subject in which the delicacy of the reader should be spared.' (*Comm. phil.* II, x; *OD* II, 433).
38 The distinction is to be found, with a remarkable example, in Aquinas, *Summa theologica*, 1a–2ae, xix.6. Gilbey, 292.

is that 'truths *de droit* wear on their face their distinguishing characteristics, and those who do not see them are not worthy of being excused. For it is cupidity, corruption of the heart, prejudice, pride – the human passions that cast them in shadow. But truths *de fait* are never perceptible by themselves; their evidence always depends on external things that can be separated, counterfeited and assumed.'[39] Ignorance always incriminates if the act done in ignorance violates the moral law. 'One is always culpable in acting according to an ignorant conscience ... The will never sins without some error in the understanding, but the error that produces the crime does not diminish it.'[40]

But factual ignorance may, at least sometimes, fail to incriminate, according to Jurieu. Perhaps it never incriminates. Jurieu's treatment of Bayle's second claim in particular, namely, that truth is relevant only if known, suggests that apparent instances of culpable ignorance *de fait* are in fact instances of ignorance *de droit*.[41] To develop the idea rather beyond anything Jurieu says, it might be that the crime one commits when one, in a drunken state, and thus ignorant of what one is doing, kills somebody, is not one of murder, for murder was not willingly committed, nor one of being drunk, even exacerbated by subsequent bad luck, but one of moral ignorance – one should have known better. (To allow that factual ignorance exculpates, but to insist that moral ignorance is not factual, tends to expand the scope of culpability and thus the grounds for persecution. Of this, more below.) For Bayle, the crime is getting drunk, and the subsequent luck, good or bad, is irrelevant; but he builds the moral weight into what is in fact known before or while getting drunk. As Kilcullen puts it: 'On Bayle's theory, someone who drinks, knowing that he may drive under the influence of alcohol and that this may lead to an accident, is very much to blame even is there is no accident, and no more to blame if there is.'[42] On the other hand, Bayle sometimes says that what is done in a state of ignorance is wrong. The woman who because of passion allows herself to be deceived by an impostor husband is guilty of the resulting carnal commerce with him, and not just of the passion that led to the deception making it possible.[43] Either way, it is not yet clear how Bayle and Jurieu really differ.

Jurieu distinguishes between his own concept of ignorance that

39 *Le vray système*, 187.
40 Ibid, 307.
41 Ibid, 189–90.
42 Kilcullen, 79.
43 *Comm. phil.* II, ix; *OD* II, 430.

exculpates an agent, as when a wife yields to an impostor husband, and Bayle's concept of ignorance that gives a right to the impostor, which he takes to be no more than an effort on Bayle's part to create a paradox for the sake of diversion. Even so, he uses the case to make the general point that being obliged to follow an erring conscience puts one in the position of being obliged to do what is explicitly forbidden by God. According to Jurieu, if the wife yields to the impostor, she is innocent because of her error *de fait*. If she does not yield, she is also innocent because it would be absurd for God to punish her for refusing a man who is not her husband. His position is that someone has a right if and only if someone else has a duty. Now, as in the case of the impostor husband, error has no rights and hence we have no duty to follow the erring conscience.[44] Bayle agrees on the mutual entailment between rights and duties, but insists that, because error dressed as truth has all the rights of truth, there is a duty on the part of the deceived wife to yield.[45]

There are two sources of error, according to Jurieu, that lead to Bayle's paradoxical result. One is to distinguish conscience and will in such a way that conscience has no obligation with respect to knowledge, and will is obligated always to follow conscience. Bayle bases duty in an intellectually blind faculty, according to Jurieu, whereas the duty to know the good is actually of a piece with the duty to pursue it. Now, at this point Jurieu seems a bit confused about what is at issue. Bayle does not disagree that we have a duty to know, or at least to seek, certain truths; his doctrine on conscience addresses the separate issue of what our duty is when, for whatever reason, we fail to reach those truths. Moreover, Jurieu does not differ in the way he thinks he does from Bayle on the rejection of separated faculties in favour of an integrated psychology. The celebrated question whether the understanding follows the will, or conversely, is a bogus one, says Jurieu; there is but one soul, called understanding when it conceives, and will when it determines itself.[46] But Bayle himself may have the most plausible version of the position that Jurieu is at best groping after: conscience as autonomous is not some internal, yet objective and other-than-self authority; it

---

44 *Le vray système*, 188–94.

45 It may well be that this connection between duty and right springs from a theory of grace and election: Those with grace as a matter of fact do what is erroneously thought to earn heaven. During the debate later in the French National Assembly over the rights of man, it was the Jansenists who insisted not only on the rights but the duties of citizens. See Christine Fauré, *Les déclarations des droits de l'homme*, 23.

46 *Le vray système*, 390–1.

is thinking or acting in good faith, which if not formally sufficient for right action according to Jurieu as it is for Bayle, is at least desirable according to him.

Another difficulty in distinguishing Bayle and Jurieu in this context stems from their views on *knowledge* of duty. Jurieu assumes not only that there is an objective action that it is our duty to perform independently of our belief, but also that we can know that action as our duty. It is one thing to know more or less obvious moral principles; it is quite another to know that an action falls under one. Such knowledge of the latter sort seems possible only if one performs the action under a description – cinematographically the same act may be either a parricide or the killing of an enemy, depending on the agent's knowledge. (Precisely this indeterminacy was the valid linchpin of Jesuit casuistry, whatever the bad-faith exploitation of it may have been. Nor did Arnauld obviate it when, against the Jesuit doctrine of philosophic sin, he argued that for sin it is sufficient to do what is wrong willingly, even if one does not know it is wrong;[47] for to do something willingly is to do it under a certain description.) With this description requirement for human agency, the difference between Jurieu and Bayle begins to evaporate, for conscience as the construer of what one does is infallible with respect to the morally relevant knowlege of what one does. Bayle's doctrine of the erring conscience is that from a moral point of view we necessarily do what we think we do. At one point Bayle seems prepared to summarize his theory of the erring conscience in just these terms. 'They once urged King Archelaus to act against someone who had thrown water on him. *It is not I whom he wetted*, responded Archelaus, *but him whom he took me for*. No philosopher reasoning on the privileges of the erring conscience ever said anything more sensible.'[48]

The other source of Bayle's error according to Jurieu is that he unduly extends the domain of conscience.[49] Jurieu does not claim, as he perhaps might, that Bayle's conception of conscience implausibly makes all beliefs and actions a matter of morality, but merely that it makes conscience decisive, with the unacceptable result that God must sometimes punish good actions and reward evil ones. Jurieu here just begs the question, of course. But in his discussion he raises an objection and then replies to it in a way that once again makes it hard, at least initially, to

---

47 See Kilcullen, 23, especially n. 56, and 37. See also sec. 13 above.
48 Art. Archelaus, rem. C.
49 *Le vray système*, 195–9.

determine the nature of the difference between his view and Bayle's. The objection is that a man who against his conscience resists a wrong action still sins – for example, a pagan who to please his Christian rulers refuses to worship his false gods and instead blasphemes them is guilty, and not just of hypocrisy. The pagan's refusal to worship his false gods is sinful, according to Jurieu, not because of the refusal itself, which is good, nor because it violates his erring conscience, which never obliges, but because 'every action without grace is a sin,' and his action is done, not from the grace of faith, but from cowardice and selfishness. This construal perhaps sounds rather like an appeal to just the sort of considerations that comprise Bayle's notion of conscience. But it is very different from that notion. Jurieu is saying that even with respect to intentions, as with respect to belief, there is a moral fact of the matter that is independent of our beliefs. The moral law calls for both actions and intentions of a certain kind. Even if we think our intentions good, they may be bad. The same contrast can be drawn even with respect to duties generated by false beliefs. Thus, there is an objective duty of obedience owed to a man whom one believes to be one's father; but the ground for the duty is just the fact of this belief (plus the relevant moral law) and not the belief, if there is one, that obedience is owed the man.[50] That is, if I believe that a man is my father, then I have a duty of obedience to him whether I believe it or not. To put it another way, believing it to be morally so does not make it morally so, as Bayle contends, but a belief is an objective fact that may be morally relevant. Jurieu wants to distinguish, as Bayle perhaps does not, between the moral *relevance* of belief and the moral *infallibility* of belief.[51]

Jurieu is prepared to justify persecution on the basis of a moral fact of the matter, including belief. The apostles have a right to preach, but not heretics, and the magistrate has the right to suppress the latter but not the former. Who judges which is which? The magistrate, at the peril of his own damnation. 'God alone is master and judge of the heart. But it is false that actions, consequent upon false thoughts of the heart, are the province of conscience and God alone. Nothing is of the realm of conscience alone but what is contained within it and does not leave it. But everything that leaves the conscience and has an effect outside it is the province of those to whom God has given the authority to rule actions and words. A mag-

50 Ibid, 188–9.
51 Infallibility in the sense that if I believe x is a duty it follows that x is a duty, although not that x is commanded by God.

istrate does not rightfully punish a fanatic who believes that all goods should be held in common, but he rightfully punishes this fanatic if he wants to act on his principles and take the goods of others.'[52] Both in the question, who judges? and Jurieu's response to it, there is a tendency to confuse two issues: the truth of a moral or political view, for example, whether heretics have the right to preach, and the result of promulgating that view, for example, whether Calvinists, who are not heretics, will be persecuted. The two come together for Jurieu because of how he views the magistrate or prince. Unless (we believe that) the magistrate has the power to determine and suppress the actions of the heretics, he thinks, society will collapse. At least in the case of the magistrate, a view about what it is right for him to do must be correct because of the results of failing to promulgate the view. Bayle, meanwhile, has a sophisticated appreciation of the distinction between the truth of a view and the results of promulgating it. Consider his response to the objection that his theory of conscience would legitimate the very persecution he was seeking to prevent by means of it. That is, if Luke 14: 23 were read by Catholics in a literal way to mean that God willed persecution, and if Catholics therefore thought it was their duty to persecute, then according to Bayle's theory it was their duty to persecute. Bayle grants the inference, but still insists that if his arguments for a figurative interpretation are sound, as he presumably thinks they are, then there is 'room to believe' that those examining them will come to a contrary view of persecution and thus a contrary duty with respect to it.[53]

19: Bayle's Reply to Jurieu

Bayle had two kinds of response to Jurieu's use of the *fait-droit* distinction. One was to diminish the significance of the distinction, first by insisting that it is the same reason in us that recognizes both errors *de droit* and errors *de fait*. Here Bayle, whether consciously or not, invokes Jurieu's own conception of an integrated psychology, the significance of which for him is that since a single conscience is the source of obligation, there is no difference with respect to obligation between ignorance of the two sorts of question. We are obliged to do what we falsely think is right (ignorance *de droit*) and we are obliged to obey a man we falsely think is our father (ignorance *de fait*). Bayle also tried to diminish the significance

52 *Le vray système*, 198–9.
53 *Comm. phil.* II, ix; *OD* II, 430. See also Rex. As has been seen at the end of sec. 16 above, however, it is a different story if the cogency of those arguments should fail.

of the distinction by reducing the scope of questions *de droit*. 'Properly speaking, there are very few questions *de droit* which do not reduce to fact, namely, whether God has revealed this or that, whether God prohibits homicide, etc., for over the question whether all that God prohibits is wrong, and all that He commands right, there is no dispute; there is dispute only about this fact, such and such thing has been prohibited or commanded by God.'[54] Just as Jurieu's tendency was to convert all morally relevant questions *de fait* into questions *de droit*, so Bayle's even clearer tendency was to treat apparent questions *de droit* as questions *de fait*. We have already seen this tendency in Bayle's response to Arnauld's use of the distinction, where the result was to upset Church infallibility. The upshot of it here is to expand the domain of what should be tolerated, for even Jurieu agrees that ignorance *de fait* exculpates.

Bayle's other sort of response to Jurieu's use of the distinction was to argue that the morally relevant consideration with respect to ignorance is simply its culpability. The kind of truth of which we are ignorant, whether *de fait* or *de droit*, makes no difference. Although matters *de droit* and matters *de fait* differ like 'black and white,' they produce (or annul) the same rights (or duties) when the ignorance is involuntary and thus inculpable. Although the woman who yields to an impostor husband because of her passion may do so out of ignorance, the ignorance is still *de fait* and no less inculpable. In the case most of interest to Bayle, heretics are not to be blamed *if they have undertaken the same investigations* as the orthodox in order to determine the correctness of their position.[55] Presumably, Bayle means that in order to be blameless the heretic must have made an effort that is in some sense responsible, and not just an effort that in some cases may have been lucky enough to yield an orthodox position. The situation might be understood in Cartesian terms. For Descartes, and many Cartesians, error occurs when we do not restrain the will's assent to what is not perceived to be clear and distinct; but sometimes we are fortunate in that our precipitate unclear and indistinct judgments none the less arrive at truth.[56] But for Bayle, unlike for Descartes, our non-precipitate judgments do not always arrive at the truth. What, then, is the difference between the heretic and the orthodox believer?

Cognitively, there is no difference between them in the sense that neither position is, in principle, defensible. For example, neither the Protestant way of examination nor the Catholic way of authority can yield any

54 *Comm. phil.* II, ix; *OD* II, 430.
55 Ibid.
56 See especially *Meditations* IV; *CSM* II, 41.

certainty. That is, neither an individual whose reading is putatively inspired by God nor an appeal to a putatively infallible Church can overcome doubts about the interpretation of Scripture. Problems just about the canonicity and translation of Scripture on the one side, and of determining the apostolic tradition on the other, defeat claims to certainty. More generally, a criterion of truth is lacking, and this is true even for those blessed with grace, which does produce conviction, but a conviction that by itself is indistinguishable from that of the heretic. As will be seen in chapter 6, grace is effectively a matter of luck, which for Bayle is in part the education we happen to receive, and education can be either good or bad, leading to error just as easily as to truth even in matters that according to Jurieu are known by all.[57] 'The prejudices of education prevent us from seeing what is in Scripture.'[58] And the difference between questions *de fait* and questions *de droit* makes no difference; 'education is certainly capable of obscuring the clarity of truths *de droit*.'[59]

Morally, there is again no difference between the heretic and the orthodox, or at least there need not be any. Grace as the basis for orthodoxy is a matter of salvation that is entirely gratuitous – as far as we are concerned, and perhaps in principle, a matter entirely of luck. The Calvinist position is that grace is a logically and morally separate domain from morality, which is a matter of good works; only grace ultimately saves, never good works, so that, although the (re-lapsed) immoral as a matter of fact are never saved, they could be. The related question of whether the moral are ever damned is rather like the magistrate's punishment of those who act according to conscience. Bayle says here that it does not follow from his view of conscience that an action done with conscience is done without crime.[60] What he must mean by such an action is one punishable by the magistrate because it is a threat to public order, as would be the bona fide efforts of atheists to proselytize, for example. God might be viewed as the magistrate who sometimes punishes bona fide actions in order to preserve Providence. This is the case of the virtuous atheist.[61]

In most general terms, Bayle's response to Jurieu is that an objective moral truth of the matter is neither necessary nor sufficient for moral action. Not all truth, but only truth 'duly revealed and announced to man'

---

57 *Comm. phil.* II, x; *OD* II, 438–9.
58 Ibid, *OD* II, 440.
59 Ibid, 442.
60 *Comm. phil.* II, ix; *OD* II, 430.
61 See Whelan (*Anatomy*, chap. 8) for Bayle's shift on whether Lucretia acts out of sinful pride in preserving her sexual virtue and killing herself when it is violated.

is of relevance.[62] But when can we take it that truth has been 'revealed and announced' to us? Co-opting Aquinas,[63] he adds that it would be imprudent to accept truth conveyed in ridiculous arguments by the impious. (The unlikely scenario is that we are asked to believe what happens to be true, indeed importantly true, but for patently fallacious reasons, and we are asked to believe it for whatever motivation of their own by bad people.) In such circumstances we do the best we can to acquire the truth, and then act accordingly. 'God proposes the truth to us in such a way as to leave it to us to engage in an examination of what is proposed to us and to enquire whether it is the truth or not. Whence it may be said that He makes no demands on us except that of carefully examining as best we can, and that He is satisfied if we then assent to objects that seem to us true and cherish them as a gift from heaven.'[64] Responsible effort to arrive at the truth, and not just good luck actually to arrive at it, is the morally relevant notion. More broadly, integrity in the search for truth, rather than the truth itself, is the basis for Bayle's moral theory.

It was noted in passing above that for Bayle a willingness to act according to conscience is *formally sufficient* for right action. That is, whatever we will to do according to conscience is *eo ipso* right. But a willingness to act according to conscience is not *materially* sufficient in that we still do not know what to do, because conscience is without content. By itself conscience provides no guidance. As doubts about her putative husband grow, the wife of Martin Guerre, for example, may well look for principles, rules or at least considerations relevant to her decision about how to respond to his demands. To tell her to follow the lights of conscience does not offer much help, for conscience is not an independent voice within one that offers such direction. But this conception of conscience as having no content may be precisely Bayle's point. A necessary condition for the morality of an action, he may be saying, is its autonomy, and his injunction to obey conscience may be nothing more than a rejection of authority.[65] (Thus the negative formulation

---

62 This is what Kilcullen (64–7) calls the argument from need for notification. He draws attention to Malebranche's view, in the *Traité de morale*, that there are an infinity of moral truths, of which only some are known to us, and to Bayle's interest in this work. Ibid, 31.

63 After an unfound secondary source, François de Sainte-Claire.

64 *Comm. phil.* II, x; *OD* II, 436. Bayle here invokes something close to Kilcullen's distinction between the ethics of belief and of assertion on the one hand, and the ethics of enquiry on the other. Kilcullen, essay IV, 139–74.

65 Kilcullen (76) makes the important point that conscience for Bayle is not an infallible agency distinct from the person, but just the person judging what is right and enforcing that judgment.

standardly given by Bayle, the sense of which is: do not act contrary to what you believe, that is, do not let yourself be imposed upon by others. The content of the judgment, meanwhile, remains open, to be decided upon in all the various ways that Bayle elsewhere discusses: grace, education, and even reason.)

20: Heresy and the Exercise of Authority

Jurieu distinguishes, as perhaps Bayle does not, between blameworthiness and failure to perform duty. *Invincible* ignorance, whether *de fait* or *de droit*, he claimed, removes blame, as in the case even of the Tartars, who were perforce ignorant of Christ. But their actions were yet wrong. One would have thought that putatively right actions would *eo ipso* merit reward, but here Jurieu draws the line between his own and Bayle's view. Such a view would empower ignorance 'to metamorphose a wrong action into a good one.'[66] Thus Jurieu does not arrive at a distinction between agent and act morality, according to which we might praise (blame) those whose action happens to be wrong (right), for, according to him, only those well-intentioned agents whose actions are also right deserve praise.

The result is that here, as elsewhere throughout his work, Jurieu is on the side of Arnauld in rejecting the Jesuit doctrine of philosophic sin. This is the doctrine that to commit damnable sin, one must sin with contempt for God known to be God. Such a view makes those ignorant of God (or of God's will) incapable of damnable sin , whereas, according to Arnauld and Jurieu, just the opposite is the case. To act in ignorance of God's will is *eo ipso* to do what is damnably wrong. The sincere heretic thus does not have the claim to toleration that Bayle asserts.[67] Bayle must have been chagrined to find his view assimilated to that of the Jesuits, but such was the charge of a typically abusive passage from Jurieu: 'Clearly [Bayle] must have learnt his abominable moral theory during the three years he spent with the Jesuits at Toulouse ... Whoever compares whatever has been said about the philosophic sin of the Jesuits and the effects of good intention according to them will see a perfect resemblance between the doctrine of the pupil and that of his masters. Except that the disciple goes further than his masters. For I know of no Jesuit who has dared to say that a man who commits a parricide with a good intention does an act which is praiseworthy.'[68]

66 *Des droits*, 238–41.
67 For the contrast between Bayle and Arnauld, see Kilcullen, Conclusion, 175ff.
68 *Courte revue* (1691), 6; quoted in Kilcullen, 15, n.32.

Despite this wide cleavage between their views, Bayle took Jurieu's concession that invincible ignorance exculpates with respect to matters of both *fait* and *droit* to represent a radical shift in position. Either Jurieu just contradicts himself, he thought, or he and Jurieu turn out to be in agreement with respect to essentials.[69] Specifically, he thought that there was agreement on the following: 1) invincible ignorance exculpates, but 2) sometimes those who follow conscience must be punished; for example, to maintain order, those who are morally blameless sometimes must be punished. Bayle also thought there was agreement on 3) that conscience always obliges, but here he was misled both by his failure to distinguish between morally infallible belief and morally relevant belief, and by his assimilation of blameworthiness to failure to perform duty.

On the crucial point Bayle goes back to quote *Le vray système* that 'conscience always obliges us, in whatever state it may be, to perform that action which is least evil. Now it is less evil for a heretic to separate from the true Church which he takes to be heretical and idolatrous than to remain in it.'[70] But Jurieu begins the sentence that Bayle quotes by denying the very conclusion that Bayle wants to draw (namely, that conscience *always* obliges): 'It is true that an errant conscience does not and cannot ever oblige a man to perform a wrong action [*un crime*] that follows from his error; but conscience always obliges ...'[71] So what is going on here? Jurieu imagines a heretic who finds it convenient to worship Christ, whom he in fact does not believe to be God. If he remains in a church that worships Christ he is guilty first of heresy, for his views have not changed; second of idolatry, for he adores him whom he believes not to be God; third of profanity, for he blasphemes in his heart him whom he eternally adores; and fourth of hypocrisy, for he acts other than as he believes. If he separates he is still a heretic and at most a blasphemer. The lesser of the two evils and thus the right thing to do is to separate. The parallel to the Protestant situation is obvious, and thus, not incidentally, Jurieu here provides an argument for the toleration of Protestants that Bayle might have appreciated. Even if Calvin and Luther were heretics and schismatics, they and their followers ought, *ceteris paribus*, to be tolerated because they were doing what was both according to their conscience and right. If Bayle did appreciate the argument, it was because he took it to be a statement of his own view of the erroneous conscience. But it is not his view. The reason why the schis-

69 *Supplément*, preface; *OD* II, 479–81.
70 Ibid, *OD* II, 479.
71 *Le vray système*, 308.

matic's act is right, according to Jurieu, is not because the schismatic thinks it is right, but because given his beliefs there is less evil in his act than in the alternative of remaining in the church. The relevant beliefs of the schismatic concern not the rightness of his schism, but whom he thinks he would be blaspheming or worshipping in the church. Once again, believing it morally so does not make it morally so; only an objective fact of the matter does, which in this case is an objective fact about the heretic's beliefs.

The fact remains, however, that Jurieu's heretic is mistaken about what is most important and that his schism separates him from the true church. Jurieu is not insensitive to the paradox, but his effort to relieve it is not obviously successful. It does not follow from his view, he says, that hidden heretics should be forced to declare themselves, to be then expelled from the church. (Jurieu's own efforts to have Bayle expelled from his church in fact belie this view.) Although it would be better for them it would be worse for the church, for such declarations would mislead the simple into heresy. It is better therefore that they be punished by God for the additional crime of hyprocrisy, and for them thus to perish for 'the good of the nation.'[72] Such a proposal seems only to heighten the paradox, for by strengthening the church the hypocritical heretic chooses the objectively right option. Perhaps the way out of the paradox is to distinguish, as Jurieu may have intended, between the actions and praiseworthiness of both the church and the heretic. By tolerating the undisclosed heretic, the church does what is in the interest of the simple and thus what is right; it is also praiseworthy. By remaining in the church, the hypocritical heretic does what is right, or at least less wrong than if he were to declare and be expelled, but he is more blameworthy than if he were to do so.

The historical denouement of the Bayle-Jurieu debate is interesting less for the adjudication, or even delineation, of their differences than for the anti-authoritarian direction in which Bayle takes his argument for toleration. The attack on authority is clear in his argument against the relevance of the *fait-droit* distinction to considerations of toleration. The context is a reply to an objection to one of his main arguments for toleration, the reciprocity argument, which, as has been seen, goes as follows. If anyone has the right to punish anyone else for their religious beliefs, if even the true church is entitled to 'compel them to enter,' then everyone acting in good faith has the same rights, including those who

72 Ibid, 308–9.

would persecute the true church; but God cannot be responsible for such a situation, and thus His injunction 'compel them to enter' must be read non-literally, that is, no one has the right to persecute.

Bayle illustrates his argument with fairly typical examples. Judges are supposed to punish the guilty and absolve the innocent; but sometimes it happens that the testimony and evidence against murderers is untenable, and when they are put to the question, that is, tortured, they hold out. In such circumstances, judges do what they are supposed to do when they absolve the murderer, and *mutatis mutandis* with respect to condemnation of the innocent.[73] The general point is that when God commands us to do certain things with respect to our neighbours, He leaves it to us to decide, in good faith, whether they satisfy the conditions for us to act. Thus giving alms to someone we believe, however falsely, to be poor or withholding them from someone we believe, however falsely, to be not in need, satisfies God's injunction. Now these examples simply beg the question against Jurieu by collapsing anything like the distinction between act and agent morality, unless the argument can be read as an argument that does not concern morality at all. Jurieu's question as to what is objectively right is, at least from Bayle's perspective, one that inevitably stirs the boundless ocean of theological controversy, for it requires that we determine which is the true church in order to know which church is uniquely entitled to persecute.[74] Bayle's argument cuts through that controversy by insisting that in such circumstances reasonable people will simply reason their way to toleration of differences. The authority of the true church is, in short, irrelevant.

He in effect argues just this conclusion in responding to an objection to the above argument. The objection is that inadvertently condemning an innocent man for murder is a case of ignorance *de fait*, but condemning an innocent man for heresy is a case of ignorance *de droit*; the one is *ex hypothesi* a case of inculpable ignorance, the other not.[75] Bayle's rebuttal is to argue that questions of the latter are no less difficult to decide than those of the former. Michael Servetus, for example, was accused of denying the Trinity. On the one hand is the question whether certain things were written or said by him; second is the status of what he denied. Since he denied that he said anything contrary to the word of

73 *Supplément*, chap. 5; *OD* II, 490.
74 Kilcullen, 92. Recall, too, Bayle's insistence that argument can change the beliefs of others and thus their duties, and thus that his argument for the autonomy of conscience will upset rather than entrench bona fide persecution.
75 *Supplément*, x; *OD* II, 497.

God, this question becomes enormously complex as can be seen from another similar case, namely, whether what Jansenius held is heretical. The disputes over what Jansenius held *de fait* show how difficult that question is. But the question *de droit* is no less so. 'I know that Jansenius's disciples did not wish to go beyond the bounds of [the Council of] Trent, or to maintain (as they perhaps would have the skill and capability to do, had they judged it appropriate) that Trent had not decided the propositions that Jansenius was accused of denying in the five propositions, i.e., they agreed that the five propositions were heretical in the sense that Rome had denied them.'[76] 'Good Calvinist lawyers,' however, would carry the case further by raising metaphysical questions (whether divine perfection better accords with human freedom or with grace that is necessary and sufficient for doing good), linguistic questions (about the relevant texts from Scripture), questions about the views of the Church fathers, and finally argumentation on both sides. Once again Bayle's general tendency is to reduce questions *de droit* to questions *de fait*; here the specific thrust is that the Jansenist case ought to be, but is in fact not, easier than the larger case of Scripture on which it depends. The upshot is not only that no view can be determined as heretical, but also that no criterion of heresy in general can be made out. To say that heresy contravenes either the decisions of the true church (as Nicole argued) or the fundamentals of Christianity (as Jurieu argued) only raises all the same questions.[77]

It is important to note that, despite his attack on authority, Bayle does not draw the theologically nihilistic conclusion that there is no difference between heresy and orthodoxy. To take the important case, either the Catholics or the Calvinists are right about the Eucharist; either Christ is really present to be worshipped on the altar after transubstantiation, or He is not and worshipping the Eucharist is an act of idolatry. Nor does Bayle say even that no view can be held, even defensibly held, on the matter. He denies this sceptical conclusion by citing the most immediate case, his own. The inability of impartial judges to decide the issue 'does not mean that I myself find in any difficulty in the dispute over the Eucharist. I am clearly convinced that the figurative sense is the true one and the objections from Catholics cause me no difficulties.'[78] His position is that no difference between heretical and orthodox beliefs,

76 Ibid; *OD* II, 498.
77 *Supplément*, xii; *OD* II, 499–500.
78 *Supplément*, x; *OD* II, 502.

not even a merely perceived difference, can be by itself the basis for persecution. To take his argument from elsewhere, the only relevant questions are *de fait*, for everyone agrees on the sole question *de droit*. But in working through the questions *de fait* reasonable people will see their way to permanently tolerating religious differences. No appeal to authority of any sort can reasonably resolve them by force.[79]

79 It is no wonder that Bayle should say that it was his overthrow of the *fait-droit* distinction that led Jurieu to embrace his view that invincible ignorance exculpates no less with respect to *droit* as to *fait* (*Supplément*, x; *OD* II, 497).

5

Idolatry

When Moses had been away for forty days on the mountain, speaking with God and receiving the tables containing the Ten Commandments, his people became disturbed: 'as for this Moses, they said, "the man that brought us up out of the land of Egypt, we wot not [i.e. do not know] what is become of him."'[1] Besides perplexity it is not clear what they felt; their reaction, in any case, was to approach Aaron, the brother of Moses, with the request to make for them 'gods, which shall go before [them].' Their state of mind at this point is even less clear, for Aaron's response was to collect the golden earrings of their wives, daughters, and sons, and to fashion from them a molten calf, before which he built an altar for their burnt offerings. '"These be thy gods," they said, "which brought thee up out of the land of Egypt."'

This behaviour was condemned at the time and forever thereafter as an instance, the paradigmatic instance, of idolatry – the practice condemned in the very first of the injunctions contained in the tables Moses was to bring down. The condemnation is not a trivial one. For idolatry was to prove the most capital instance of heresy – the crime of those who chose to believe other than as they were supposed to believe. To take a spectacular example, when two millennia later the witches went to the stake in their tens or hundreds of thousands, their crime was heresy – they had worshipped the Devil. Thus the text cited to justify the extermination of witches connects them with idolatry and, not incidentally, bestiality.[2] The treatment of witches as idolaters was not unique. As we shall see, the

---

1 Exodus 32: 1–4.
2 Exodus 22: 18–20. The authorized term 'witch' in fact translates *maleficium*, evil-doer. The estimated numbers of witches executed between 1500 and 1700 vary widely, but 'spectacular' is the word to describe the phenomenon, since witch trials and executions

treatment of Catholics and Protestants at each others' hands was cast in the same terms and was hardly less spectacular.

21: The Problem of Idolatry

But what kind of error is it to worship false gods? Deliberate self-deception about who God really is seems implausible as an explanation of such behaviour. Even evil for its own sake, if it is ever comprehensible, is hard to understand in this case: perhaps one can like Augustine steal pears just as a moral violation – for the hell of it, as it were – but what makes one's act an act of worship if one knows that the object of the act is not God? For Locke, the idolatry of the Jews, who alone lived under a theocracy, was the crime of treason; God Himself was the author of their civil laws and was 'in a special way' their king.[3] But one still wants to know what led to such treason; literally, *what were they thinking of?* Explanations that make idolatry a deliberate, voluntary act seem problematic, for what could be the motivation? Yet something like these explanations must be true if the First Commandment is to be a moral injunction to something other than just knowing the truth about who God is. Thus Locke, citing Galatians 5, takes idolatry to be a 'work of the flesh' along with adultery and fornication.[4] Similarly for Jurieu, the Socinians make the mistakes they do because they have false ideas of God, and these false ideas spring from their cupidity. In an example that opens another dimension to these questions, he says that the Socinian claims to good faith are like those of papists who say that the Commandments do not prohibit adoration of images. For Jurieu, idolatry is a matter of 'culpable unregulated passion.'[5]

As part of his case for toleration, Bayle argued against Jurieu that education is the principal determinant of belief, that not all error springs from the corruption of the heart. Jurieu's view on toleration (that heretics should be persecuted) would be plausible, according to Bayle, only if all error were connected with cupidity, but some errors obviously do not have this connection. The example he gives is transubstantiation. It will soon be seen that, for Bayle, it is an example, not just of an error unconnected with passion, but of idolatry itself. Meanwhile, how might

were often public spectacles. The charge of witchcraft often involved those of idolatry and bestiality, among other crimes.

3 *Epistola de tolerantia*, 116–19.
4 Ibid, 62–3.
5 *Des droits*, 231–3.

an error about transubstantiation have been thought to be connected with passion?

Some Catholics had tried to attribute the Calvinists' refusal to accept this doctrine to their pride. That is, Calvinists had been taken to hold their particular view just because it is particular to them, or, perhaps, to persist in what they know to be an error because they are constitutionally unable to acknowledge it as such. But this explanation in terms of passion fails, according to Bayle, for it construes Calvinists as deliberately holding views contrary to what they believe God to have revealed. 'Now, this thought cannot enter the mind of anyone, not even the evilest demon, because every mind with an idea of God means by the word "God" a Being who knows things with certainty and is incapable of deception; and never did the demon who spoke to Eve the contrary of what God had said believe himself to speak the truth. He knew full well that what God said was true.'[6]

This important question will be reviewed at the end of this chapter, but for the moment, the argument seems to be that while passion might lead one to hold a view that is false, one cannot know that a view is false and still hold it, even through passion. (The inability to *acknowledge* error because of passion is not an instance of actually believing what one knows to be an error.) The passion explanation of idolatry would have the idolater know that God is incapable of error and yet take His command to worship Him and nothing else to be invalid. Bayle's citation of God's command not to worship anything but Him and His inability to deceive with respect to this command, or to anything else, is rather misleading. His point is that in committing this crime, the idolater must know God to be God. Even passion cannot lead one to believe that he who is known to be God is not God, and knowledge of God seems to be a condition of idolatry. In Bayle's view, then, acting as if one believed something other than God to be God, for example, bowing down before a golden calf without believing it to be God, would not be an act of idolatry. Again, we may ask, how is idolatry possible? For if Bayle rejects passion as an explanation of idolatry, he also seems to regard deliberate self-deception as impossible and all other deception as irrelevant as explanations of idolatry. How so?

Idolatry is the worship of x, where x is not God. It is worship of x not merely as if x were God in the sense of deliberate contrary-to-known-fact pretence that x is God. It is not a hollow gesture. Rather, idolatry is committed in the conviction that x is God, with the attitudes and actions

6 *Comm. phil.* II, 10; *OD* II, 439.

appropriate to that conviction. But if it is understood in this way, idolatry presents the following dilemma. If the Israelites acted in the knowledge that the calf was not God, then their act was not one of idolatry. On the other hand, if they acted in the (presumably false) belief that the calf was God, then either, once again, their act is not one of idolatry, given that idolatry is an act for which one is responsible, or idolatry is not an act for which one is responsible, and it is hard to make sense of its condemnation. Even if their false belief is culpable, they are responsible only for it, and not for the idolatry that results from it – at least according to Bayle, who would otherwise have to sacrifice his views on toleration.

This dilemma is not faced by Jurieu, who, as will be seen, thinks that there is an objective fact about what the Israelites did that makes their act one of idolatry. Their knowledge or lack of it is irrelevant to their crime. Moreover, Jurieu has a straightforward response to the perplexing question raised above about what the Israelites were thinking, what they were about, what their intentions were. The question in fact is ambiguous. It may be the question as to *why* they engaged in idolatry, that is, what were their motivations? Jurieu's response would be that their motivations, although attributable to passion, were irrelevant to the moral significance of what they did. The question might also be about the cognitive conditions for their action, that is, *how* must one be thinking in order to engage in idolatry? Once again, Jurieu just denies the relevance of the question. What matters is not what the Israelites were thinking, but what they did. The price that he pays is to make worship the very sort of empty ceremony that he criticized in Catholicism. For Bayle, the dilemma above is a real one; worship is, though ceremonial, not empty, and thus he must deal with this question, or at least recognize its significance, in both of its versions. For him, to answer the first version would violate the biblical injunction of not to judge. That is, to specify the motivations of the Israelites would make it possible to condemn them, even as they appeared to have been by God Himself. At any rate, it is the question in its second version that is the more interesting.

22: Transubstantiation

Idolatry is of colossal significance for understanding Bayle, who condemns the practice in very harsh terms.[7] One might speculate about the

7 Regrettably, the article Aaron, the first of the *Dictionnaire*, disappoints anyone looking for a discussion of idolatry. Bayle is content there to correct the mythology that had grown up around the episode related in Exodus 32. Some of the overlay concerned rel-

source of the vehemence of his condemnation of idolatry. Sometimes Bayle creates a worthy target and hits it with good and effective ridicule. For example, the exploitation by the Catholic clergy of the credibility of their laity is a frequent target; at one point Bayle hits his target by drawing attention to the money-making schemes of the relic business. He points out that the same saint, or even the same part of the same saint, is to be found idolized in several monasteries and churches.[8] But sometimes his concern seems exaggerated and his judgment distorted, at least from the perspective of modern sensibilities. The article Francis of Assisi is one of the *Dictionnaire*'s most disappointing in its grossly unsympathetic treatment of a figure whose simple piety and independence of thought ought to have appealed to Bayle. That Francis represented for Bayle only another example of medieval Catholicism's superstition and obscurantism is attributed by Labrousse to the enduring effect of the excesses of Jesuit idolatry to which the Catholic Bayle was exposed.[9] Perhaps this sort of psycho-biographical account might be more plausibly mobilized with respect to the article Abraham, whose subject is said by Bayle to have been the first man to go into voluntary exile because of his religion, specifically his refusal to engage in idolatry.[10] Abraham might be read, of course, as a surrogate for Bayle, who also went into exile because of his refusal to engage in what he thought was idolatry.

More important by far than these speculations is the deep structural significance of idolatry for Bayle; for according to him it is the most basic error of Catholicism, the differentia between it and Calvinism. Bayle largely ignores the extensive debates between the camps over

---

atively minor detail, such as whether the calf was of solid gold or only gilded; some of it is typically quaint, such as the story that for refusing to join in their idolatry, the people spit on Hur so much as to suffocate him, or the story that the ashes of the calf after Moses had burned it and mixed it with water stuck to the beards of those worshippers who drank from it, thus producing guilty beards, as it were. The general thrust of this material, if there is one, is to exculpate Aaron. For example, some authors had claimed that Aaron had been threatened by the people, whose demand for the calf he tried to avoid by making them contribute their earrings to its production (alas, 'those intoxicated by superstition and idolatry will sacrifice everything to it'). Since some of this material had found its way into translations of the Bible, Bayle's concern for setting the record straight is the more understandable

8   Art. Abbey, rem. B.

9   *Pierre Bayle* I, 86.

10 Remark A. Here Bayle seems inclined to agree with Jurieu's explanation of the phenomenon, calling idolatry a 'natural propensity' (remark C).

doctrines of grace and insists instead that the only doctrine of significance separating the two is transubstantiation.[11] As defined by the
Council of Trent, the Catholic doctrine is that 'the body and blood with
the soul and divinity' of Christ are 'truly, really and substantially
present' in the Eucharist. The operation of the sacrament is *ex opere operato;* what this means is that the Eucharist is not just a symbol for Christ,
but his actual presence on the altar, independent of what anyone may
believe, even the priest who utters the words of consecration, who,
according to Bossuet, need only to have the intention of carrying out the
rite as prescribed by the Church. According to Calvin and his followers,
on the other hand, the body of Christ is in heaven and nowhere else,
although it exercises its power through the Eucharist, which depends on
the faith of the recipient.[12] Most theologians in the period, both Catholic
and Protestant, agreed that if the Catholic position on the real presence
of Christ in the Eucharist was correct, adoration of it was called for.[13]
But if the Calvinists were right, then even Arnauld agreed that Catholics
were guilty of idolatry in their adoration of the Eucharist.

It seems clear, then, that in the attacks on idolatry that appear
throughout his work, Bayle was aiming at Catholicism. Or it should
seem clear. In the *Continuation des pensées diverses sur la comète,* however,
Bayle insists that in claiming that atheism is no worse than idolatry, he
does not mean to include papism in the latter. But this disclaimer serves
only to occasion the ironic observation that his Protestant opponents
criticize him for his claim when they themselves say that they would
rather be Jews or Mohammedans than papists since they would then not
have to worship wood or stone, or a plaster God. Jurieu in particular is
quoted at great length and in gory detail on just how dreadful Catholicism really is. In short, Bayle disavows nothing but the directness and
style of the attack on Rome, and not the attack itself.[14]

11 'This is the doctrine of the Roman Catholics: take from it transubstantiation, for
   instance, and put the Trinity in its room and the most orthodox Protestant divines subscribe to it.' Explanation III; *Dict.* V, 834.
12 Some context for these questions is provided by Armogathe, who in *Theologia Cartesiana,* 36–40, catalogues seven accounts of the Eucharist attacked as false by Bellarmine.
   Bayle is quoted, without source, as saying that the question of the Real Presence
   'belongs to the deepest and most abstruse part of philosophy, and demands much
   meditation and discussion.' Bayle's view is that in fact the Eucharist is beyond philosophical explanation.
13 See Jurieu, *Le janséniste,* 143.
14 *CPD,* lxxv; *OD* III, 295–6. Later, Bayle responds to the objection that paganism is preferable to atheism because in worshipping false gods it worships the true God at least

What, then, of the original *Pensées diverses*? Writing Bayle's biography much later, Desmaizeaux took at face value Bayle's effort to calm allegedly widespread concern, but newspaper accounts and correspondence from the period belie his account. Prat points out that the comet of 1680, by way of contrast to comets even as late as the one of 1654, did not cause any great fears[15]. Rather, the comet whose significance Bayle was only nominally concerned to undo might be read as a symbol for the relics, images, holy sites, apparitions, and other paraphernalia of Catholicism so abhorrent to Calvinism. His specific argument might be summarized that a comet cannot by itself portend evil in men's lives, because 1) men have free will that could counteract any such portent, and 2) there is no causal connection of any significance between the comet and anything in their environment. The same applies to the influence, whether good or evil, of the Catholic paraphernalia. Moreover, if a comet did portend, it would do so only through a miracle by God; but then God would be confirming almost all men in their idolatry. Only Christians know how to appease the true God; in the attempt to do so, all others prostrate themselves before idols, sacrifice to them, and consult demons.[16] That Catholics are to be included in the latter group is clear in Bayle's denunciation of the pagan practice of 'attributing their misfortunes to the neglect of some ceremony rather than to their own vices.'[17] And when he marvels at the monstrous credulity of ancient Rome with respect to auguries, he undoubtedly intends the credulity of modern Rome.[18]

One must remember that the *Pensées diverses* was supposedly written by a Catholic, and that perforce Bayle's strategy was subtle and indirect. Likely, not even Jurieu was initially bothered by this early work.[19] But in the *Dictionnaire*, the starkness of Bayle's attack on idolatry was not to be missed, even by the Protestant community of Holland, in response to

---

by worshipping personified attributes of Him. This construal, he says, would justify the worst practices of Rome – the relics, the Mariolatry, the false traditions, etc. *CPD*, cxxxi; *OD* III, 372–3. Whether God could even be partially represented in this way (what or whom exactly do the pagans worship?) is the main issue to be discussed below.

15 *PDC*, ed. Prat, intro. vi ff.
16 *PDC*, lvii, lx.
17 *PDC*, lxix; *OD* III, 46.
18 *PDC*, lxvii.
19 Jurieu was not informed of the author's identity until after the fact. To what extent this episode is a part of the psychological explanation of his later antagonism is an open question. See *Pensées diverses*, ed. Prat, xix.

the first of whose criticisms Bayle published an Explanation of his preference for the morals of some atheists over those of most idolaters. His
Explanation took nothing back. Reserving the performance of virtuous
action to those in the true church, he insisted that the actual sources of
good behaviour in men – love of fame and fear of shame rather than of
God – operate as well in atheists, who at least are spared the instruction
of false religions. As he had argued in the *Continuation* atheism is preferable to paganism on two counts: 1) it is more easily converted to the
truth; 2) it is less of an offence to the true God. In fact, paganism is a
worse form of atheism. It would seem that the essence of the genus,
atheism, consists in failing to honour God for failure to recognize Him.
One species denies the existence of all gods, the other of the true God;
the difference between them, fidelity to false gods, worsens the latter.[20]

Beyond these strictly theological and political concerns, the issue of
idolatry, specifically with respect to transubstantiation, provides a handle on a number of more obviously philosophical concerns in and
around Bayle – for example, his near-obsession with Spinoza. He thinks
that the Catholics' doctrine of the Eucharist, which requires that the
same body be in more than one place, entails, whether they know it or
not, a kind of Spinozism: 'all things reduced to one only created thing.'[21]
The ontological havoc that would be wrought by the doctrine was an
early discovery of Bayle's. In the foreword to the *Receuil* of 1684, he
observed that the doctrine as defined by Trent required not only that
'Christ be present everywhere there are consecrated hosts, but also that
all the parts of His body penetrate each other.'[22] Now, he gets this observation from the Jesuit La Ville, whose piece attacking the Cartesian
account of the Eucharist Bayle published in the *Receuil*. La Ville had
argued that its inability to accommodate the doctrine as defined showed
that the Cartesian ontology of body as extension is false. Bayle accepts
the logical connection, but argues in the opposite direction that it is the
doctrine that is false. (Whether ironically or not, Bayle muses that the
Cartesians could bring peace to all of Christianity with their view, and,
indicating his own fideistic inclinations, that Calvin himself would not
have broken with the Church had it not so precisely defined the doctrine, 'which should never be done in things mysterious if schism is to
be avoided.')

20 *CPD*, lxxxiii; *OD* III, 308–9.
21 Art. Pyrrho, rem. B; n.16.
22 Unpaginated.

Philosophical interest in the ontology of the Eucharist ceases rather quickly, for religious faith in the sacrament, regardless of the sect and its belief, is soon invoked and philosophy becomes, at most, the hand-maiden of theology. There is another issue, however, better connected with the questions at the outset of this chapter, that seems endlessly rich. To ask what the idolaters were thinking of is also to raise the more general issue of intentionality, namely, the property of the mind, or of its thinking, that allows it to be *about* something else. (The more usual sense of intending, namely, purporting or designing, might involve this property, but is distinguished from it below.) This is, of course, an important property. Indeed, some have argued, even recently, that its aboutness or intentionality is what sets consciousness apart from all else. Thought can be about a candle, but the candle is not about anything. As we have seen in chapter 3, Bayle joined Malebranche in resisting Arnauld's version of this thesis. An indication of the richness and relevance of intentionality here may be had from David-Augustin Brueys.[23]

Brueys was one of the few who denied the generally held view that the real presence of Christ in the Eucharist entailed adoration of it. 'Is proximate adoration more potent,' he asked, 'than distant adoration?'[24] Because divine, Christ is everywhere, thus never either farther or closer. In addition, 'with regard to the soul, an object is neither closer nor farther away, and in order better to act, it has no need for its object to be at a certain distance from it.'[25]

Brueys here raises a question that was soon to bedevil Cartesian theories of ideas. Given that the mind can know only what is present to it,

---

23 Brueys (1640–1723) was born a Protestant and was trained for the practice of law, which he soon relinquished in favour of literature and theology. He initially defended Calvinism but then converted and became a prolific defender of the opposite side. (In the *Traité de l'Eucharistie*, however, he raised the idolatry issue only indirectly in arguing that St John Chrysostom clearly adored the body of Christ on the altar, 243–50.) Bayle, of course, noted these efforts. E.g., to Minutoli, 6 October 1692; *OD* IV, 682, and especially *NRL* August 1685, iv; *OD* I, 676. Some, including Jurieu, thought that he was the author of the *Avis aux refugiez*, such was the confusion generated by that work. *NRL* October 1685, iv; *OD* I, 676. See also below, and especially *NRL* August 1686, i; *OD* I, 611–15. The motivations for his abjuration were impugned by Jurieu, with some justification, at least after the fact, for he received a royal pension for his polemical efforts. After the death of his wife, whom he had married 'plus par inclination que par raison,' he entered orders under the hands of Bossuet. This status did not prevent him from pursuing a successful career as a playwright at the end of what must have been a colourful life. *Oeuvres de théatre*, I, ix–xxiii.

24 *Réponse*, 193.

25 Ibid, 194.

what kind of presence is required and what is the role of ideas in establishing that presence? Arnauld argued that Malebranche had mistakenly assumed that physical presence is required, with the result that ideas for him were a *tertium quid* standing between the mind and physical things, which were therefore unknowable.[26] It is ironic that Brueys's anti-adoration premises should be repeated, even if in a different context, by a member of Port-Royal, where the Eucharist was adored, literally twenty-four hours a day. Perhaps this is an indication of the depth and abstruseness alluded to above.[27]

There is a more concrete issue that emerges from this immediate context – the question of toleration. The Protestant theologian Jean Daillé (1594–1670), it seems, had anticipated Brueys's position at least to the following extent; 'even if Christ Himself were present in the Host,' said Daillé, 'the Calvinists should not be *forced* to adore it, for their consciences tell them (rightly or wrongly) that they would be committing the blasphemy [really, the idolatry] of worshipping bread.'[28] This view finds its culmination in Bayle, for whom intention in both senses of the term is paramount, and contrasts with the position of Jurieu, for whom there is an objective act of idolatry that is punishable regardless of intention. For both, the issue is one of authority. In Bayle's case, it is the authority of the individual conscience, for only it can decide upon the appropriate object of its worship. In Jurieu's case, the issue is the authority of the Church. For it was the Catholic view, not only that Christ is present in the Eucharist, but that theirs was the only Eucharist, because Calvinist ordination was invalid. Unlike the Anglicans, but like the Lutherans, the Calvinists had broken the apostolic succession, and therefore their ministers did not have the power of consecration. The issue, then, was a special focus for the debate over the identity of the true Church.

Despite his rejection of the Real Presence, Brueys recognizes that Christ was adored at His birth in Bethlehem by the shepherds and at His ascension by His disciples, and that God was adored by Moses in the burning bush and by the Jews in the ark. He explains these episodes as

---

26 For Arnauld's argument see Nadler, *Arnauld and the Cartesian Philosophy of Ideas*, secs. 11–12, and for a defence of Malebranche against the *tertium quid* consequence, see Nadler, *Malebranche and Ideas*; for an alternative reading of the kind of presence Malebranche invokes, see Lennon, 'Malebranche's Argument for Ideas.' For the most recent round, from five among the most important commentators, see Kremer, *The Great Arnauld*, part 2. Brueys's work precedes the opening of the Arnauld-Malebranche debate by two years.

27 Note 12 above.

28 Rex, 168, emphasis added.

instances where God is adored in places 'where He manifests His glory.'[29] To say that God is especially adorable in certain places, however, might mean only that adoration actually occurs in certain places. God's glory is manifested, according to Brueys, simply when people congregate to worship Him. 'Where two or three are gathered together in my name, there am I in the midst of them' (Matthew 18: 20. Such an invocation – a kind of performative whose performance makes it so – may be like transubstantiation itself.) As for the notion of a church, such a conception comports with regarding a church as an actual building, picked out in a metaphysically arbitrary way for practical purposes – a kind of ecclesiastical nominalism, with a contractual model of authority. Such a plain conception certainly contrasts with the Catholic view of the Church as the mystical body of Christ, with its resultant powers not only of transubstantiation but of infallible authority in the interpretation of Scripture.

Jurieu argued something like Brueys's position by distinguishing two kinds of adoration and presence:

Internal adoration consists in movements of the heart, in the infinite annihilation of ourselves in the presence of the infinite Being; external adoration is in genuflection, prostration and other sensible signs to which usage has attached the idea of internal adoration. There is also internal and external presence of God. The internal presence of God is a presence of virtue, essence and action whereby He operates in all creatures. External presence consists in certain extraordinary visible signs that God gives of His operations in certain creatures. Now, each kind of adoration naturally and ordinarily has a connection with the presence of the same order. That is, internal adoration should correspond to internal presence; and because God is present everywhere, He should be adored in all creatures with an internal adoration and an annihilation of self before Him who is, and operates, in all the creatures in the world. Likewise, external adoration must be reserved for the places where God manifests Himself with an external presence, i.e., by certain external and extraordinary visible signs.[30]

Jurieu clearly avoids the Catholic conception of a church. But the upshot of his own view seems less ecclesiastical nominalism than ecclesiastical historicalism – God is to be worshipped externally only at certain sites in the Holy Land. Moreover, Jurieu gets himself into trouble over idolatry,

29 *Réponse*, 195. The Host, of course, is not an instance of such glorious manifestation.
30 *Le janséniste*, 161–2.

which occurs, he says, only when external adoration is preferred to internal adoration. Here Jurieu seems to be concerned, not with idolatry, but with what for him is Catholic hypocrisy, shallowness, or just plain silliness over ceremony. The question of idolatry is precipitated by his notion of internal adoration, the 'annihilation of self before Him who is, and operates, in all the creatures in the world.' How does one worship God in the stone and not the stone itself? Arnauld had previously raised just this question for Jurieu, accusing him of either Nestorianism or Socianism.[31] If Jurieu is more willing, as he says he is,[32] to worship the divinity in a piece of bronze than the real presence of Christ's humanity in the Eucharist, then either 'the humanity of Christ is not the humanity of the divine Word [Nestorianism], or the divine Word is not God [Socinianism].' Perhaps Arnauld catches Jurieu in a moment of hardly atypical hyperbole; but in order to reply to the dilemma, Jurieu must distinguish as objects of intention God from the bronze and Christ from His body. How he or anyone else might do so is considered in the next section.

23: Jurieu and Bossuet

The dispute between Malebranche and Arnauld was a generally intramural affair in that they agreed at least that the essence of a thing must be apprehended in order for that thing to be known. When we have the clear and distinct idea of a thing we have its essence, and hence everything we find in that idea we can truly assert of the thing – the basis for both disputants of their common Cartesian methodology. The earlier dispute between Descartes and Gassendi, however, was anything but intramural. Here was an extended point-by-point confrontation of diametrically opposed perspectives. The fulcrum of their opposition can be understood as the issue of the divisibility of essences, specifically whether in order to know God knowledge of His whole essence is required.[33] Gassendi's model is one of accretion; we gradually come to know God as we come, through experience, to know His attributes. Descartes's model is a binary one; we innately have the whole idea of God, and to add or subtract from this idea would make it the idea of something necessarily other than God. We come to know God better only by making explicit what is already implicit in this idea. (The model for the

31 Arnauld, *OA* XII, 539.
32 *Préservatif*, 258.
33 See Lennon, 'Pandora.'

connection is the axiom-theorem connection.) Gassendi thus stands charged either (charitably) of not understanding his own idea of God, or (provocatively) of idolatry. The dilemma is of great consequence. The question may be how we know God but at stake is how we can know, or even think about, anything.[34]

There is also at this time an important moral dimension to the narrower question of how we know God. As a foil to his discussion of Bayle's theory of toleration and the erring conscience, Kilcullen draws attention to Arnauld's criticisms of Jesuit views on philosophic and theological sin. The moral stakes are high, for the Jesuit thesis was that only theological sin merits eternal damnation. It occurs essentially when an offence is committed against God known under a certain description. It is 'an offence against a person of infinite dignity known as such [*cognitae qua talis*],' 'against God under the description [*sub ratione*] of highest and infinite good.'[35] What this would mean, and what it did mean for Jesuit casuists, is that damnable sin is difficult to commit. The Israelites in the desert, for example, needed to know in some strong sense whom they were offending; in Cartesian terms, they would have needed the one clear and distinct idea of God. Not incidentally, Arnauld rejected the Jesuit distinction. For him, all sin is theological sin in the sense that even, perhaps especially, acts committed in ignorance of God are sufficient for damnation. A shorter route to the same conclusion would be to invoke the Cartesian doctrine: all sin is theological because no act is committed in ignorance of God, the idea of whom is innate. For Gassendi and Bayle, by contrast, it is possible to have a very imperfect idea of God, or even none at all.

A version of the Descartes-Gassendi dispute emerges in the Catholic-Protestant disputes over idolatry and church authority. Very roughly, the idea is that there was a competition between realist and nominalist conceptions of the church. According to the Catholic realist conception, there is a fixed doctrine that defines the true church's fixed essence, as it were.

34 The issue between Malebranche and Arnauld is whether ideas are in the human mind as modifications of it (Arnauld) or in the mind of God as exemplars for creation (Malebranche). A point at which this dispute ceases to be intramural is when, according to Arnauld, Malebranche makes God material by placing in Him the essence of extension. At this point, Arnauld says, Malebranche takes up the Gassendist cause against Descartes. For the subtleties of this issue, see Ndiaye, *La Philosophie*, chap. 2, pt. 2.

35 Arnauld, *Seconde Dénunciation du péché philosophique*, OA XXXI: 49, 51, quoted in Kilcullen, 18. Whether the Jesuits actually held the view was, of course, itself a matter of controversy; see Kilcullen, esp. 16–17, nn. 33, 39.

According to the Protestant nominalist conception, doctrine develops over time and with it the church emerges as a kind of construction. Obviously, a great deal is stake in the confrontation between these two views, especially the nature of church authority. Historically, for present purposes, the best example of the confrontation is that between Jurieu and Bossuet.[36]

Jacques-Benigne Bossuet (1627–1704) was a churchman. Quintessentially.[37] His two most important works are likely the *Discours sur l'histoire universelle* (1681) and the posthumous *Traité de la connaissance de Dieu et de soi-même*, but he fails now to be better known for failure to be known even in the period for a single identifiable work, position, or idea. Yet no one then spoke for the Church in France more than the Monsieur de Meaux, as he was called after his bishopric. The little pun, Monsieur Deux-mots, belies his stupendous literary output, which itself is an accurate reflection of his political and intellectual importance in the period.

Bossuet's *Exposition de la doctrine de l'Eglise Catholique sur les matières de controverse* was written in 1668 for Turenne, whose abjuration of Protestantism it is supposed to have achieved. The work was enormously successful, both in its dissemination, with translations into Latin, English, Flemish, Italian, and German before 1680, and as a Catholic apologetic. In addition to Turenne, Mademoiselle de Duras came to doubt her Protestantism after reading the work and arranged a discussion between Bossuet and Claude, after which she, too, abjured. Nor were these the only conversions. The Marquis de Courcillon, and later, the Abbé de Dangeau, who was the grandson of the celebrated Protestant Duplessis-Mornay, were among those converted by it.[38] It was in

36 For the problems raised earlier for Catholicism by the work of Ockham, the *locus classicus* of nominalism, see Ozment, 60–3.

37 He was tonsured at eight, named a canon at thirteen, but was ordained only at twenty-four, the same year that he received a doctorate after theological and philosophical studies in Metz and Paris. His talent for preaching was noted at an early age – an episode at the Hôtel de Rambouillet at age sixteen is frequently cited in the literature – but he seems to have shone more for eloquence than for doctrinal or moral reform. For example, his funeral orations for noble celebrities are among his best-known contributions.

38 Bossuet's first published work was the *Réfutation du catechisme de Paul Ferry* (1655), which is also supposed to have led to several Protestant abjurations. Despite his endorsement of the Revocation of the Edict of Nantes, one senses Bossuet to have been conciliatory, optimistic, trustworthy, broad-minded, undogmatic, and reluctant to take hard stands. He was chosen by Péréfix to intervene with Port-Royal on behalf of the Church and was respected by Arnauld and others there; to negotiate with Leibniz and others from the House of Brunswick in an abortive attempt to reconcile Catholicism and Lutheranism;

response to this work that Jurieu wrote his *Préservatif contre le changement de religion, en Idée juste et veritable de la religion catholique romaine
opposée aux portraits flattés que l'on en fait et particulièrement a celui de M.
De Condom.*[39] Noguier, Bastide, and in the work already noted, Brueys
were among other Protestant authors responding to Bossuet, who continued the debate with the first two but succeeded in converting the last.
Brueys reports that he was led to his conversion by reading Bossuet's
book but not before attempting to refute it.[40] An important text from
these debates for the issue of idolatry is Bossuet's *Histoire des variations
des Eglises protestantes* (1688), which was attacked in England by Burnet
and in Holland by Basnage and by Jurieu. The latter's *Lettres pastorales*
began to appear in the same year, and they were responded to by
Bossuet in the six *Avertissements aux Protestants* (1689–94) that began to
appear before the completion of Jurieu's attack. Since Bossuet accused
him of Socinianism, Jurieu left off in order to publish his *Tableau du
Socinianisme* (1691). It was an unfinishable controversy, with material
appearing even posthumously.

The exchange between Bossuet and Jurieu is typical of the stand-off
between their camps over a much longer period of time. The aim of
Bossuet's *Exposition* is to reconcile their differences, but on terms that
involve no change in his own position. His argument is that the differences either are overcome or are seen to bear only upon inessentials.
Even with Bossuet limiting himself to the teaching of Trent, the amount
of material is massive, the issues are numerous, and the argument is,
both historically and conceptually, complex. Sorting might be achieved,
with an eye to present concerns, by viewing it all as concerned with the
proper conception of the divinity.

This sorting is certainly relevant to Protestant charges of idolatry with
respect to images, relics, and saints. Bossuet's response here is clearly to
emphasize divine omnipotence.[41] But he is less clear when addressing the

---

and to mediate between Louis XIV and the Pope over the *droit de régale*. He was partisan but not excessively polemical or bitter in dealing with the French Protestants –
except with Jurieu, whose personal attacks exasperated him. Only at the end of his life,
in dealing with Fénelon and the Quietists, does a sharp edge emerge in his work.

39 Bossuet was at the time still bishop of Condom, hence the reference in Jurieu's title.
The OED finds 'condom' applied no earlier than 1706; Robert tells us that *préservatif*,
the current word for condom, was first used at the beginning of the twentieth century.
The assumption that Jurien was not perpetrating a pun is thus entirely safe.

40 *Examen*, avertissement unpaginated.

41 'The [Church] does not permit the recognition in the greatest saints any degree of

question of justification (which, he thinks, at first had been the main point of difference but then no longer was). Citing Trent, he makes it obvious that grace is necessary for salvation, but less obvious whether it is also sufficient. 'Our sins are forgiven us gratuitously through divine mercy because of Christ ... We are said to be justified gratuitously because nothing preceding justification, neither faith nor works, merits this grace.'[42] What happens after justification remains indeterminate. Speaking for himself, he says that 'free will can do nothing that leads to eternal happiness except in so far as it is moved and elevated by the Holy Spirit.'[43]

The most important and most difficult of the controversies, according to Bossuet, is the question of the Real Presence. This difference ought to be non-fundamental, even according to the Calvinists themselves, because they see no fundamental difference between themselves and the Lutherans, who, although they do not draw all the consequences of their doctrine (specifically worship of the Eucharist), do teach the doctrine of the Real Presence.[44] Even so, he argues in strong terms against the Calvinists. Denying the Real Presence and opting for a figurative reading of the words of consecration, the Calvinists claim that one sacrifice of Christ was enough and thus also reject the Mass. They are therefore on the slippery road to Socinianism, which takes the same position on the Incarnation. Christ need not have been divine in order to lead us to salvation.

To our own age, which sacrifices nothing but chess pawns, Bossuet's argument is, to say the least, obscure. The background to it is the long history of religious attempts to sacrifice – literally, to make holy. One reached a divinity, typically in propitiation, by offering an animal through its destruction, typically on an altar. (Thus the burnt offerings of the Israelites before the molten calf.) The Christian version, or conscious fulfilment, of this rite sees the death of Christ as propiation for Original Sin; the Catholic doctrine is that the Mass is a repetition of this sacrifice in a non-bloody, but also non-symbolic, way because Christ is really present on the altar and is really consumed in the rite of communion. The Socinian position rests on an appeal to rational simplicity and

---

excellence not coming from God, nor any consideration in its eyes except by their virtues, nor any virtue that is not a gift of grace, nor [any special knowledge in them], nor any power to assist us except by their prayers, nor any blessedness except through submission and perfect conformity to the divine will.' 31.

42 Ibid, 42. See also 55–6.

43 Ibid, 47.

44 Ibid, 146–52. This state of affairs is annoyingly attributed by Bossuet to Providence, which he sees as calling for the *rapprochement* of Calvinism to the Church.

economy of means. No such self-sacrifice or involvement by an omni-potent deity would be necessary to achieve the aims of creation. The stand-off here is between a dialogical conception of a divinity whose Providence works only through time and a monological conception that allows all to be fixed a priori. In these terms, it is clear that the Calvinists, despite Bossuet's criticism, are on the Catholic side, and that as per Bossuet's main thesis, their differences from Rome are non-fundamental. How, then, did they respond?

Jurieu's *Préservatif* is perhaps his most pathetic and desperate work, written in the conviction that his church was faced with extinction in France. His condemnation of the French use of 'iron, fire, violence and punishment to achieve conversion' reads as coming from one who is as deeply moved as anyone writing on the topic, not excepting Bayle, whose sang-froid enabled him to employ indirect stratagems that were in the long run more effective. For Jurieu's tactic was always confronta-tional. However sincere Bossuet's attempt at reconciling differences, Jurieu's response was to emphasize them. The list is long and not unusual: relics, images, prayer, satisfaction for sin, indulgences, purga-tory, communion under a single species, the use of Latin, etc. Some of these differences have lately been shown by Vatican II to have been of little significance. Others are more important and Jurieu insists on them. One such is the doctrine of the Real Presence, whose falsity for Jurieu entails that Catholics commit idolatry. Although Bayle was later to agree with Bossuet that this is the only difficult hurdle between the camps, Jurieu takes that position to be only a Catholic stratagem.[45] For there are other important differences, notably the Catholic doctrine of grace, which before Trent might be said 'without exaggeration' to have been Pelagian and since then at best ambiguous.[46] Most important is the question of the role and authority of the Church and of the Pope.

45 *Préservatif*, 218.
46 Ibid, 150–76. Brueys also accused Bossuet of ambiguity; if Christ's death alone is suffi-cient for salvation, then any recourse to human actions of the sort Bossuet allows is a contradiction. *Réponse*, 92. According to Bossuet, at least in the case of those who sin beyond original sin, Christ's satisfaction needs to be 'applied' through human actions. '*It is for us* to receive ... with actions of grace each part of His benefice.' *Exposition*, 68. After his conversion, however, Brueys's account also became ambiguous if not contra-dictory. Sometimes he seems to say that good works are themselves a gift of grace, that is, that God does all, sometimes that a man who is saved must do something after grace in order to distinguish himself from the damned. *Examen*, 111, 118–20. Brueys then received from Jurieu the same treatment that Bossuet had. *Suite du pré-servatif*, see especially 84–7.

The connection between authority and idolatry can be seen as follows. Just as there is a fixed essence that is needed to know God and without which all attempts to worship God fail and result in idolatry, so there is a fixed essential doctrine that defines the true Church and needs to be believed in order to belong to that church, that is, in order to be saved. Without acknowledging it as such, Bossuet took this Cartesian line in his *Histoire des variations des églises protestantes.* 'The faith never varies in the true Church' according to Bossuet, because 'the truth initially comes from God in its full perfection.' All that the Church does is to write down and better explain, even if with new language, what was believed from its beginning. The conception he employs of doctrinal definition and elucidation is very much that of the elucidation of Cartesian innate ideas. The upshot, acccording to Bossuet, is that Protestants are mistaken in their views just because their ideas change. Jurieu in his *Lettres pastorales* responded to Bossuet in just these terms. For him, 'God's truth is established only in parcels,' 'piece by piece,' and the history of Christianity even among the Fathers of the early church is one of gradually corrected error.[47] This conception of doctrinal definition is the analogue to Gassendi's account of how we form the idea of God, or of anything else.

Bossuet's reply in his *Avertissements aux protestants* accuses Jurieu of encouraging revolt under the pretext of endorsing freedom, of authorizing fanaticism, and of Socinianism. These are not Monsieur de Meaux's best pages. At one point, Jurieu seems to be regarded as a Socinian only because of the toleration he shows them and because he fights against them weakly and with bad arguments.[48] But Jurieu's pages occasioning them were not his best either. The larger question is, of course, the nature of the true church, here whether in some sense the Socinians belong to it. Jurieu's view is that they do belong to it, because they believe in Christ as the redeemer even if they reject his divinity, but they are still not saved. The relevant principle is that it would be a merciless and frustrated God who allowed His word to be preached among people all of whom are damned; but Socinians are so few in number that none of them are saved – unlike the principle, which, with 'so small an exception,' is saved.[49] Aside from the atrocious logic, Jurieu's position is another instance of his conservatism, or perhaps pragmatism: numbers

---

47 See F. Lachat, 'Remarques historiques,' in Bossuet, *Oeuvres* XV, i–xiii.

48 *Oeuvres*, XV, 233. Earlier Bossuet had called him a Pelagian because, like the original Pelagians, Jurieu complains that the larger part of Christianity has gone astray. Ibid, 222–3.

49 Ibid, 230–3.

make a difference in practical social matters like toleration and salvation; there are thresholds, which once reached have to be lived with. (His argument for toleration of Calvinists in France, it will be recalled, is simply that they are established in sufficient numbers there.) But he also evidences an anti-essentialist conception of a church: one need not believe all or even its fundamental doctrines in order to belong.

Bossuet's essentialism, meanwhile, is clear in these exchanges. An instance of it occurs in his response to Jurieu's *Tableau du socinianisme* with respect to the discovery of religious error. For Bossuet an error is clarified or determined when it is 'refuted by Scripture, the faith of centuries appears contrary to it, and it is finally condemned by the authority of the Church and its Councils.'[50] For Jurieu, according to Bossuet, none of these produces clarification, at least not necessarily, and in fact can serve only to entrench error; instead, clarification for Jurieu comes from 'philosophical ideas we have *today*. But, according to Bossuet, faith is not for today, it is for all time: the faith does not await formation or governance by philosophical ideas: it is permissible to be a poor philosopher as long as one is truly faithful – now as in previous centuries, and the reason for this is that faith takes the place of philosophy for Christians.'[51] Bossuet does not explicitly make the charge here, but Jurieu stands accused, this time more plausibly, of Socinianism.

Earlier, when Jurieu argued against Arnauld, the charge of Socinianism was even more obvious. The Catholic 'way of authority' is the way of tyranny, according to Jurieu. It is naturally resisted by the human mind, which 'is free and can resolve to yield only to the lights of reason.' Thus, the attempt to convert a freethinker by appealing to Scripture as established by the authority of the Church does no good, for he rejects that authority. This is why, according to Jurieu, the reformed church urges the 'way of examination' that makes the individual the judge of Scripture on the basis of its divine characteristics. 'He then regards his conviction as his own doing.'[52]

50 *Oeuvres* XVI, 103.
51 Ibid, 103–4.
52 *Esprit de M. Arnauld*, 85. The next chapter debates the issue, begun in *La politique* and *L'Apologie*, of who is more Socinian than whom. Because they were regarded by many Catholics and Protestants alike as Calvinists, the Jansenists' anti-Calvinism was virulent and of early date. St Cyran was prevented by imprisonment and subsequent death from fulfilling his intention to write against the Calvinists. But beginning in 1659, Arnauld and Nicole exchanged blows with Claude, leading to a proliferation of insult. (Since Port-Royal was 'committed to the perpetual adoration of the Holy Sacrament,' it was appropriate that the first work should be Arnauld's *Tradition de l'Eglise touchant*

Despite his rejection of an essential church, Jurieu held that there was and is a 'pure faith' with respect to which the Church doctors with their 'stiff, vain speculations' erred because of their philosophical ignorance. This pure faith lay instead with the 'people,' and thus the opponent of toleration was also a populist of sorts. His position, argued against Nicole, is that any church, like any society, has the right to elect its own leaders, and that thus the argument that the Apostolic succession has been interrupted is without basis.[53] Once again, Jurieu's conception of the church comports best with the communal, developmental, parcel-by-parcel account of the reception, or even the generation, of truth as per the Gassendist model.

24: Protestant Responses to a Catholic Convert

Brueys was one of the more noteworthy converts from Protestantism to Catholicism whose abjurations were at least occasioned, if not directly brought about, by the work of Bossuet. Two years after attacking the book that in fact led to his conversion, Brueys adopted the strategy of Bossuet's *Exposition*. In his *Examen* he investigated the significance of the differences separating Catholics and Calvinists, including the issue of transubstantiation. There were three important replies to this work, and Bayle took note of all three.[54] He has great praise for Jurieu's effort, and he begins by noting Jurieu's previous 'complete victory' over Bossuet. Daniel Larroque he regards as something of a spiritual youngster, but one who is able to follow Brueys step for step, pointing out his gross errors with both delicacy and sarcasm. Argument in more general terms comes from another youngster, Jacques Lenfant, who like his coreligionists argues successfully and with learning, according to Bayle.

---

l'*Eucharistie*.) The title of Arnauld's *Réflexions sur ... le préservatif contre le changement de religion* (1682) is self-explanatory. Bossuet seems to have been pleased by the work, exclaiming in a letter to Mme de Morton that 'if his [own] Exposition had led only to this work, his efforts in producing it would have been compensated.'*OA* XL, 515–91. Bossuet cited, *OA* XII, xliii. Jurieu's *Le calvinisme et le papisme* (1683) attacked Arnauld's *Apologie pour les catholiques* (1681–2), which had responded to Jurieu's depiction of Arnauld and the Dutch Catholics as 'seditious,' with Arnauld ready to appeal to the Dutch authorities. De Neercassel, the archbishop of Utrecht, advised him only to publish a brief letter. In fact Arnauld did nothing – until 1691 when he was back at it, attacking Jurieu's *Justification de la morale des Réformés* with the *Défense du ... Calvinisme convaincu*. The degeneration in the quality of this exchange was extreme.

53 See *Unité*, esp. 449–92.
54 *NRL* March 1684; *OD* I, 22.

The latter two authors evidenced the deism that was increasingly characteristic of their own and future generations. Certainly there are indications of it in the *Considerations générales sur le livre de M. Brueys* (1684) of Lenfant.[55] He argues a figurative interpretation of the words of Consecration on the basis of the idea of the Christian religion derived from Scripture: 'It represents this religion as simple, detaching men from everything material and sensible, dispensing them from locally and temporally bound considerations and leading them everywhere to a reasonable and spiritual worship conforming to the nature both of God and of man ... Now, these words, *this is my body*, taken literally, absolutely destroy this idea of simplicity ... and lead men to I-don't-know-what worship that is enigmatic, corporeal, unreasonable, and entirely opposed to the nature of man and of God.'[56] Quite apart from his own positive beliefs, his negative attitude towards the Real Presence is one shared by Bayle and others, who see the view as of a piece with relics, images, ceremony, and the other perceived paraphernalia of debased Catholicism.

The same attitudes appear in Larroque,[57] but his *Le Proselyte abusé* (1684) also engages philosophical issues of some interest with respect to the Eucharist, even if he seems not to understand the Catholic doctrine he criticizes. He quotes the Council of Trent that Christ is in each species of the Eucharist (bread and wine) and in every separated part of each species. But if Christ is in each separated part, he reasons, the Eucharist does not represent a single body, but a multiplicity of them, and that would be a false sign. Larroque either ignores or is ignorant of the Catholic doctrine

---

55 Lenfant (1661–1728) studied at Saumur and then in Geneva, where he was denounced as a Socinian. Later he was ordained in Heidelberg and wound up in Berlin, where he was elected to the Academy of Sciences. He left a considerable bibliography, most of it in church history. E. and E. Haag, VI, 549–52. He was encouraged to publish the *Considerations*, his first work, by Jurieu and by Bayle. Bayle was a friend and correspondent, who for example consoled him on the death of his father. 9 July 1686, *OD* IV, 630.

56 Ibid, 107.

57 At least initially. A minister son of a minister, Larroque (1660?–1731) was chased by the Revocation to England and then to Holland, where he was involved with the *NRL*. However, he returned to France and abjured in 1690. He then got into trouble and was imprisoned for five years, yet wound up serving in government. E. and E. Haag, VI, 367–8. Bayle counted himself among his friends over a long period of time and defended him, against Jurieu, even when he returned to France to abjure. God, and no man, is the judge of Larroque's actions, according to Bayle, who remarks that while 'the true religion has advantages infinitely above the others, there are still cheats and people of honour in all religions.' For an obvious reason, it is revealing when Bayle asks whether by 'changing religion one loses all the qualities that make an honest man.' *La chimère de la cabale*, *OD* II, 715.

that the Eucharist is not a symbol representing anything but is the body of Christ, the same body present in all instances of the sacrament. He also seems to take it as an argument against that view that Christ should be reproduced as many times as the consecrated Host is divided or as a result of the priest's intention in consecrating a Host to divide it later. But, according to the Catholics themselves, even a division of the Host for the benefit of an unexpected communicant, for example, yields no less a Real Presence. This result is intended to be part of the view itself and is not an unforeseen consequence of it that can be used as a *reductio ad absurdum* of the view. On these sorts of issues, Larroque's discussion is a dead end.

A far more fruitful domain concerns idolatry and intentionality. After his conversion, Brueys had claimed, unexceptionally, that Catholics do not adore the bread and wine, but Christ under the species or appearances of bread and wine. Larroque responded by digging up a text from no less than Bellarmine himself: only Christ is adored and 'this adoration also appertains to the symbols of bread and wine in so far as they to some extent form a unity with Christ whom they contain [*ut quid unum cum ipso Christo quem continent*], just as those who adored Christ on earth did not adore him alone, but also to some extent the clothes He wore; for they did not require Him to be naked in order to adore Him nor did they separate Him in spirit from his clothes when they adored Him.'[58] This searchlight theory of intentionality, as we might call it, is, 'ridiculous,' according to Larroque; it is as if when asking a favour of the king we also ask it of his clothes, since he was not naked when we asked him.[59]

The searchlight theory views the mind's intentionality as a kind of seeing eye: what it sees is what it gets, but all and only what it sees. The mind might be thought of in crude physical terms as having the sort of organ described by various optical theorists, beginning with Plato. Rays, or pencils to use Molyneux's contemporary term, are emitted from the

---

58 *Disputationum*, 774.

59 *Le proselyte abusé*, 144–7. Larroque is not quite fair. At the beginning of the sentence that he quotes, Bellarmine explicitly denies that the external symbols are to be worshipped and asserts that they are to be venerated just as those of other sacraments are; that is, there is nothing intrinsically more special about the appearance of bread and wine in the Eucharist than the appearance of (what in fact is) water in Baptism. What is important here, however, is the theory Larroque introduces, whether held by Bellarmine or not.

The metaphor of the searchlight for a theory of intentionality seems first to have been used by R.F. McRae in his account of Descartes and Leibniz; see esp. 70. It is used also by R.A. Watson; for criticism of the theory itself, see his *Representational Ideas*, 64. For an illuminating account of Descartes, Berkeley, and Hume in terms of the searchlight, see Hausman and Hausman, esp. 113 ff.

eye that touch, or even interact with, objects in their path, which are thereby seen. The mind may be immaterial, but it has an analogous ability to scan what is somehow in its path and thus to be aware of it.

It is instructive here to turn briefly to Arnauld, the philosopher who in the period most worried about intentionality. The searchlight theory had earlier occurred in Arnauld's *Réflexions sur* [Jurieu's] *Préservatif* [against Bossuet].[60] Human bodies have pores filled with matter that is not part of themselves – presumably because they are not part of the organic whole; thus, in adoring the humanity of Christ, the Apostles adored such matter. The idea seems to be that as the matter in the pores in Christ's body falls within the mind's scan of that body, so the appearances of bread and wine fall within the mind's scan of that same body in the Eucharist. Arnauld gives other examples of the same phenomenon: Moses adoring God in the burning bush or St Elizabeth worshipping Christ in the womb of the Blessed Virgin.

It is not clear, however, whether this theory is Arnauld's own, or the Lutheran position or a *reductio ad absurdum* of it, or even Jurieu's position according to Arnauld. (The context is the question whether Catholics or Lutherans draw the correct inference concerning adoration, given the Real Presence.) Elsewhere, however, Arnauld makes it clear that intentionality is a primitive, inexplicable feature of the mind. But while we cannot ask why the mind is aware in this way, we can ask why it is aware of one thing rather than another, and here Arnauld's theory of ideas, which he thinks is also Descartes's, becomes relevant. The idea of a thing, which is that thing in so far as it exists in the mind, directs the mind's awareness or attention to that thing rather than some other. I think of the sun rather than the moon because I have the idea of the sun, that is, the sun itself, existing in my mind.[61] This theory is ambiguous with respect to the searchlight theory of intentionality, for ideas might be viewed as filters, which allow the apprehension *only* of the object, for example the sun or Christ's body, or as lenses that focus not only on the objects but on all they contain, for example the wings of Icarus or particles of dirt.

Arnauld's solution to the problem of abstraction suggests still another model, different from either the filter or lens models (although it is not one that he appealed to in this context). The problem is how we are aware of something in general rather than in particular, of circularity rather than this or that circle. For the realist Aristotelian scholastics, the mind is

60 *OA* XII, 539.
61 See Nadler, for example, *Arnauld and the Cartesian Philosophy of Ideas*, esp. secs 13–14.

able to abstract the circularity present in each circular thing. For the nominalist Arnauld, there is no such entity, circularity, to be abstracted. His solution (and not incidentally that of his reader Locke) was in terms of partial attention. When I am said to be aware of circularity, I attend to only part of a particular circle, namely its shape, and ignore the rest, for example its colour. Here, the searchlight picks out an object, illuminating it for awareness, which then focuses on only an aspect of what is illuminated. The mind should then be able to ignore the hem of Christ's garment and concentrate on Christ himself.

Whatever his own theory may have been, Jurieu made just this point, or one close to it, in his reply to Arnauld. Recall that the purpose of Arnauld's example of the adoration of extraneous matter in the pores of Christ's body was to show how the appearance or accidents of bread and wine might be adored in adoring the substance of Christ's body that underlies these accidents. Jurieu attacks the analogy on the basis of the mind's ability to attend. The particles in the pores of Christ's body, he said, were unknown to the apostles because they were uninstructed in the Cartesian philosophy. 'Neither with their eyes nor with their mind did they attend to this matter; how could their mind attend to this matter?'[62] The particles are not in the searchlight at all, hence the mind cannot focus on them in any sense. But Catholics, says Jurieu, attend with their eyes and mind to what they adore. The moral-theological question is why they do not restrict their attention to Christ; the philosophical question is how they might be able to do so.

A handle on these questions may be had by returning to the thread of Larroque's criticism of the Catholic convert Brueys. In the *Examen* Brueys tried to respond to a version of the general position he had previously taken as a Calvinist in his *Réponse* [to Bossuet], namely that even granting the Real Presence, adoration of the Eucharist is unjustified. The specific objection, undoubtedly to be found in previous anti-adoration literature, was that transubstantiation might for some reason fail with the result that the Catholic, thinking Christ to be really present on the altar, would be in fact worshipping only bread and wine. (We can think of transubstantiation as a kind of performative whose felicity conditions might not be met – for example, the priest might be an unordained impostor, without the power of consecration.) The objection is, of course, irrelevant. The potential for idolatry that it points to as an unhappy consequence of the doctrine does not entail that the doctrine is false, and if the doctrine is true then the

62 *Le janséniste convaincu*, 174–5.

only way to avoid that consequence is either never to perform consecration or never to worship. In any case, the Catholic Brueys's response was to cite the case of Mary Magdalen and Mary the mother of James, who went to Christ's tomb to worship, ignorant that He had already risen; they no more than the deceived Catholic should be guilty of idolatry. His point seems to be that the real presence of Christ is not necessary to avoid idolatry and that intention, in both senses of the term, is sufficient. This was the premise, of course, that he had previously cited against the adoration of the Eucharist. That is, previously he had argued that the Eucharist should not be adored in an effort to adore God because the intention to adore God is by itself sufficient for such adoration. Now he is saying that for the same reason it is safe to adore the Eucharist in the face of the danger that it might not be the Eucharist after all. The view common to both his positions is that while there is an objective fact of the matter, whether Christ is really present or not, it does not matter to the moral status of those who adore or fail to do so. In fact, it is hard to see how it matters at all.

Brueys's position on the morality of adoration is, of course, a specific instance of the general position that Bayle was then developing on conscience. Larroque rejected Brueys's position; Jurieu rejected both Brueys's and Bayle's position. For both Larroque and Jurieu, intention is not sufficient and, in a sense, not even necessary for proper adoration, which depends on an objective fact of the matter, that is, Christ's presence, and our knowledge of that fact. According to Larroque, Brueys just begs the question with his example of the two Marys. Circumspection is required in so important a practice as adoration, and they failed to exercise it. What is more, even if Christ had been in the tomb, they would have been no less guilty, for they did not yet know Christ to be God – as is indicated by their arriving to embalm Him on the second day of his death when the prophecy called for Him to arise on the third, which shows that they thought of Him as a mere man. Only when they encountered the risen Christ did they, as the Gospel of St Matthew recounts, fall to the ground and worship Him. Biblical exegesis aside, Larroque here sets two conditions for proper adoration to take place: local presence and knowledge that is stronger than mere true belief. Christ must be present, and in some sense we must know Him to be present. Adoration would thus seem ruled out for all but a few historical figures such as the Magi.

But the significance of even proper adoration is discounted by Larroque, who argues Brueys's original position. Even if the two Marys recognized the divinity of Christ in the tomb, why adore Him there rather than in heaven, 'since the divinity is everywhere and especially there?' The sensory evidence of the divinity's presence does not give us greater certainty of it, and the hankering after it is in fact a sign of the weakness of the human spirit, 'which is happy to place false gods before Him.' Thus it is a mistake to worship Christ in the Sacrament even if He is present in it.[63] Larroque is inclined to take a dim view of the worship even of the historical Christ. The explanation is likely the incipient deism he shares with Lenfant.

Brueys's reliance on intention in dealing with the problem of the unexpectedly absent Christ – absent from the altar, absent from the tomb – requires him to deal also with the biblical text that began this chapter. He wants to say that the deceived Catholic who intends to adore Christ in the Sacrament innocently believing Him to be there really adores Christ. 'But, it will be said' – as undoubtedly it had already been said – 'the Israelites were idolaters although they intended to adore God, whom they believed to be in the golden calf.' His answer is that the Israelites, newly led out of the land of superstition and idolatry, were expressly forbidden to worship God under any form whatsoever; not only did they worship God, but they did so under a form relating directly to the idolatry of the Egyptians, who worshipped a calf under the name of Apis.[64] Their sin, then, was a violation of the first Commandment ('Thou shalt have no other gods before me') in its second clause ('Thou shalt not make unto Thee any graven image, or any likeness *of any thing* that *is* in heaven above, or that *is* in the earth beneath, or that *is* in the water under the earth.)'[65] Catholics, meanwhile, are obviously not forbidden to worship God, and they do so in a sacrament that was instituted by Christ and that 'presents Christ Himself.'[66]

Larroque attacked the relevance of intention by asking 'what greater sin would there have been in adoring the divinity under the form [of the god Apis] rather than another, if the correctness of intention is a valid excuse?'[67] But this question only addresses the grossness of the sin, and not Brueys's major point that the Israelites were not guilty of idolatry. This

63 *Le proselyte abusé*, 155–63.
64 It is not clear what Brueys bases his interpretation of the prohibition on. Deuteronomy 9: 16, for example, only repeats Exodus 32: 8, that in making the golden calf, the people of Moses had 'turned aside quickly out of the way which the Lord had commanded [them].'
65 Exodus 20: 3, 4.
66 *Examen*, 142–7.
67 See *Le proselyte abusé*, 163–5.

point is attacked instead by Jurieu, who agrees with Brueys that the Israelites, fearing only god, adored the calf only as the image and likeness of God. Yet they were idolaters, for intention is irrelevant. Whoever adores the sun intending to worship God is guilty of idolatry.[68] For Jurieu, the Israelites violated the first commandment, the same sin committed by Catholics. The two kinds of violation also occur with similar intentions.

The golden calf was the fruit of misguided piety and ignorant zeal that sought visible images of its God to excite its devotion; the Sacrament, by supposing the Real Presence and adoration, is the product of ignorant devotion that would draw help in ascending to God from supposing its God to be locally present on the altar. The golden calf was adored by the people on the false supposition that the God who led them out of Egypt had taken up his dwelling within, according to the crazed imagination of the Egyptian idolaters who believe that through the virtue of consecration the gods had entered their statues;[69] the Sacrament is adored by the people in the supposition that Jesus Christ had entered and had been drawn there by the virtue of consecration. The adoration of the golden calf was a formal violation of the prohibition to them of representing God under images in order to adore him in these images; the adoration of the Sacrament formally violates the prohibition against adoring the divinity by adoring such creatures as the sun ... it is therefore against the first commandment.[70]

As part of his position on intentionality, Brueys had distinguished two kinds of adoration: one, adoration properly speaking, which is a self-annihilation before the Creator; the other, a feeling of respect evidenced daily before kings. On the basis of behaviour they cannot be distinguished. Thus it is an internal issue, on which we should not judge.[71] Once again, Jurieu disagrees. 'We know nothing about the inner man except by external signs. Actions are visible words to which we should relate it. They are established by nature and by usage to signify the inner movements of the soul, and we should stop at that. God Himself, who knows the inner man with the help of actions and words, none the less judges of [the idolatry of] worship rendered Him by the outward aspect, without regard for the inner.'[72] As in the case of erring conscience, there is, for

68 *Suite du préservatif,* 75–6, 109.
69 Here Jurieu has a reference to the *Asclepius* of Hermes Trismegistus. For the background, see F. Yates, *Giordano Bruno,* chap.1.
70 *Suite du préservatif,* 126–8.
71 *Examen,* 74–7. See also note 59 above.
72 *Suite du préservatif,* 74.

Jurieu, an objective fact of the matter that fully determines the moral significance of an action. Later he was to make explicit the connection between idolatry and the culpable erring conscience. 'We cannot be under an obligation to follow the erring conscience because idolaters intend to adore the true God, the infinitely perfect being; the Israelites by adoring the golden calf intended to adore the God who had led them out of Egypt; nevertheless they were idolaters and God punished them as such.'[73]

To summarize Jurieu's position, then, the Israelites intended to worship God but failed to do so. The failure was the result of a mistake of the sort always attributable to the corruption of the heart. This is the language, of course, which Jurieu was to use against Bayle, who had other explanations of such mistakes – for example, in terms of education – which do not inculpate. The biblical text supports Jurieu's account, for the Lord says to Moses in so many words that his people have 'corrupted themselves' and have made a golden calf. The mistake itself was the belief that the way to worship God was to worship the calf. (The text is also clear that the calf was worshipped.)[74] One way to read the position is that the original purposive intention contained an aboutness intention that was superseded by another aboutness intention with a different object, with the result that the purposive intention was frustrated. When the Israelites tried to worship God by worshipping a calf, they thereby worshipped 'only a phantom of their imagination'[75] that is, a false god who is worshipped in this way. Their failure to reach the true God for the purpose of worshipping Him or for any other purpose, is of the same sort that, according to Descartes, necessarily follows from the idea of God as Gassendi claimed to conceive it. In any event, there is, for Jurieu, an objective fact of the matter, independent of intention in either sense, according to which an action is an instance of idolatry or not. However plausible this position may be with respect to the morality of other actions, it is a curious one to be taken on idolatry by one who criticizes the emptiness of Catholic ritual. For what seems to count for Jurieu is just that – ritual. The emptiness of Catholic ritual must be attributable, not to ritual itself, but to the fact that they have the wrong ritual.

---

73 *Le vray système*, 193. On the other hand, as has been seen, a heretic commits a greater crime by remaining within the Church than he would by separating from it. For he is not only a heretic, but also an idolater, because 'he adores Him whom he believes not to be God. He blasphemes in his heart the God whom he externally adores' (ibid, 308). Either Jurieu contradicts his previous position or he confuses idolatry and blasphemy.
74 Exodus 32: 8.
75 *Le vray système*, 305.

Brueys was not one to let such responses go unnoticed. He did not reply to Lenfant, whose work he just might not have known, but he did reply to the two others. Like Bayle, Brueys comments on Larroque's youth, and he deals mainly with Jurieu.[76] After defending himself against the personal attack of Jurieu that he is a wastrel, that he is a base-born opportunist, etc., Brueys focuses on Jurieu's case with respect to the Eucharist. First, Jurieu obfuscated the real issue, according to Brueys, and never properly replied to the question *de fait*, namely, whether Trent ever authorized worship of something other than Christ. Jurieu addressed this question only with an inappropriate comparison between worship of a body like a tree or the sun and worship of appearances, or accidents, like those of bread and wine.[77] Brueys does not develop the point, but what he wants is a sharp substance-accident division. Catholics are not idolaters, for they worship Christ under the accidents of bread and wine; the idolater is Jurieu, who in claiming to worship God worships a created substance.

The question *de droit*, according to Brueys, is whether it is permissible (contrary to Jurieu) to worship God in a place where He gives no external sign of His presence.[78] His own answer to this question is ambiguous. The premise is that, according to Scripture, God evidences His love and mercy towards us in the Eucharist, in which He gives Himself to us, but not in any creature such as a tree or the sun. Whether the Eucharist is thus an external sign or not, worship of it is appropriate; but any worship connected with a tree or the sun is idolatry. It might be noted that this question *de droit* seems to reduce to a question *de fait* in so far as it is a Scriptural issue. But both sides agree on what words are to be found in the text, namely, 'This is my body.' The important question is to their meaning and who is in a position of authority to determine that meaning, which is indeed a question *de droit*.

Brueys also attempts to rebut a version of the searchlight theory that he finds in Jurieu. This is an argument to the effect that 'as the sovereign adoration that falls on the divinity of Christ is the same that by way of reflection [*par voye de rejaillissement*] falls on human nature, so that ado-

---

76 *La réfutation de deux réponses faites à l'Examen*, appended to the *Défense du culte extérieur*. Bayle rather sarcastically reviewed Brueys's *Défense du culte* but not the *Réfutation*. He castigated Brueys's failure in the earlier work to make clear that the conversions then being obtained in France were the result of force, particularly through the practice of dragooning. *NRL* December 1685, x; *OD* I, 442.
77 Ibid, 449.
78 Ibid, 446.

ration that falls directly on the flesh of Christ falls likewise by reflection on the accidents of bread and wine.'[79] But at this point there is a stalemate. Brueys asks whether Catholics are therefore accused of adoring the chalice holding the Sacrament, or whether the Apostles adored the clothes of Christ. His position is that Trent decreed that the object of worship by the Magi in Bethlehem and by the apostles in Galilee should be the object of worship in the Eucharist. But how their worship takes place is left unclear and the same questions that began this chapter reappear. Jurieu's position is that even granting the Real Presence, Catholics do not make the 'mental separation' between adoring Christ and adoring the Sacrament; they are like the Israelites who worshipped the calf. Brueys's response is that no one would be so stupid as to worship bread; Catholics cannot be guilty of idolatry because they say in good faith that they worship only God. Heretics, according to him, are condemned only when what they say is contrary to what the Church teaches – for example, when the Arians say that Christ is not God.[80] This response raises the question debated by Gassendi and Descartes as to whether the word 'God' in such circumstances of disagreement is nothing but a homonym. This extension shows, perhaps, the bankruptcy of essentialism: which idea is the correct one? If the question remains in principle always open to discussion, to amendment, etc., essentialism is false; if not, then there is an intellectual stand-off. From all that we have seen, Bayle should reject essentialism.

25: Bayle and the Divine Dialogue

The Council of Trent defined its doctrine of the Eucharist such that Christ is everywhere wholly present in the sacrament. The ontological implications of the doctrine were indicated at the beginning of the seventeenth century in a text that went through some twenty editions. *La Physique ou science des choses naturelles* (1603) of Scipion Dupleix (1569–1661) argued against Aquinas and in favour of Scotus that matter can exist without form because in the Eucharist accidents exist without subject, which is 'more repugnant'. He also argued that the same body can be in different places at the same time and that several bodies can be in the same place at the same time. Although this cannot happen naturally, it does happen in the Eucharist, for the Son of God is in every instance of

---

79 *Suite du préservatif*, 116; *Défense du culte extérieur*, 456.
80 Ibid, 457–63.

the Eucharist, and in every part of each instance.[81] Now, as has already been seen, these are also the terms in which Bayle understands the doctrine of Spinoza. If there is only one substance, then the one substance, which is material as well as spiritual, can be simultaneously in more than one place; indeed, it must be in all places.

This dialectic explains Bayle's unusually vehement and consistent denunciation of Spinoza's doctrine: it is an ontology that supports, and is supported by, the doctrine of the Real Presence. 'The Spinozists,' he says, 'might profit from the doctrine of transubstantiation; for if they will consult the writings of the Spanish scholastics, they will find an infinity of subtleties for somehow answering the arguments of those who say that the same man cannot be a Mohammedan in Turkey and a Christian in France, sick in Rome and healthy in Vienna.'[82] But the dialectic fails to explain Bayle's prior denunciation of the Real Presence as an instance of idolatry. There are two parts to this latter explanation. One is the interpretation of the crucial words of Scripture, 'this is my body.' The question of this interpretation is treated in chapter 3 above as the question *de droit* as to the Church's authority. The other part of the explanation relates to the issue of intentionality as discussed above in this chapter. In the terms used above to discuss that issue, Bayle is ambivalent and perhaps even contradictory. (In exasperation, one may be inclined to take literally Bayle's exasperated comment on the Malebranche-Arnauld controversy over the nature of ideas. 'This dispute,' he said, 'shows us that the way in which we know objects is inexplicable, and can provide us with great lessons in humility.')[83]

An example of Bayle's ambivalence is his treatment of purposive intention. In a text from the *Commentaire philosophique* that was discussed above in chapter 4, Bayle claims to extend religious toleration 'as far as anyone.' Bayle none the less would show 'not the least quarter to those who insult the divinity in whom they profess to believe, even if it be the least of the dung divinities of which Scripture speaks.'[84] He cites Grotius, Grotius on Cyril, and Seneca to the effect that those who *believe* themselves committing sacrilege are punishable. Whether the sacrilegious man and his judges are of the same religion makes no difference; what is important is that he was acting contrary to conscience, and with

81 Bk. 2, chap. 5, 131–2; bk. 4, chap. 6, 261–2. I am grateful to Roger Ariew for pointing out these texts to me and for making the point above.
82 Art. Spinoza, rem. DD; for one of the subtleties, see ibid, rem. M, III.
83 *NRL* April 1684, ii; *OD* I, 26.
84 *Comm. phil.* II, ix; *OD* II, 428.

respect to this, it seems, all must be of the same view. Here is the argument. '[God] as the legislator of the laws of morality is the one principally offended by their transgression. Now, the most necessary and indispensable of these laws is that which prohibits doing what one believes to be evil or impious.'[85] Whether or not 'the God whom they know be a fiction of their mind,' if they believe him to be the true God, then in offending him they offend the true God. Thus there is no difference between a Jew pillaging the temple of Jerusalem and a Greek pillaging the temple at Delphi. The upshot is, or should be, that if the Israelites in good faith believed that they were worshipping God in what they were doing, then they were innocent. This position comports perfectly with Bayle's later view of conscience as autonomous.

The position seems explicitly contradicted, however, by what he had said earlier about idolatry. In the *Critique générale de ... Maimbourg*, Bayle makes it clear, and does so at length, that intention to the contrary is not sufficient to excuse idolatry; or more precisely, that while intending to adore the one true God one may nonetheless commit the sin of idolatry. It is not likely, he says, that the Israelites should have passed from knowledge of God their liberator to total ignorance of Him by worshipping a mass of gold in the form of a calf. 'They had the intention of honouring God under the shape of a golden calf, and yet their good intention did not prevent them from being idolatrous; thus the good intention of Catholics does not keep them from being idolaters if they adore the Sacrament without Christ being there.'[86] Absent the Real Presence, Catholics are guilty of idolatry, regardless of their intentions – just as they are according to Jurieu. Bayle thus goes on immediately to discuss what Brueys was later to call the question *de droit*, which Bayle understands as the question whether Scripture reveals the Real Presence as clearly as it does the Incarnation, or if not, whether there is a church 'endowed with infused knowledge' that enables it to interpret the obscurities of Scripture to this effect. Bayle's answer on both counts is obvious.

The contradiction is eliminated if the idolatry in question is an objective fact of the matter, but one for which the idolaters are not culpable. Good intention in the sense of purpose is the domain of conscience, which is sufficient and independent of all else. But conscience does not guarantee a successful intention in the sense of aboutness. Whether this view is in fact Bayle's view – whether it is even intelligible – is an open

85 *OD* II, 429.
86 *Crit. gen.* IV, xxviii; *OD* II, 133.

question (how can purpose succeed, that is, succeed, not in being fulfilled, but even in being a purpose to do x rather than y, without aboutness?).[87]

Even if an objective act of idolatry runs against Bayle's doctrine of an autonomous conscience, it may be supported by his account of the source of error. Here he rejects Jurieu's view that all error springs from the corruption of the heart – basically the Cartesian view that all error is a function of the will, and thus culpable. This view would be plausible, according to Bayle, only if all errors were connected with cupidity. But, as we saw at the outset, the issue of transubstantiation is not connected with cupidity for Bayle and is, rather, his counter-example to Jurieu's thesis that all error springs from corruption of the heart. One side or the other gets it wrong as an objective fact of the matter, but not as a result of anything they are responsible for. (Education is the determinant of such beliefs.) Good intention would seem to be irrelevant.[88]

The same text yields a second point of relevance that has already been examined above. Even the dispute over transubstantiation might be a matter of passion if the Calvinists hold their view as a matter of pride. But they do not, according to Bayle, for that would be for them to hold views contrary to what they believe God to have revealed. 'Now, this thought cannot enter the mind of anyone, not even the evilest demon, because every mind with an idea of God means by this word a Being who knows things with certainty and is incapable of deception; and never did the demon who spoke to Eve the contrary of what God had said believe himself to speak the truth. He knew full well that what God said was true.'[89] That is, even those who are prepared to act contrary to what God has revealed do not, if they understand who God is, believe that what God has revealed is false or could ever possibly be false; for God is veracious. Now, this argument might assume something like Descartes's view that in order to know God at all, one must have the one and only true idea of God, that if one thinks of a being as capable of deception, one is therefore not thinking of God at all. The argument might minimally assume a version of Descartes's view, namely, that to know God at least some of His quali-

87 In the recent literature on intentionality, Ruth G. Millikan has argued (244–5) that the 'classical' account of intentionality (think of Descartes or Arnauld above) mistakenly conflates the following: seeming to think about x, actually thinking about x, seeming to know what x is, and actually knowing what x is.
88 *Comm. phil.* II, x; *OD* II, 439.
89 Ibid.

ties must be known – if not all that comprise his essence, at least a cluster of its components.[90]

Did Bayle subscribe at least to a cluster theory? Not necessarily; for even in his argument concerning divine veracity, he commits himself to much less than this. If one knows what the word 'God' means, or perhaps better, if one know what others mean by the word 'God' who have a proper idea of God, that is, if one has a proper idea of God oneself, then one has a grasp of at least certain qualities of God. But this leaves open the possibility that, contrary to the cluster theory, one could know God without any idea of Him at all. And it is just this possibility that Bayle seems to allow when he argues that the pagan pantheon did not personify the attributes of the one true God.

The view is that pagans were not atheists but imperfect believers, and that their gods were attempts to represent such various qualities of God as they were able to grasp. (This may be what according to Tournemine the Chinese were attempting to do.) Recall that one argument against the view is the moral consideration that it would exculpate the worst practices of Rome with respect to relics, Mariolatry, etc.[91] Another argument is based on empirical grounds: the religious practices of the pagans are an indication

90 As it happens, there is, or may be, an early expression of this cluster theory, as it is
    called in the recent literature on reference. (For the recent expression, see Searle.) It
    occurs, curiously, in a piece criticizing Bayle's views on knowledge of God. The Jesuit
    R.J. Tournemine, in his 1710 preface to Fénelon's *Démonstration* (unpaginated), argued
    that there has never been a true atheist, that 'the idea we have of ourselves is so per-
    fectly joined to the idea of God that we cannot at all develop the former without being
    struck by the force of the latter.' Against Bayle's claims that there are atheists, which he
    takes to be a show of arguing the pro and con of all questions, Tournemine argues in
    the alternative. First of all, Bayle's reports of barbarous people deprived of all knowl-
    edge of God are based on false information. Even crediting them, such people are men
    'only in shape, lacking reason as much as religion.' Nor are they ignorant of God so
    much as just 'forgetful' of Him, even like some Christians, for when questioned in the
    proper way, they come to believe in God. Even the enlightened Chinese of whose pro-
    fessed atheism Bayle speaks are not atheists. 'It is true that they are mistaken about the
    essence of God; they conceive of the divinity as I don't know what virtue spread
    throughout the universe, especially the material sky, His principal instrument. After
    all, to err in this way is not to deny the existence of God; it is not to be an atheist. Idola-
    ters have the most debased ideas of God and are not atheists.' These enlightened Chi-
    nese attribute to the divinity the same attributes we do: creation, conservation of the
    universe, and providence. 'So little are they atheists that their error could not have
    entered their minds except by accommodating our natural idea of God and giving to
    the chimerical *Li* the traits of the divinity.' The position seems to be that everyone has
    some idea of God, that this idea need not be of His essence, but that it is always suffi-
    cient to know God, at least that He exists.
91 See n. 14.

that they believed there are real distinctions among their divinities, which they therefore could not have viewed as aspects of the one God. Moreover, previous attempts to interpret the pantheon in this way have failed. 'The philosophers, mainly the Stoics, wanted to reduce the mythology of the poets to a measurable system, even before the birth of Christianity ... They sought I-don't-know-what allegorical sense in terms of which they would formulate a system based on the teachings of physics ... [But they can be accused] of the same mistake found in those who adore nature. If they adore it in a single being they adore only a definition or abstraction of their mind; if they adore something existing outside their understanding, they adore as many beings as there are particular natures. For there exists no universal nature, but only the nature of this or that thing, and thus there are really as many distinct natures as there are individuals.'[92]

Bayle here rejects both the Jurieu-Gassendi position and the Bossuet-Descartes position, including the cluster-theory variant. For God is not known by any idea at all. Outside the mind there are only individuals – particular natures as he calls them – and these do not answer to our ideas, which are universals – definitions or abstractions as he calls them. Not incidentally, this nominalism is consistent with, and in fact helps to explain Bayle's comment on the Malebranche-Arnauld dispute over the nature of ideas. Recall that the moral of the story for him is one of humility, that the way objects are known is inexplicable. But this is not to say that they are not known at all, for he continues: 'The dispute can teach us above all that while we know with great certainty the existence and immateriality of our soul, we have no idea of it. This is what apparently will be found best proved in [Malebranche's *Reply* to Arnauld]'[93]

The same conclusion emerges from the long discussion of Simonides' response to the request from Hiero, tyrant of Sicily, for a definition of God.[94] As reported by Cicero, Simonides asked for a day to think over the question; at the end of the day he asked for two more days, and so on, each time, doubling the time needed, and explaining, finally, that the more he considered it, the more obscure it became. Bayle imaginatively reconstructs Simonides' reasoning to show the inconceivability of a God with the attributes He is supposed to have – first and most importantly the power of creation, but also freedom and wisdom that limit each other, and the responsibility for a world that contains evil. The catalogue is a familiar one, leading either to atheism or to some way other than by rea-

92 *CPD*, cxxi; *OD* II, 374–5.
93 *NRL* April 1684, ii; *OD* I, 26.
94 Art. Simonides, rem. F.

son and ideas of knowing God. Reason leaves every such question in the balance, which is tipped only by 'grace or education in childhood.'[95]

Bayle rejects ideas of all things outside the mind; in this, the case of knowledge of God is not different from that of the soul or of anything else. But there is a special reason why God must be known as an individual. Only as such is He a transcendent participant in a dialogic exchange that is not written out in advance. This is perhaps why Bayle, like Larroque, gives little evidence of willingness to worship the historical Christ, let alone the Eucharist. The importance of Christ is less the presumed presence of divinity than the word of God in a fairly literal sense. The attempts of the philosophers above to know God through an idea of reason miss the whole point; 'they started with the gods of the poets, living and animate gods, and they substituted other gods having neither life nor knowledge.' By their construing Juno as the air, for example, prayer and sacrifice became ridiculous, for she would hear and know nothing. This is a material atheism that would be acceptable even to a Spinozist.[96] Moreover, Spinozism, which obliterates differences between individuals and denies miracles (in particular, God's interventions in human history and creation itself), also makes dialogue impossible. The Spinozists, claiming to worship God, in fact worship nature. Catholicism does the same with a God silent upon the altar. Bayle exhibits the same animus towards Spinozism that he does towards transubstantiation, not only in the intensity of the animus, but in its object.[97] Both are instances of idolatry.

95 Not incidentally, Bayle draws attention to 'the most subtle Cartesians' (read: Malebranche), who deny that we have any idea of the soul: through experience we know that it thinks, but we do not know its nature. Not knowing what a mind is, Simonides would not have affirmed God to be one. It might be noted that Malebranche too denies that we have an idea of God – not because He is inconceivable or unintelligible, but because no idea of Him is needed since He is perfectly intelligible by Himself and in fact is the ground for the intelligibility of everything else. See Malebranche, *The Search after Truth*, bk. 3, part 2, chaps. 6-7. For more on Bayle's view of God as incomprehensibile, see art. Sadeur, rem. C, which incidentally is a typically offbeat text from Bayle.

96 Art. Jupiter, rem. N.

97 The notion of change employed by Catholics to describe transubstantiation is, according to Bayle, the same notion employed by the Spinozists. When Catholics say that bread is changed into the body of Christ, they mean that the substance of the bread is annihilated and replaced by that of Christ; when the Spinozists say that the one substance, God or nature, does *not* change they mean that is not annihilated and replaced with another. But the ordinary notion of change has it that substance changes through changes in accidents that it acquires and relinquishes. Thus the Spinozists really allow change in God and the Catholics no change in the bread. Art. Spinoza, rem. CC.

6

Providence

The nest of concepts to be discussed in this chapter much occupied the attention of the seventeenth century. Pascal at mid-century invented the modern probability calculus – as the story goes, in order to divide the stakes in an interrupted game of chance. Gassendi around the same time was arguing, on behalf of a theologically acceptable atomism, that if the Epicurean world were finite, chance could not account for its order and Providence would have to be reintroduced.[1] Towards the end of the century, these concepts of probability, chance, and related notions were, for additional sorts of reasons, receiving even greater attention, and Bayle's writing on central issues was shaped by them in profound and surprising ways. How so?

It would seem that the notion of Providence is, no less than Leibnizian essentialism, at odds with autonomy, conscience, and polyphonic interpretation. In Popper's terms, anyone committed to Predestination in particular is committed to historicism and the closed society in a fairly literal sense. For the world thus has a denouement describable only as fatalist, according to which, most notably, some people are saved and some damned. Even so, Bayle avoids at least the most pernicious aspects of historicism. For one thing, no one but God knows what His providence is, and therefore no mortal is in a position to dictate religious, or any other, views on the basis of it. Bayle is very much aware of the dangers of fatalist views and of the ruses of those who 'make others believe that the heavens are a book in which God has written the history of the world.'[2] But most importantly, whether people are saved or not,

---

1 See Osler.
2 *CDP*, lxxvi; *OD* III, 49–50. *CDP*, lxxx; *OD* III, 51. *CDP*, lxxxii; *OD* III, 52.

whether they belong to one religion or another, is of no relevance in how they ought to be treated. (This is just the doctrine of toleration.) Such questions are, from Bayle's perspective, effectively a matter of chance. Although current and important in a variety of ways at this time, the concept of chance was, like the *fait-droit* distinction, philosophically charged and, like it, requires a broad context to be appreciated.

26: Lotteries

In August of 1686, Bayle reviewed Jurieu's *Jugement sur ... Grace.*[3] In his review, Bayle cites a line from earlier Jansenist disputes to the effect that questions of grace are like an ocean in which there is no bottom and no shore, and he recounts Jurieu's argument that none of the many systems dealing with grace is able both to preserve the idea of an infinitely sovereign deity and to answer the difficulties in Augustine's position, which is to say Calvin's position, with which Jurieu therefore remains. Bayle takes Jurieu's argument to be theorectically weak, but sufficient for practical purposes. To remain with the view that one happens to hold 'is to act according to common sense and the incontestable principle of the natural light that *immobility is preferable to change*. Among bodies it is an inviolable law of nature that they never change states unless the reasons for change are stronger than those for not changing. The same must be true for minds, so that even if it is only chance or caprice that has placed us in a given sect, it is better to live and die in it if the others are no better.' This conservative recommendation rather resembles Descartes's provisional morality in both its statement and motivation. Having demolished the house of human knowledge, Descartes was in need of a dwelling while his job of epistemological reconstruction was in progress. Not unlike the Pyrrhonian sceptics, he opted for the locally held positions. 'The first [of four rules] was to obey the laws and customs of my country, holding constantly to the religion in which by God's grace I had been instructed from my childhood.'[4]

For Bayle the *faute-de-mieux* recommendation to adhere to locally held positions has particular significance given his own two conversions and presumable changes on issues such as grace. If difference in belief about grace distinguish Catholics and Protestants, and these beliefs can-

---

3 *NRL* August 1686, art. iv; *OD* I, 620.
4 *Discourse on method* 1; *CSM* I, 122. This is one of the very few instances in which Bayle clearly follows either Descartes or the Pyrrhonians.

not be rationally justified, then it is best, according to Bayle, to rest with the religious lot that one has drawn by chance (*le hazard, ou le caprice*). In addition, Bayle holds that quite apart from *beliefs* about grace, the *distribution* of grace itself cannot be understood and may, at least as far as we are concerned, be taken as if we had drawn lots. That is, from our perspective, both what we happen to believe about grace and whether we have grace, whatever we may believe about it, turn out to be matters of chance. Thus, as both religion and salvation can be understood as matters of chance, the lottery is more than just a metaphor in dealing with Bayle on these topics.

The Old Testament evidences many instances of the use of lotteries or games of chance to determine a range of issues such as the choice of kings or the division of land. The basis for this use is reflected in Proverbs 16: 33: 'The lot is cast into the lap; but the whole disposing thereof is of the Lord.' Now, in the seventeenth century, there were two general considerations that were appealed to in the condemnation of gambling. One was that it is unproductive (and in many cases actually destructive); the other was that it is an unwarranted invocation of the deity.[5] To call upon God to decide the division of stakes is, as it was put, to tempt God and to do so in a trivial matter. In this sense, gambling is a perverse manipulation of Providence. Significantly, it is difficult to distinguish lotteries understood in this way from petitionary prayer, even on the basis of triviality, for prayer seemingly can be for a trivial or even immoral purpose.

Not all prayer is petitionary, but the paradigm of prayer is largely petitionary. His apostles ask Christ to teach them how to pray and they are instructed not just in praising God, but in asking their daily bread, forgiveness for their sins, and deliverance from temptation and evil.[6] Non-formulaic or incompletely formulaic prayer might be used to ask for all sorts of things. Keith Thomas reports that according to Thomas More, Welsh and Irish thieves prayed before going out to steal, and, in an example of particular relevance, he quotes Thomas Browne: "'Tis not a ridiculous devotion to say a prayer before a game at tables."[7] Such prayer was generally a way of dealing with the environment, including of course the supernatural, which was a more frequent and acceptable object of petition, and in particular as it related to one's salvation.

5 See Brenner, *Gambling*, chap. 1, sec. 1.
6 Luke 11: 1–4.
7 Thomas, 135.

(Given the necessity and sufficiency of grace for salvation, such prayer needed to have been understood by Calvinists as pure supplication and not as anything of merit. Even so, it is hard to imagine Bayle praying. For him, *les jeux sont faits*.)

One form of petitionary prayer was divinitory – praying for guidance before making a decision, for example, whether to take a trip. And one version of this prayer was casting lots, with a long history in Christianity both of practice and condemnation. Here, Thomas quotes Gibbon: 'From the fourth to the fourteenth century, these *sortes sanctorum*, as they were styled, were repeatedly condemned by the decrees of councils and repeatedly practiced by Kings, bishops and saints.'[8] (This history was, of course, of a piece with the decision-making practices of trial by ordeal or by combat. In all three cases, the judgment rendered was thought to be God's.) The basis for the condemnation of casting lots was, as John Weemse wrote in 1636, that 'when a man hath other means to try by, then it is tempting God to use lots.'[9]

An important statement of this condemnation based on the Providence argument, as we may call it, comes from William Perkins (1558–1602).[10] In *Cases of Conscience*, Perkins raises the question of whether recreation is lawful for a Christian man, and answers that it is[11] for rest and for delight.[12] Games are of three sorts. There are games of 'wit and industry,'[13] 'mixt' games of wit and luck, where 'hazard begins and skill gets the victory,' as in some card games (these are not to be condemned, but are nevertheless better avoided), and games of chance, 'in which hazard onely bears the sway, and orders the game, and not wit; wherein also there is (as we say) chance, yea, meere chance in regard of us. Of this kind is dicing.' These games of chance are unlawful, for three reasons: They stir up passions and distemper the mind; they are usually motivated by greed; but most importantly because 'games of meere haz-

---

8 Ibid, 139.

9 *A Treatise of the Foure Degenerate Sinnes*, 79; quoted in Thomas, 121.

10 Important because according to Thomas (123, fn. 1), Perkins was an an authority for Jean Barbeyrac's opponent Pierre de Joncourt, the only late seventeenth-century author actually to have clearly used the Providence argument. See below for more on these two authors.

11 See *Works* II, 1210–43. As a young man at Cambridge, Perkins apparently had been something of a hell-raiser until he heard himself pointed out on the street as 'drunken Perkins.' *Dict. Nat. Biog.*

12 Ecclesiastes 7:18, 'Be not too righteous.'

13 'Shooting in the long Bow ... Wrastling ... Musicke ... and draughts, the Philosophers game.' (141).

ard are indeede lots; and the use of a lot is an act of religion, in which we refer unto God, the determination of things of moment, that can in no other way be determined.'[14]

The Providence argument was soon under attack, and continued to be throughout the rest of the century. Thomas Gataker in his *Of the nature and use of lots: a treatise historical and theological* (1619) sought to refute the view that 'in every lot ... there is an extraordinary and immediate hand and providence of God present.'[15] A lot, that is, 'a casualtie or casuall event purposely applyed to the deciding of some doubt,' may be any of three kinds. To be sure, Gataker condemns one kind of lot, apparently on intrinsic grounds as a violation of Providence. These are 'extraordinary' or 'divinitory' lots, wherein the effort to determine what otherwise cannot be known surpasses the natural powers of those casting them and of their instruments. Thus, Abraham's servant selects the proper wife for Isaac by praying to God that it be the woman who quenches his thirst and waters his camels as well (Genesis 24: 12–15). Some of these lots reported by the Bible were authorized by God, hence lawful, others not. None thereafter was authorized, hence all are inappropriate, superstitious efforts to elicit special acts of Providence. But there are also two kinds of 'ordinary' or 'divisory' lots for dividing something by entirely natural means. One is the 'serious' kind for 'the division of lands, chatels, bargains, exercises, offices, imployment, and the like.' A second kind is 'lusorious,' which involve games in some way. Neither kind is illicit, specifically because neither involves any special Providence.[16]

Gataker's work set off a series of attacks and replies, including his own second edition, over the next half century. No less than Voetius (Gisbert Voet, 1589–1676), nowadays mainly known as a thorn in Descartes's side, first attacked Gataker in 1636 with a *De sortibus*, and was ultimately led to argue (in the negative) the question raised by his student Martin Schook as to whether it is permissible to drink to someone's health.[17] Not the drink, obviously, but the implicit appeal to Providence was the obstacle to Voetius's *prosit*.

Whether for the Providence argument or for other reasons, gambling was almost universally condemned in this period. Despite this sort of

---

14 Ibid. There are four components in such an act: 1) a 'causal act,' casting the dice;
   2) 'applying' the act to some question of importance; 3) recognition of God as judge;
   4) supplication that God decide.
15 Advertisement to the reader, unpaginated.
16 Ibid, 2, 315–16, 347, 60, 150.
17 See Barbeyrac's preface to the second edition of his *Traité*.

condemnation, 'gambling was everywhere in France during the seven-teenth and eighteenth centuries,'[18] – and not just in France. A particu-larly relevant source on the nature and frequency of gambling is the *Critique historique, politique, morale, economique et comique sur les lotteries, anciennes et modernes, spirituelles et temporelles des états et des églises*, trans-lated from Italian and published in French in 1697. It was written by the blowhard buffoon, Gregorio Leti (1630–1701), who has a number of con-nections with the larger story here.[19] However clownish his work gener-ally, Leti's *Critique* seems basically accurate; it certainly resonates with the *Zeitgeist*. Everyone, everywhere, he says, talks only about the lottery – priests in their sacristies, lawyers in their offices, students in school, etc. – even the author was enticed by family into buying some tickets ('RIP to a hundred ducats'). But the lottery is not some aberration. Nature itself is a lottery, he says, endowing some with good looks and others with the Devil's own ugliness.[20] Childbearing is a lottery – a royal couple wanting for nothing, in perfect health, and doing all that is neces-

18 Thus does Grussi begin his book, (7), a very useful work for information on currency (16), vocabulary for games, (14–16), how gambling was organized (chaps. 2–4), its role as an instrument of control in the politics of Louis XIV, (60 ff.), the ruin often caused by gambling (150–53), etc.

19 A Protestant, born in Milan, later living in Switzerland, England, and Holland, who was the father-in-law of Leclerc. Bayle initially took him quite seriously. He cites Leti's maxim, from his *Theatro Brittanico*, that the religion of a historian should not be known from his work, and observes that Leti adhered to it himself. He also summarized Leti's scathing denunciation of Louis XIV's decree concerning the conversion of Protestant children. *Nouvelles lettres* VIII, 8; *OD* II, 213. But Bayle's respect deteriorated. As Gigas put it, 'This Italian of rather dubious honesty, expelled from one country after another, his head full of his own greatness and always beating the drum for his own numerous publications, impugned the practices of the *Nouvelles de la république des lettres*' (xxv). Although Bayle had given remarkably good reviews of two of his works, Leti was not satisfied, and Bayle ended with a low opinion of him. To Minutoli, 18 February 1692; *OD* IV, 756. Letters to Bayle from Duclos, Minutoli, and Turrettini certainly do not show much respect at all for Leti. Bayle certainly knew the *Critique*. On 29 August 1697 Bayle wrote to Dubos that the *Critique* had gotten Leti in trouble with the Walloon Church in Amsterdam and that Leti had to make amends (Gigas, 108). A month later, Bayle had to write to Leclerc, having already written to Leti, denying that he was the author of the *Considerations sur la critique des Lotteries*, criticizing Leti on, among other grounds, anglophobia and francophilia. Leti and Leclerc were difficult to dissuade, however. Only after Leti had published a *Recueil* of letters in his favour with a preface in response to the *Considerations* did the author identify himself as Pierre Ricotier, who under his own name published *Reflexions sur la dernière preface*. To Leclerc, 30 Septem-ber 1697; *OD* IV, 756–7; and to an unidentified recipient, 9 December 1697; *OD* IV, 763.

20 Leti, 22, 39.

sary find themselves sterile, while a mere shepherd, the first time ... And so on, throughout all of nature. The distribution of grace, which he understands in terms of goods in this world, is a lottery,[21] as is the creation of the world, at least as far as the Fall is concerned. The church is a lottery, as are government, health, and so on, by which he means that they undergo various unpredictable vicissitudes.

As to the proper, institutionalized lotteries, Leti reports that in England and Holland they were established to support the war effort. Since money to supply the ships so effectively pirated by the French is not found in the woods or the sea and does not fall from the sky, it had to be extracted, he says, from the guts of the people.[22] The model and inspiration seems to have been the London lottery set up by Parliament in the spring of 1694.[23] The lottery spread to Holland, first to Amersfort, where real estate was offered as prizes, and then, elsewhere, as individuals held their own lotteries to rid themselves of less valuable property – silversmiths and jewellers, for example, and finally, in Amsterdam, hairdressers, who put up outmoded headdresses.[24] In July 1695, the Walloon Church of Amsterdam undertook to establish a lottery to pay for the two thousand people it fed and otherwise supported daily.

27: The Legitimization of Gambling

At the end of the seventeenth century, gambling was common, important to a variety of interests, and yet vaguely objectionable. A certain literature emerged in the effort to come to terms with the phenomenon. The clear tendency, especially among Protestant authors, was to construe gambling, specifically the lottery, in naturalistic terms, to undo the

21 Ibid, 56–63.
22 Ibid, 31–2.
23 The lottery was based on a fund of a million pounds, raised from 100,000 tickets, at 10 pounds each. Each ticket was to earn ten per cent interest for sixteen years; in addition, 500 tickets were to be drawn, worth an additional amount of 1,000 to 10 pounds each. Since the aim was to raise money for the king, those with winning tickets would only collect interest on them. Leti's account of this lottery, (161–2) is corroborated by Ashton, *History*, 49–50. (More than a third of the tickets went to foreigners, and, as luck would have it, the first winner was Mme Lecoq, wife of the former counselor to the French, who had fled the Revocation to London.)
24 According to Ashton, the first recorded lottery in England, projected in 1566 and drawn in 1569, already had prizes other than money: silver and gold plate, and cloth (*History*, 5). The total distribution of the universe might very well be, as Leti would have imagined, a lottery.

Providence argument by reversing its significance, and to relocate gambling in a larger context of religious and commercial activities. This literature invariably drew attention to the dangers of gambling, but nearly all of the objections to gambling were of an instrumental nature. Gambling was thought to be wrong, not intrinsically, but because of its ill effects. Although much of the literature was concerned to refute the Providence argument, that argument seems actually to have been endorsed by no one aside from the little-known Pierre de Joncourt (?–1725), Protestant theologian and pastor, member of the *Refuge* from the Revocation, whose profile would suggest an attack on the argument, but whose *Quatre lettres* (1713) defended it against the attack of La Placette (of whom more below).

An important source for the argument is the *Traité des jeux et des divertissements* (1686)[25] by the Catholic Jean-Baptiste Thiers.[26] The quality of his presentation of the argument is less than sophisticated – for example, he argues that gambling is permissible because there are rules governing it[27] – but Thiers provides for use by later authors a very long catalogue of condemnation of games of chance by Christian and pagan

25 Bayle treats this book at some length, in the lead article of *NRL* for January 1687. The conclusion of his treatment of what it has to say about games of pure chance begins with a typically Baylean ironic poke at Rome, but ends, it would seem, by showing Bayle in sympathy with its position: 'According to the principles of the Roman communion, ecclesiastics who play cards must fall into disgrace since Sanchez and Escobar [Jesuit casuists cited by the *Traité*] find this to contain a mortal sin – they in whose moral balance it is difficult to find weighty sins. We find here an ample collection of canon and civil laws that have been passed against *brélans*, or the gaming houses. This shows on the one hand that a remedy for the evil has always been sought, but it appears on the other hand that no success has been achieved. The disorder is thus too inveterate; it would be better therefore not to commit the majesty of the state to prohibitions that are not carried out and that, to tell things as they are, would be carried out quite well by employing proper means.' *OD* I, 735.

26 Thiers (1636–1703) was primarily a theological polemicist, but he also published a great deal on unusual topics, including the history of wigs (designed to show that ecclesiastics should not wear them), the morality of carriages, relics (specifically, the holy tear of Vendome), merchandising at church doors, etc. He was the author of the *Critique de l'histoire des Flagellans et justification des disciplines volontaires* (1703), which criticized Boileau's *Historia Flagellantium*, which Thiers takes to be, not a history of the twelfth- and thirteenth-century sect, but a condemnation of discipline, in the strong sense of the term, which he undertakes to defend. Such liberal views on gambling as are to be found in Thiers do not spring from laxity.

27 For example, one cannot gamble money not belonging to oneself, or with people who can ill afford the potential losses, such as slaves, children, the mad, the blind, and administrators of church funds.

authors, civil and canon laws, Church councils, etc. His own position, as well as almost all those he cites, focuses on instrumental considerations. There are two exceptions, who offer objections in principle. One is the Protestant theologian, Lambert Daneau (1530–96), who argued that in earlier times playing cards had pictures of false gods on them instead of kings and queens.[28] Perhaps, he says, this is why Petrarch, Aquinas, Agrippa, and others assert that 'games of chance are the invention of the Devil and that those who play cards sacrifice to the Devil.'[29] Elsewhere, however, Daneau clearly endorses the Providence argument.

Gambling is expressly forbidden by God, who regulated it in this third commandment, thou shalt not take the name of the Lord thy God in vain. Now, whoever draws lots for ridiculous and insignificant things and uses it only for the useless pleasure of man – doesn't he take God's name and Providence in vain? For drawing lots is one of the main testimonies of God's power (as is written in Proverbs 16: 33 and 18) in so far as He rules and governs immediately by His hand, His power, and Providence. But we should not employ lots in this ridiculous way as if to tempt God and to see His concern with the world; thus, in things of great consequence where His will must be known, as it were, extraordinarily – as in the division of goods, the choice of a magistrate, and such things in order to avoid disputes and rigged elections – and not in things of no moment, as if we were to make God the valet of our pleasures and tried to learn whether He cared about them.[30]

The other author cited by Thiers who offers an objection in principle to gambling is Jean Taffin, minister of Amsterdam. His *De emendatione vitae*[31] asserts that 'games of chance are evil for Christians because they are condemned by the third commandment, which prohibits taking the name of the Lord in vain, in that drawing lots is used for a frivolous thing, and cannot be used without offending God's Providence.'[32] This is clearly an instance of the Providence argument, indicated as such.

A third source in Thiers for the argument is, possibly, François de

---

28 Not incidentally, Klaits (71) credits Daneau with what seems to be the first French-language book on witches, in 1564. His only reference is to Fatio, whose only plausible reference is to Daneau's *Briève remonstrance sur les jeux de sort* (1574). Daneau was also the translator of Tertullian's treatise on idolatry (1565) (Fatio, 106–7).

29 Daneau, 171.

30 *Les jeux de sort*, p. 24–5.

31 French translation, *Traicté de l'amendemente de vie*, 2d ed., 1596.

32 Bk. 2, chap. 19; cited by Thiers, 176.

Sales, whom Thiers cites for many instrumental considerations, but also as regarding gambling as 'simply and naturally evil and blameworthy.'[33] Perhaps this was the text that Jean Barbeyrac later claimed to get from Thiers for the view he attributed to François de Sales, namely, that games of chance are a 'manifest profanation' in that they necessitate particular acts of Providence.[34] We shall soon return to Barbeyrac, who was perhaps the most important theorist of gambling who sought to undo the Providence argument. Meanwhile, we can note that François de Sales does not give, and Thiers, who quotes him accurately, does not say that he gives, the version of the Providence argument reported by Barbeyrac, who was probably attributing to a likely source an argument that was, if no longer accepted, still in the air at the outset of the eighteenth century. Instead, François gives three reasons why gambling at dice, cards, and the like, which is naturally and simply evil and culpable, should be prohibited. First, reason is offended that chance should reward someone who merits nothing by skill or industry. That the payoff is by mutual agreement, he says, does nothing to alter the unreasonableness of the agreement itself. Second, the point of games should be recreation, but the 'sad, sombre, and melancholic' occupation of gambling is, on the contrary, stressful and violent. Third, such joy as there is in winning is entirely at the expense of those who lose.[35] François's preference, rather, is for taking some air, walking, playing a musical instrument, hunting, sports like handball, etc.[36] More important here, in any case, were arguments against the intrinsic evil of gambling, which came, typically, not from Catholics like François de Sales, but from Protestants. A good reason for this will be seen below.

The Providence argument was indirectly attacked by Leclerc.[37] His *Reflexions sur ce que l'on appelle bonheur et malheur en matière de lotteries et sur le bon usage qu'on en peut faire* (1696) was occasioned, as he says, by the proliferation of lotteries due to the prodigious success of the English lottery two years earlier, and by the hubbub of discussion that the lotter-

---

33 Thiers, 168.

34 Barbeyrac, *Traité*, 22–30.

35 François de Sales, *Introduction à la vie devote*, Paris, 1686, 348–9.

36 Ibid, 346–7.

37 Jean Leclerc (1657–1736) was a Remonstrant, accused of Socinianism by the Jesuits' *Journal de Trévoux*. In addition to those of Locke, works of Stanley and Burnet were translated by Leclerc, whose three *Bibliothèques* (*universelle*, *choisie*, and *ancienne et moderne* were a lesser, if longer, NRL). His *Parrhasiana ou pensées diverses* (1699, 1701) occasioned Bayle's last polemic.

ies were generating. He ends the book with an endorsement of the Dutch lotteries then being conducted on behalf of the poor, and with a recommendation for generosity.

The theoretical thrust of Leclerc's book is to naturalize the phenomenon of gambling. For example, he tries to show that the use of the terms good or bad luck in describing an 'I-know-not-what belonging to certain people who win or lose at games, war, etc.' is inappropriate. All that is true of them is thay they win or lose consistently.[38] Especially given the naturalistic usage of his father-in-law, Gregorio Leti, what Leclerc is denying here is explicitly the doctrine of grace as something supernatural possessed by the elect. If the distribution of grace is, as Leti thought, a distribution of goods of this world, and if the 'luck' of such distribution refers, not to those receiving the goods, but only to the distribution itself, then there is nothing true of the elect other than that they are the elect. Whether this conclusion, apart from its naturalistic interpretation, is precisely the one sought by Calvinists, or the one to which at least some of them may have been committed, even despite themselves, is an interesting question. That is, not just from our perspective, but intrinsically or from God's perspective, salvation may be no more than a lottery.

At a minimum, what Leclerc says about luck can be translated into an argument against supernatural grace. More specifically, he wants to argue that there are four possible senses in which the terms 'lucky' or 'unlucky' might be applied to mean something more than just consistent success or lack of it. They might mean influenced by: destiny or fate; chance; good or evil angels; or God Himself. He takes the first two to be 'pure chimeras,' both of them defeated by human freedom. His discussion is none too cogent, however. First, he fails to distinguish fatalism from determinism. That is, he does not distinguish between saying that every event necessarily occurs *regardless* of the circumstances, and saying that every event necessarily occurs *because of* the circumstances. He then argues that because we are ignorant of the circumstances, that is, of the universal chain of causes, that chain does not exist. Secondly, chance is made to depend entirely on voluntarism. A chance event occurs when bodies that otherwise always behave mechanically are interfered with by minds, which have freedom, that is, the ability 'to do or not do something ... to determine themselves in [only?] indifferent or absolute

---

38 It is worth noting that the French terms that Leclerc uses, *bonheur* and *malheur*, often are used in just this sense.

things, or things they regard as such, through pure caprice and without any reason, unless it be their willing, and without there intervening anything to engage them necessarily to judge or will.'[39] This self-sufficiency of the will to make a difference in the environment is a clear indication of the Pelagianism expected of some one with Leclerc's Socinian-Armininian-deistic inclinations. (By contrast, when Bayle construes salvation in such a way as to be construed as a matter of chance, he means precisely that the human will has no role in it whatsoever.) As to chance, it is a 'negative idea' in that when we shake the box of lots and draw a name of which we say that it was drawn by chance, we mean only that the occurrence was not merely mechanical.

Of the other two possibilities for aleatory influence, appeal to angels is without foundation and basically a pagan view, according to Leclerc. But the appeal to God cannot be dismissed as easily. The effect of Leclerc's discussions of divine influence is to eliminate the difference between chance and other events – there is nothing special about any event that privileges it as an *entrée* for God's intervention. There are no oracles, and Leclerc addresses the issue in just these terms.[40] If drawing lots were the instances of particular Providence that people take them to be, all kinds of questions could be decided just by writing alternative answers on papers and drawing one of them – for example, to determine whether a lost object was stolen by a domestic.[41] Such an effective procedure would surely be of use in eliminating atheism, he says with irony. Moreover, if God always intervenes in what we called chance events, then there are 'infinitely more' miracles in gaming houses, on behalf of people who are unworthy of them, than in the Old and New Testaments combined. Here, of course, we have an argument, and one that reverses the Providence argument. The same premise that is cited by the Providence argument to show that gambling is evil is here cited to show in effect that gambling is without moral or religious significance.

The same tack was taken by Jean Barbeyrac[42] in his effort to show

---

39 *Réflexions*, 52–3.
40 Nor was he the only one in the period to employ this image in establishing the sufficiency and reliability of human faculties. See Lennon, 'Lady Oracle.'
41 *Réflexions*, 107–8.
42 At the Revocation Barbeyrac (1674–1744) left France with his parents for Switzerland, where he studied first theology and then law. He taught literature at the French college in Berlin beginning in 1697, history and civil law in Lausanne (1711), and public law in Gröningen, where beginning in 1714 he directed the academy. He was also a member

that gambling is intrinsically indifferent and thus legitimate in principle. To be sure, in his *Traité du jeu, où l'on examine les principales questions de droit naturel et de morale qui ont du rapport à cette matière* (1709; well-enough received for a second edition, 1737), Barbeyrac draws attention to the instrumental evil resulting from gambling. The larger part of the work details circumstances in which gambling should therefore be prohibited, and includes horrific stories of people who gamble away their wives, children, teeth, fingers, hair, freedom, and even their lives (the Huns, according to St Ambrose).[43] If anything, Barbeyrac's pragmatic concerns are more obviously urgent than in other works of this sort, which he takes to be too abstract and based on exaggerated principles designed more for angels than for men.[44] Nevertheless, Barbeyrac opposes the Providence argument, citing Leclerc's *Reflexions* against François de Sales as reported by Thiers. The number and circumstances of the miracles that would have to occur in gambling houses show gambling not be an instance of particular Providence. In addition, the results of cards or dice are determined, according to Barbeyrac, no less closely than the behaviour of a rolling ball – even if, as in the case of events covered by insurance contracts, we do not know the causes. On the other side, games of skill are affected by what is called chance, as when a small stone affects a tossed ball. The naturalizing, morally neutralizing picture is thus complete.[45]

The unresolved contrast between approbation in principle and condemnation in practice is striking in Barbeyrac, as also in others. His reference to insurance contracts may provide a clue to understanding this

---

of the Prussian Academy of Sciences. Best known perhaps for his work on Puffendorf, Barbeyrac was 'a prolific writer, but one with the faults of this quality.' *Nouvelle biographie universelle* (Paris, 1852) III–IV, 441–2. Barbeyrac has gotten a much better shake recently from Rétat (39–43), who, while recognizing that Barbeyrac never produced a systematic work, sketches for him from minor works and the prefaces to his translations a coherent system of some interest.

43 *Traité*, 294–6.

44 The work was occasioned by a perceived excess of gambling: 'books on morals are always in season; but they are never more so than when they help to correct the century's disorders least attended to. Games are of this sort, and I don't know whether the abuse of them has ever been more common. They infect all ages and levels of life; they increase daily, but hardly can go further. Few take note, and gradually talk of them ceases; and bravery is needed to directly oppose so rapid a torrent. Let us try, however, leaving to chance what will happen. Let's do what depends on us and not worry about the rest' (xxv–xxvi).

45 *Traité*, 22–30.

contrast. For Barbeyrac, gambling is a kind of contract. Gambling is an agreement requiring, in addition to the game itself, all that is required by what Grotius and Puffendorf call a *contrat onéreux*: freedom of engagement, equality of conditions, and fidelity of execution.[46]

According to Barbeyrac, 'If I can promise to give my goods to someone as I wish, absolutely and without condition, why will I not be permitted to promise and give someone a certain sum in case he is luckier than I or more adroit with respect to certain movements on which we agree? ... Each is free to make the right that he gives another to require this or that thing of his to depend on a given condition or event as seems good to him, even chance events.'[47] This argument may represent the converse of a monumental explanation of the rise of capitalism in the sixteenth and seventeenth centuries. The Weber-Tawney thesis has it that making money, especially by means of money, which was condemned by the Third Lateran Council (1175), and by the Councils of Lyons (1274) and of Vienne (1312), was legitimized three centuries later by Protestant theories of grace. The problem is what may be called the paradox of predestination. If the Pauline doctrine of justification by faith alone is to be interpreted to mean that grace is necessary and sufficient for salvation, then good works are irrelevant, even to the point that antinomianism reigns. That is, if we are antecedently saved by grace, then nothing we can do one way or the other can alter our predetermined lot. (The paradox is highlighted when I consider how to act. If I realize that my lot is already decided, then I might as well have an immoral good time of it. But if I do so, I thereby demonstrate that my lot is damnation. Of this, more later.[48]) The historical solution to this paradox was that one demonstrates one's salvation after the fact of predestination by material and financial success of just the sort that had previously been condemned.[49] (Perhaps a way to put the thesis is that interest, that is,

46 Ibid, 104–5. Much of the work consists in explaining these conditions as applied to gambling. La Placette, who, as we shall see, was also concerned to undo the Providence argument, was also to make the connection to contracts. Agreeing to pay if a certain face of the die comes up is like an insurer agreeing to pay if a certain cargo is lost (ibid, 59).

47 Ibid, 12–13. Puffendorf is cited for support, and Paschasius Justus and Jean Samuel Stryck are also cited as condemning gambling as a kind of theft. Barbeyrac agrees that no one gambles to lose, and that the loser is unhappy, but the contract is as valid as any other, and one may ask, as with any other regretted contract, why it was entered into.

48 The more recent version of this paradox is treated as Newcombe's paradox. For a particularly good account of it, see D. Olin.

49 For Tawney, the key notion is less grace that the vaguer notion of a calling (176, 199–204). For his differences from Weber, see 261–2, n. 32.

non-productive earnings, is a model for human effort, which in terms of salvation is also non-productive.) By the end of the seventeenth century, it may well be that business ethics drove theories of grace, rather than conversely. That is, the need to legitimate the gambling inherent in contracts gave credence to friendly theories of grace, and indeed, this may have been the dynamic a century earlier as well. Whatever the order of dependence, there is likely a connection, perhaps one of co-dependence.

Now, for Bayle, although religion and salvation are both matters of chance, they are not to be naturalized. It comes as no surprise, then, that in this work that argues for its naturalization, Barbeyrac also argues a very different conception of Christianity from Bayle's. Against Bayle's dour, tragic pessimism, Barbeyrac argues the optimistic liberalism of Locke and Leclerc. 'Christ was far from representing God His Father to us under the frightful idea of a hard and cruel master who constantly leads us into unavoidable snares by surrounding us with an infinity of objects that flatter the senses, and by none the less prohibiting us from giving in to the least part of our desires and inclinations.'[50] As part of this conception, he argues the predictable package of Socinian-Arminian-deistic views, beginning with the near-coincidence of Christian and natural morality. In one of his arguments, Barbeyrac cites Leclerc for a premise that Bayle himself had previously illustrated at length beginning with his first work, namely, that there is hardly any virtue not praised, nor any vice not condemned, by some pagan author. And he cites Locke's *Reasonableness of Christianity* to the effect that Revelation was needed in order to promulgate a universal law – whose validity, presumably, is independent of that Revelation.[51] Another argument given by Barbeyrac for Revelation is that, although men are naturally capable of arriving at morality through reason, they do not do so because of practical considerations. One might say that Revelation functions for Barbeyrac as experience or natural revelation does for a Cartesian such as Malebranche, namely, as a practical shortcut. In both cases, God provides directly what in principle we could obtain for ourselves.

For Bayle, religion, morality, and salvation are, as we have seen, all conceptually separate domains – which is why he can accept, indeed defend, the principle later taken up by Leclerc concerning the atheist's morality. Among these opponents of Bayle, the thrust is to naturalize, or at least rationalize, these concepts and to collapse their differences, espe-

---

50 *Traité*, 44.
51 Ibid, 32–6.

cially if salvation can be understood in the fashion of Leti's happiness in
this life. A good example is Barbeyrac's treatment of the three virtues he
takes to be sufficient for defining a Christian:[52] piety, temperance, and
justice. The list alone give the flavour – no defence of flagellation here –
but the details particularly exhibit the significance of his concerns. Piety
gets the shortest treatment, which is designed mainly to show that
excessive vigor is not enjoined by the Gospels – we need not and should
not all be monks or hermits.[53] Temperance consists in controlling
desire,[54] which has three sorts of object: esteem, which is permissible so
long as it is realized that God's glory supersedes all other; riches, which
in themselves are indifferent – here Barbeyrac reads like a manifesto for
the Weber-Tawney thesis on the rise of capitalism; and pleasure, whose
moderate enjoyment has instrumental value, amply recognized by
Scripture. Finally, justice consists of two parts: rendering each his due
and loving one's neighbour, the latter being what distinguishes Christians from the Greeks, Romans, and Jews.[55] Here Barbeyrac explicitly
criticizes Bayle's fideist pessimism, citing the *Nouvelles lettres*[56] to the
effect that there is an opposition between the laws of reason and those of
charity. It is worth relating at length Barbeyrac's citation of Bayle, for it
places both Bayle's pessimism and his scepticism in a certain perspective. Reason may indicate near- universality of evil motivation, with
negative consequences for toleration, but faith points in a different
direction.

This proposition, that man is incomparably more inclined to evil than to good
and that incomparably more evil actions are performed than good ones, is as
certain as any principle of metaphysics. It is therefore incomparably more probable that the secret springs that have produced [some action with apparently
nothing evil about it] are corrupt than that they are decent [*honnêtes*]. Thus reason would have it that if we knew simply that an action has been done by a man,
that is, if we do not know the heart of the person who has performed it, we
should judge that it is incomparably more probable that this action has bad
motives than good ones. And yet the laws of charity would have it that, unless
there is a very probable knowledge of the wrongness of an action, we judge
rather that it is good. Thus charity leads us to do just the opposite of what reason

52 Based on the Epistle to Titus 2: 11–12.
53 *Traité*, 71–81.
54 Ibid, 43.
55 Ibid, 62–3.
56 Lettre XII, para. 12.

would have. This is not the only sacrifice that religion orders us to make of our reason.'[57]

Barbeyrac agrees with Bayle's premise but rejects the conclusion that faith and reason are at odds. In his view, nothing about the morality of a particular action follows from the general principle. Reason would have us *suspend judgment* and not judge on the basis of simple possibility, to which a contrary possibility may be opposed. Here the sceptical tables are turned on Bayle, who, according to Barbeyrac, fails to distinguish between 'abstract possibility' (Barbeyrac uses 'possibility' and 'probability' interchangeably here) and the 'fact of the real event.' Here is his argument:

The comparison [Bayle] makes with lotteries will explain my view and at the same time will serve to overturn [Bayle's] argument. When one reasons on the basis of simple possibility, it is truly more probable that an individual [*un particulier*] will lose in the lotteries than that he will win. But when one asks whether a given individual [*un tel*] will win or lose, one must not thereby be led to believe that he will lose rather than win. For it is certain that someone must win and that each one can be the lucky one to whom the lot falls. Yet, with respect to him who actually will win, it is true to say, as of every other, that it is more possible for him to lose than to win. Thus the greatest degree of possibility is not the rule for judging the fact or event itself. In general, even what is more likely is not confirmed in the event rather than what is less likely; far from this, it was long ago noted by Agathon, according to Aristotle [*Rhetoric* II, 24, 1402a10] that many unlikely things occur in the world, and Bayle elsewhere [art. Agathon, rem. F] accepts this view.

Before Barbeyrac is credited with having at least faintly anticipated the lottery paradox, it should be noticed that while it is true that, given any detail in the description of what happens, what happens is under that description often unlikely, this is not to say, as Barbeyrac does, that what happens is always or even often unlikely. Moreover, Barbeyrac goes on to reject all relative frequency theories of probability: the previous frequency of an event is irrelevant without some additional reason that it will occur, for example, a disposition of the agent. But the same is true of the gambling tables, where our author of a treatise on gambling would be in deep trouble. Barbeyrac concludes, in any event, that without an additional reason, common sense prescribes suspension of judgment, which, as it happens, is just what the Evangelical laws of charity enjoin. Thus, contrary to Bayle, reason and faith are not at odds. He quotes Paul, 'judge not beforehand,' (I Corinthians 4: 5), and buttresses his rationalist optimism with La Bruyère's adaptation of Descartes's rule on clarity and distinctness, namely, that it should be extended to judgments about people.[58] That is, just as Descartes recommended that we should not accept a proposition as true unless it is perceived as indubitably true, and otherwise suspend judgment, so according to Barbeyrac we should suspend judgment about the moral status of others unless the evidence for the judgment makes it indubitable.

On the face of it, Barbeyrac's seems the more liberal, tolerant attitude. But his criticism of Bayle is partly based on a misconception. Bayle's concern is not with the likelihood of occurrence of beliefs or events. Even on the question of grace – that is, who will be saved and how – his opinion is that the competing views themselves are and can be of no practical concern – only the debate over them can be. Rather, his concern is, as we have seen at length, with authentically engaging other autonomous beings. His basis for toleration is that only thereby can there be any behaviour to engage, *even if the behaviour that results from it is thought to be wrong.* Barbeyrac, like Locke at points, seems prepared to tolerate behaviour only because for all we know it may be right. Like Jurieu, he seems prepared to persecute heretics, if *per impossibile* they were known to be such.

Support for reading these authors' attention to gambling as involving much broader social, theological, and metaphysical concerns comes from still another Protestant critic of Bayle, Jean La Placette.[59] His *Traité des jeux-de-hazard* (1697)[60] argued against Joncourt and 'several others,' probably including Leclerc, that chance is not an empty word devoid of meaning. Its ordinary meaning, which can legitimately be used in explanations, according to La Placette, is the intersection (*concours*) of two or more contingent events, each of which has its causes but none, at least none that is known, for the interaction. This is Barbeyrac's notion, just

---

58 *Caractères* (Brussels, 1697) 429.
59 Jean La Placette (1657–1736) also left France just before the Revocation. He preached for a year in Königsberg before winding up, first in Copenhagen, then in Utrecht. He published many works dealing with moral issues, seemingly from a non-rigourist perspective. He is described as a 'cold and dry theologian,' but one read by, among others, the Jesuits, who regarded his attacks on Bayle as showing the inability of Protestants to rebut the sophisms of Bayle (Rétat, 32, 95, 170n).
60 In *Divers traités*, 2d ed. 1699, 3rd ed., along with a *Défense* against objections, 1714.

noted, of the small stone unexpectedly altering the path of a tossed ball. Neither author considers, however, that perhaps no event is the product of a single cause or chain of single causes, that every event is the product of an intersection of causes.[61] Thus, while the concept of chance is hereby naturalized, either all events are chance events (the tendency among these authors is to discount Providence anyway) or, from the perspective of the whole, all are necessary (not incidentally, La Placette found it important to argue against Spinoza[62]). Once again, the description of what is taken to be an event is paramount, not just for relative probabilities, but for all modal notions. For Bayle the context for description is in the first instance historical or narratological, which gives a very special meaning to what is necessary, for instance.

But La Placette's interest in chance derives not from stories, or even from physics or metaphysics. As he explains in the preface to his *Traité*, he was originally interested in the gambling controversy because of his concern with the general question of restitution, the two most difficult cases of which are interest and gambling. The relevance of the gambling question as an instance of the Weber-Tawney connection seems obvious.[63] La Placette's particular contribution here is twofold. His discussion of the theoretical objections to gambling includes additional theological doctrine that supports the connection, and his discussion of the practical objections suggest an explanation of what may often have been at issue in such objections.

In practical terms he regards gambling as 'one of the most pernicious inventions of an evil mind,' and he details at length its evil consequences.[64] Even so, he was interpreted as approving of gambling. In particular, his treatment of chess seems to have raised eyebrows. In his *Défense* (1714) he explained that games in themselves that are quite innocent can have pernicious consequences. In the case of chess, the game is too time-consuming, does not divert and relax, and generates pride and other inappropriate emotions.[65] One gets the sense that the complaint here, reflective of much in the literature against gambling, is one of *non-productivity*.

---

61 Nor does Aristotle, who has a similar notion of chance, but one limited to events involving living things. See Ross, 75–8.

62 *Eclaircissement*, Amsterdam, 1709.

63 La Placette's treatise on games of chance was published with a treatise on interest. The first chapter acknowledges that usury is universally despised but then goes on to argue that it is 'necessary in the present state of the world' (*Divers traités*, 74n).

64 *Traité*, 7, and chaps. 7–11.

65 Ibid, chap. 19. Published with the 1714 edition of the *Traité*.

Gambling at dice or cards is non-productive, whereas gambling in the market, or on insurance contracts, is most certainly productive, at least in the aggregate. (Lotteries were generally viewed as an instance of gambling on an insurance contract.) If this is at all plausible, then the misinterpretation of La Placette becomes explicable. But he also ends his *Défense* by claiming that he has the advantage over Joncourt that while they agree that gambling should be condemned on extrinsic grounds, they disagree on the instrinsic grounds. How is this an advantage? One suspects additional motivation for a preacher to be raising such an abstract fuss.

La Placette's criticisms, in the *Traité*, of the theoretical objections to gambling are fairly standard. He attacks the Providence argument as employed by Daneau and others and does so in a way tending towards a naturalistic elimination of Providence. But he also addresses the argument from these authors that in gambling one person wins only at the expense of another. One of his considerations here is revealing. The morality of gambling, he argues, depends crucially on intention; if the intention is diversion, it can be innocent, 'for the aim of winning and profiting is not always criminal. If it were, commerce would not be permitted for Christians, which no one has claimed.'[66] He also connects the issues of particular Providence and transubstantiation in an interesting way. He endorses the gambling-house reversal of the Providence argument found in Leclerc, but also argues that miracles can be neither numerous nor perpetual because of divine wisdom, which establishes admirable general laws that are violated only for some special and widespread effect, for example, in order to gain credibility for Scripture. The age of miracles was over for Protestants once Scripture was established. This is one reason why they reject transubstantiation.[67] Another version of this difference of Protestants from Catholics is invoked by La Placette's response to Joncourt's claim that God always acts with a special volition when lots are drawn. He points out that reception of all other revelations from God depends, like the sacraments, on our attitude – without faith, devotion, and piety, there is nothing. Catholics take a passive attitude and believe that the sacraments are effective regardless of intention; for example, whatever his purpose or state of mind, the words of consecration from an ordained priest produce the divine presence on the altar.[68]

66 *Défense*, 251.
67 *Traité*, 241–50.
68 There is more to this story, of course. Joncourt replied to the attack on the Providence argument by La Placette and Barbeyrac with *Quatre lettres*, published in 1713, and Bar-

Even if La Placette's (and Barbeyrac's) treatment of gambling were not a part of the active, non-miraculous Protestant version of Christianity that grounded the rise of capitalism, his treatment would certainly be of a piece with the liberal package of views found in Barbeyrac, Leclerc, and others opposing Bayle. Once again it is not surprising at all that an author such as La Placette should attack Bayle's fideism. In his *Réponse à deux objections*, (that is, from Bayle on the problem of evil and the Trinity) he argues that while faith may be above reason, it can never be contrary to reason.

What is the upshot? To be sure, Bayle may have found the lottery an appropriate model in a number of related domains (grace, religion, toleration), and he may have, thereby and in other ways, contributed to the general legitimization of gambling in his period (even if he seems not to have addressed the Providence argument as such, his insistence on the inscrutability of God's ways was at odds with any such appeal to Providence). But Bayle's dialectic of legitimization, as we might call it, was of a radically different sort from that of Leclerc, Barbeyrac, La Placette, and, in fact, all others. They were concerned to broaden the concept of gambling by naturalizing it (and thus legitimizing gambling itself). Bayle was concerned to broaden the concept by supernaturalizing it, far beyond anything premised even by the Providence argument.

28: Miracles and Mechanisms

Robinet's thesis is that Bayle's thought underwent a broad evolution, from favouring Malebranche's occasionalism, through attraction to Leibniz's pre-established harmony, to finally drawing close to Arnauld's views.[69] On the last stage, however, Robinet offers very little by way of documentation or even commentary. He may be summarized as offering three points of contact between Arnauld and Bayle, of which only the last seems to be of interest. One is an anti-rationalist conception of faith, which certainly characterizes Bayle and certain members of Port-Royal, such as Pascal, but to a much less extent Arnauld. Another is

---

beyrac in turn replied with a *Discours sur la nature des sorts*, published with the second edition of his *Traité* in 1737, and, perhaps, in certain editions of his translation of a work by G. Noodt on the power of sovereigns (1714). In addition, there was an exchange between Barbeyrac and the editor of the *Mémoires de Trévoux*. See preface to the second edition.

69 In 'L'aphilosophie de Bayle ...' Its title is a typesetter's nightmare, but this is an exceedingly penetrating article.

the critique of Leibniz's principle of the best as inconsistent with human freedom, which Arnauld had argued in criticism of proposition 13 of his *Discourse on Metaphysics*; but Bayle would not have seen these texts, which were not published until much later. On neither count, therefore, does the Arnauld-Bayle connection sketched above seem in need of expansion. Finally, there is the account of miracles. Here the contact is clear, documented, and important.

The liberal Protestant Jaquelot had argued that there are few miracles in the world because 'the order of the universe is something of infinitely higher importance than the health and prosperity of a good man during the brief duration of this life'; that is, God does not exercise particular Providence on behalf of the moral because to do so would upset the regularity of His ways, which is a higher value. Said Bayle: 'This view is rather brilliant. Malebranche set it out and he persuaded some of his readers that a simple and very productive system better agrees with God's wisdom than a system that is more complex and proportionately less productive, but less capable of avoiding irregularities. [I] was among those who believed that Malebranche thereby produced a wonderful solution; but it is almost impossible to credit this solution after one has read Arnauld and considered the vast and immense idea of the sovereignly perfect being.'[70] Bayle goes on to elaborate this Arnauldian idea of God such that a multiplicity of miracles might be possible because God's wisdom and goodness are thoroughly compatible, even if in ways incomprehensible to us.

One might speculate that the background concerns of Arnauld and Bayle in this issue are, if not incompatible, yet rather different. Arnauld is concerned with the process of salvation, which for him occurs according to individual, that is, imponderable, choices on God's part, and not, as Malebranche thought, according to general choices inscribed in laws for the distribution of grace, which could be manipulated in Pelagian fashion as natural laws are manipulated for material goods. For Bayle, the concern with issues of Providence is always dominated by the problem of evil. Malebranche's solution to that problem, for example, offers a kind of closure that Bayle cannot accept. If there were a rational, that is, mechanical, a priori, explanation of why an omnipotent God both permits evil and is incapable of it, He would be programmed in a way incompatible with dialogue, with being a person. To put it briefly, from

70 *RQP*, civ; *OD* III, 825. Arnauld was also a source for Bayle of others' views on Providence, e.g., Maimonides. See art. Rorarius, rem. D.

a Baylean perspective the Malebranchean line above on divine intervention commits the Leibnizian Fallacy.[71] Despite these differences in their background concerns, however, Arnauld undeniably led Bayle away from Malebranche.

In his early *Pensées diverses*, Bayle had invested in Malebranche's view of Providence as set out in the *Traité de la nature et de la grace*. 'Nothing gives us a more elevated idea of a monarch than to see him, having established a law, maintain it towards all and against all, without allowing the prejudice of an individual, or preferences for a favourite, to apply any restriction to it.'[72] The plagues and famines inflicted on the pagans are not a result of particular volitions, but of the general laws for the communication of motion – laws that God adopts in the interest of simplicity and fecundity. 'Undoubtedly Malebranche will be written against and will be given occasion to clarify this new system, from which, it seems to me, many useful things might be drawn.'[73]

Malebranche was written against, of course, and tried to defend his system. Bayle reviewed his *Lettres* (1686) written in response to Arnauld's *Réfelexions philosophiques et theologiques* and concluded with praise for Malebranche's mechanistic account of particular volition in the construction of the world.[74] He relates that Malebranche distinguishes between God's particular volitions, which apply to every particular event, but which are not always efficacious, and His general will, which is always efficacious. Particular volitions that are efficacious

71 Indeed, Leibniz's best-possible-world doctrine may well have been derived from Malebranche's conception of God as divine strategist. See C. Wilson, 'Leibnizean Optimism.' Ironically, however, Bayle may have been first attracted to Malebranche's occasionalism as an antidote to Leibniz's metaphysical mechanism. See Lennon, 'Mechanism As a Silly Mouse.' See also Norton, according to whom Leibniz does not eliminate the problem of evil so much as relocate it as a conflict among divine attributes, which from a Baylean perspective is tantamount to Manicheism.

72 *PDC*, ccxxix; *OD* III, 139.

73 *PDC*, ccxxxiv; *OD* III, 141.

74 *NRL* April 1686, art iii; *OD* I, 531–7. In the same year, Bayle reviewed Robert Boyle's *De ipsa natura* (1686). Bayle applauds Boyle's rejection and ridicule of the ordinary concept of nature, which is supposed to abhor the vacuum, etc., and which cannot account for irregularities such as earthquakes, which are thus taken to be miraculous. To attribute them to Providence will not do either, because 'it ordinarily acts in simple and general ways for the good of the whole rather than of parts,' which is just the opposite to the ordinary notion of nature. 'This distinction is based on common sense, for it is more permissible for a cause whose end is universal to override the interest of an individual than for a cause whose only interest is a particular man.' Here Bayle takes physical mechanism to enhance Providence. *NRL*, December 1686, art.iii; *OD* I, 707.

always violate general laws and are miracles; they occur when demanded by order and occur such that the least change has the greatest possible benefit. To Arnauld's complaints about the intelligibility of simplicity given the inscrutability of God's aims, Bayle seems to accept Malebranche's response that without some notion of the perfection of creation, admiration for it (and presumably thereby for God) would be an illusion. But Bayle shows awareness that some critics of Malebranche, unnamed, would find his system tidier without any miracles at all. Perhaps this realization provoked reconsideration by Bayle of Arnauld's objections.

In any event, at the end of his life, in the *Réponse aux questions d'un provincial*, Bayle comes finally to criticize Jaquelot's account of the motivation for creation by appealing to Arnauld's criticism of Malebranche's essentially similar account. Both accounts, according to Bayle, deny divine freedom and omnipotence; he thinks that, in fact, they both yield a 'Stoic fatalism' that denies human freedom as well. Adam had no choice but to sin as part of God's plan. According to Jaquelot, God is motivated to manifest His glory and to do so in the most suitable way, which involves the fall of man. Arnauld's argument is that if God is obliged, as He is according to Malebranche, to create the most perfect work and to do so by the simplest means, which already strips God of His freedom of indifference, then He is also stripped of His freedom whether to create at all. Nor is this all. 'What most embarrasses our reason is its demand that we preserve all the attributes of God in their entirety, without sacrificing some in order to maintain others.'[75] The principal attribute that reason assigns to divinity is goodness, which raises the question as to why not all men are saved. Malebranche tries to reconcile divine goodness, according to which God would will all men to be saved, with the fact of damnation by arguing that universal salvation would require particular volitions, which would be incompatible with divine wisdom. But even by attributing to God conduct that bears the character of His attributes to the extent compatible with that of other attributes, Malebranche's account, according to Arnauld, upsets the first article of the Apostle's Creed, namely, that God is omnipotent.

Bayle unequivocally rejects Malebranche's position and throughout seems prepared to accept Arnauld's. But for him it is not just a matter of our ignorance with respect to God's ways. Instead, there may be no a priori solution to the problem Malebranche had dealt with. 'We were

75 *RQP*, cli; *OD* III, 812.

seeking light that would draw us out of our predicament by comparing the idea of God with the state of human kind and, lo and behold, we encounter elucidations that cast us into deeper shadows.'[76] Later in the same work, Bayle again cites Arnauld's *Reflexions* to the effect that God has not made human reason the judge of what is more or less worthy of His wisdom. One argument that Arnauld advances there that Bayle would surely have accepted is our certainty, on grounds other than the problem of damnation, of the incommensurability between human reason and divine wisdom. According to Arnauld, the Chinese, relying only on reason, would correctly say that a saviour come in glory would be worthier of divine wisdom than the crucified Christ.[77]

But, quite apart from Arnauld, another argument might be that divine wisdom is displayed in its most important aspects only a posteriori, in dialogical response to what *we* do. That is, Providence is not to be conceived in the fashion of the Leibnizian Fallacy, as a deductive system from which God stands apart, even from its premises, but rather, in the fashion of Bakhtinian polyphony, as a system in which God is both author and participant. Providence is not a scenario, written out in advance, that provides us with all that we say and do. Even if what we say and do necessarily serves God's ends, it does so in the way that Dostoevsky's characters serve his, with polyphonic negotiation among autonomous beings along the way.[78] The intended argument developed over previous chapters is that, although Bayle did not put his conception of Providence in these terms (indeed, could not have done so) his writing leads us to just this view.

That the world exhibits such Providence is for Bayle a matter of what he calls faith; how it does so is what he calls a mystery.[79] His language is, unfortunately, technical and theological; the view that it expresses, however, is as deep as any to be found in his work. Certainly, the view is central to it.

---

76 Ibid, *OD* III, 811–13.

77 *RQP* clxi; *OD* III, 839.

78 In this sense, Bayle would, and effectively did, reject Malebranche's theodicy according to which Christ would have come even if Adam had not sinned. The Oratorian's view is that God creates through no rational necessity, but from love. This love is for Himself, and is expressed as His glory. However, no finite universe can testify to His glory; only if made divine by the Word can it do so. Hence the Incarnation, an event conceived by Malebranche independently of the Redemption.

79 *CPD*, cii; *OD* III, 327.

29: Grace and Chance

It is a revealed truth that not all men are saved.[80] Thus grace is *non-universal*. It is also *necessary* for salvation, otherwise men would, as according to the Pelagian heresy, save themselves. However much atheists and pagans may be capable of maintaining a workable society, they are incapable of meritorious action, that is, 'according to the theology of St Augustine, they have never performed an act of virtue according to a good principle for a good end.'[81] 'A very strong argument for the necessity of grace' that Bayle gives runs as follows: other men can only *persuade* us of the truth; they cannot make us *embrace* it. In particular, only God can make us embrace the truths of the Gospel 'by adding to the illumination of our mind a disposition of the heart that makes us find more joy in the exercise of virtue than in the practice of vice.'[82] The exercise of virtue does not *merit* salvation, but is none the less an invariant concomitant of it. Of this justifying faith, more below.

Grace is also *sufficient*. Here again Arnauld shows the way. The Spanish Jesuit, Juan Cardinal de Lugo (1580–1660) had theorized that the atheism of American savages is culpable because they are given extraordinary grace and special illuminations of God's existence that they reject.[83] Bayle endorses Arnauld's point that 'an hypothesis designed to amplify God's mercy in fact is better able to amplify the idea of His rigour because these graces and inner illuminations serve only to worsen the state of these unfortunates; God knows very well that they will have no other result than [their damnation].' Bayle also makes the same point by appealing to a Protestant theologian, Frederick Spanheim, according to whom, 'a much weaker idea of God's goodness is given when we speak of a universal grace destined for all men, but which the greater part will be unable to accept, than when it is admitted that God destines His grace only to those to whom He has resolved to give the strength to accept it.'[84]

---

80 *CPD*, clxi; *OD* III, 812. Bayle cites Arnauld citing Malebranche. Origen had held that all men are in fact eventually saved, and Bayle was very interested in his views. But his interest in Origen focused on two points, both negative: as a failed attempt to solve the problem of evil, and the Church's persecution of Origen. See art. Origen.

81 *PDC*, cxlvi; *OD* III, 94.

82 *PDC*, clvii; *OD* III, 101.

83 *CPD*, cii; *OD* III, 326–7. See *Dictionnaire*, art. Lugo, rem. G. Here Bayle reports him to have been credited with the doctrine of philosophic sin.

84 *CPD*, cii; *OD* III, 327. On Spanheim, see art. Spanheim.

Thus Bayle accepts the Calvinist position that grace is non-universal, necessary, and sufficient. But he is not much moved by the details of this fascinating, if desiccated, issue. On the contrary, both early and late he showed distaste for the debates over grace and, if anything, regarded them as undecidable. Writing to his father from Geneva on 21 September 1671, he observed: 'People are greatly divided over the question of universal grace. The discusssion begins with the professors, for it is the most learned who make the first play in affairs of this sort. Then the ministers, from whom it spreads into all the houses of the city, all on one side or the other, right down to tradesmen who are asked whether they are for universal grace or particular. Thus are born factions, cabals ... until the Republic itself is threatened ... From my reading and pitiful judgment, the question is itself of very little consequence for salvation; we can indifferently be for one opinion or the other with nothing to lose or gain; both are to be found in Scripture.'[85]

Later in the *Dictionnaire* he complained that, with all that has been written on the topic, we are no better off, no more enlightened, and that such will always be the case. Repeating a remark cited in his review a decade earlier of Jurieu's book on grace, he observes: 'Someone has said that matters of grace are a sea in which there is no bottom and no shore.' The question comes down to whether Adam sinned freely, in which case Omnipotence is violated, or not, in which case Adam was not culpable. We have a mystery in either case: the foreknowledge of future contingents, or sin without freedom. Never, according to Bayle, has such bad faith been evidenced as on this question. He thinks that there are two possibilities, with neither being acceptable. Either outside forces leave the soul free to act (Molinism) or not (Thomists, Jansenists, Calvinists), with the Jansenists scrambling to avoid Calvinism, the Thomists to avoid both, and the Molinists to avoid denying Augustine.[86]

One reason why Bayle would not have been interested in the theoretical debates over grace is that for him grace as a bare and inexplicable causal factor has no theoretical relevance. Instead, its relevance is entirely practical, not just in the sense that it is the difference between heaven and hell, but also that it determines the salvific value of conduct. 'What is properly called grace is faith operating through charity,' that is, 'justifying faith, which makes us love God, obey His commandments,

85 *OD* I, 9–10. (Edition of Trévoux, 1737).
86 Art. Jansenius, rems. G, H.

and cherish the truths of which He persuades us.'[87] This is the conduct of those who are saved and who exhibit, though do not earn, their salvation by it. But grace does not give us religious truth; at least, it does not justify belief. In this same passage he condemns the heresy judges whom Jurieu was prepared to recognize. *Even if they judged correctly as a result of efficacious grace*, according to Bayle, they would be no more justified than if they had done so through good luck. They would be like the judge who, 'having slept through the presentation of the case and waking with a start, responded as his decision, "Let him be hanged"; when told the case dealt with a dispute over a field, he replied, "Let it be plowed."' Even if the judge's pronouncement had been, as luck would have it, appropriate, 'the chance encounter with truth does not make a judge's conduct correct.'

It is not just with respect to belief that the effect of grace is, as far as we are concerned, like a matter of luck. In the Apocalyptic case of salvation, there is no fathoming of God's ways. Again following Arnauld, he concludes that the most appealing accounts of predestination are those that multiply its difficulties. 'To adore in silence this profound abyss is best.'[88] Perhaps another way to express Bayle's lack of interest in the theoretical debates is that all parties to them assume a mechanistic account of salvation, or at least an objective calculation of facts as its basis. For Bayle, salvation is obviously more like clemency from a judge, which requires luck.[89]

30: Religion, Morality, and Chance

Not only is salvation, as far as we are concerned, a matter of chance, but also religion. Bayle clearly takes this position, most notably in the *Commentaire philosophique* and the *Dictionnaire*. In an argument that was to have important consequences for Hume's general theory of belief, Bayle rebuts the argument from Nicole and other Catholics that the Protestant way of examination can never yield certainty in the interpretation of Scripture. The same is true, he says, of the Catholic way of authority. It is true that 'the way of examination will never lead us to the criterion of truth, which is an idea so clear and so distinct that we have a lively sensation [*nous sentions vivement*] that the thing cannot be other than it is,'

---

87 *Supplément*, xxiii; *OD* II, 524.
88 *CPD*, cii; *OD* III, 327.
89 Consider the French word *heureux*, which means blessed, saved, happy, and lucky.

just because of doubts about translation, lexicography, etc., and thus that matters of Scripture do not have 'the irrestible evidence with which we know that the whole is greater than its part.' But the same reasons that militate against certainty in the way of examination do so against any attempt to establish the Church's infallibility, which would be the basis for the Catholic way of authority. The result is that 'neither by Scripture, nor by the natural light, nor by experience can Catholics know with certainty that the Church is infallible; and if it were infallible, those who believed so would have a true opinion only by a stroke of good luck, without being able to give any necessary reason for it, or being able to see in their soul any marks of truth that another who believed the contrary would not experience to the same extent.'[90] That Catholics are actually mistaken about the infallibility of the Church, and Protestants right, as Bayle thinks, is thus effectively a matter of luck.[91]

If religion and salvation are both effectively matters of chance according to Bayle, morality is decidedly not. Our performance of duty, which is the basis for his theory of toleration, requires that we know, in a strong sense of the term, what our duty is. At the core of Bayle's position is the paradox of predestination, which he makes no attempt to solve. (On the contrary, he revels in its intractability.) The relevant version of the paradox, once again, goes as follows. Those who are saved are saved independently of anything they may do; none the less, those who are saved behave as if their behaviour earned their salvation, that is, they behave morally. How, then, to behave? If I behave immorally, I know that I am not saved; but behaving morally does not earn me salvation, not even in the sense of satisfying a necessary condition for it. Bayle's view is that one should behave morally, on the basis of a different kind of consideration. Perhaps he faintly sees that the very question rests on a mistake[92] – that asking for a reason to perform what we know to be

90 *Comm. phil.* II, x; *OD* II, 438.
91 In art. Nicole, rem. C, Bayle argues that Nicole's case on behalf of the way of authority is 'the high road to Pyrrhonism.' All the reasons that Nicole gives in his works against the Reform, that it is temerarious to join it unless all the reasons for and against it are examined, apply as well to the acceptance of the Church. Bayle's resolution of this stand-off is a pragmatic one – the same one that under his influence Hume was to employ, namely, we believe what we do because of education. See Lennon, 'Taste and Sentiment.' What, then, of Bayle's *arguments* for his position? He believes, as he does with respect to toleration, that anyone considering them will come to his position. But that he has this belief, along with the arguments, depends on his education, that is, on grace or chance.
92 See Pritchard's once-celebrated article, which argues just this case.

binding is like asking for a reason to believe what we know to be true. He in any case buries the question in an appeal to a certain kind of life based on the conviction that to act morally is what it means to accept the authority of God. However irrelevant that way of life, including all its duties, may be to salvation, performance of those duties requires that if we believe that x is a duty, then we have a duty to do x. Anything less makes morality a matter of luck.

Bayle's view is that only his conscience theory of morality saves morality from the lottery it is on Jurieu's objectivist theory. 'The turpitude of an action at the tribunal of divine justice is not measured by the real quality of the subjects it is about, but by their objective qualities [in the Cartesian sense, that is, qualities that are objects of the mind's attention], which is to say that God considers only the act itself of the will.' So if a man tries to kill someone he believes to be in a coach and instead fires on a statue placed there, he is guilty of homicide. 'Willing to move the arm at the moment that one believes its movement will be followed by the death of a man comprises the whole essence of homicide. The rest, namely, whether a given man is really killed or not, is but a pure accident, in which God, the infallible and sure judge of all things, does not consider as something attenuating or aggravating the sin.'[93]

Unless we are able to appeal infallibly to the inner sensation of conscience, if instead there is a cleavage, as Jurieu thinks, between what we think is right and what objectively we ought to do, we are caught in a paralysing Pyrrhonism exactly analogous to the scepticism generated by the *fait-droit* distinction. The solution to both is identical. Just as we know what we mean, so do we know what we ought to do – on the basis of good-faith judgment, not blindly, but after taking into account what we in good faith take to be relevant. 'The sole certitude that we have that the actions that appear to us right and pleasing to God should be performed is that we have the inner sensation in our conscience that we should perform them.' Otherwise, the risk of damnation is too great to do anything. 'No wise man should do something when he believes that by doing it he will expose himself to eternal damnation; to behave wisely therefore, he should live like a statue, and yield nothing to the instincts of conscience.'[94] Nor is an appeal to faith of any use in this crisis. Bayle insists that his view does not eliminate grace as the basis for adhering to revealed truths. But the resulting faith is not self-

93 *Comm. phil.* II, x; *OD* II, 428.
94 Ibid; *OD* II, 441.

guaranteeing. 'Faith does not give us any marks of orthodoxy other than inner sensation and the conviction of conscience, a mark that is found in the greatest of heretics.'[95] Thus Bayle is not a fideist in the usual sense that faith yields truth; for the relevant truth is that the conscience, whether determined by faith or in some other way, has a certain belief that should be acted upon. Bayle's solution to the sceptical dilemma may not work – living like a statue cannot be any more likely in the interest of salvation than anything else – but the element of chance that he sees Jurieu's theory as injecting into morality is clear.

To be sure, Bayle's view incorporates an element of chance, but it is irrelevant to our duties. He argues the case, on behalf of toleration, that error and difference of opinion do not necessarily spring from corruption of the heart. As we have seen, cupidity and sensuality for him have no role to play in the differing views on the Real Presence or the Trinity, for example. Nor is it a matter of pride, as the Catholics charge, that Protestants hold their views; for no one would knowingly reject the word of God *recognized for what it is* on such a ground. Instead, it is the prejudices of education that prevent one from finding in Scripture what is there. Now, the education one gets is entirely a matter of chance. Someone born in China has one set of views; the same person born in England would have another.[96] But this difference in moral views makes no difference in their bindingness. Though the Englishman and the Chinese may have contradictory beliefs about what one ought to do, each is obliged to do as he believes.

31: Fatalism, Chance, and Creation

Like the history of the world to date, the doctrine of grace offends the sensibilities of our liberal egalitarianism. As some people are, for reasons beyond their control, beautiful, intelligent, healthy, rich, famous, and happy, and others are ugly, stupid, sick, poor, obscure, and miserable, so some people for reasons beyond their control are saved and others damned. Nor should this parallel between the orders of nature and grace be very surprising, for the latter may be understood as an attempt to explain the former – may indeed be viewed (recall Leti) as a description of it.

An interesting version of the view is that immortality consists in the

---

95 Ibid; *OD* II, 439.
96 Ibid; *OD* II, 439–40.

fact that whatever is true of a person at a time is eternally true of that person for that time. No matter what else happens to me, including my death, it always will be (is, and has been) true of me that at this moment I am writing. (The same sort of Leibnizian predicate-in-subject analysis is true of all other things, of course, including inanimate objects like the pen in my hand, but perhaps the differences ordinarily emphasized between people and pens will suffice to ground the more interesting version of my immortality. Whether it can avoid the Leibnizian Fallacy is another question.) To put it simply, annihilation does not (contrary to the worries of the *Phaedo*, for instance) entail mortality, for our lives as a whole turn out to be immortal. In these terms, the order of grace does not shadow or parallel the order of nature, but rather informs it and invests it with significance. Indeed, the same may be true even if we ignore these metaphysical speculations and assume the simple naturalism of a Gregorio Leti. The order of grace just is the order of nature.

Bayle sometimes gives evidence of thinking in these terms. For example, he observes that Epicurus, whose morality was relatively unproblematic both in theory and in practice, has yet suffered near-universal infamy, and then comments: 'We must recognize here as in other things the empire of fatalism. There are people who are fortunate [*heureux*] and there are people who are unfortunate; this is the best explanation that can be given of their different lots [*fortune*].'[97] Early in his life Bayle was prepared, it would seem, to count himself among the fortunate, trusting in Providence as he experienced the troubles and vicissitudes of a hounded existence. Such is the impression he gives in a letter to his brother as he arrived a refugee, penniless, and under a false name, in Rouen. But after the death of that same brother, in prison because of Bayle's writings, he never again invoked Providence in personal terms.[98]

On the face of it, the concept of Providence seems open to interpretation in the fatalist terms that Bayle suggests, and it thus seems liable to Popperian objections, both moral and cognitive, against historicism, of which it may even be a paradigm case.[99] The usual way of framing the issue is in causal terms: no matter what causal mechanisms I may mobilize, my fate is such that certain future states will be true of me. (Certainly, Leibniz tried to avoid any fatalistic implications of the above

97 Art. Epicurus, rem. N.
98 Labrousse, 199–200.
99 See Popper, *The Poverty of Historicism*.

notion of immortality by insisting that the built-in predicates of a subject are the sufficient reason for everything truly asserted of it; that is, what I do is *caused*, not *fated*.) Bayle rejects mechanism[100] and, perhaps for the same reasons that he does so, he would frame the issue, not in causal terms, but *semantically*: no matter what I do, the whole of history, and my part in it, will have a certain *meaning*. Bayle seems to accept this form of fatalism at the cosmic level; but can he accept it at the individual level? And how then does Providence comport with the polyphonic outlook attributed to him above? Bayle does not think that Providence can be reconciled with human freedom, a problem that he sees as of a piece with the problem of evil. 'That a God, infinitely good, infinitely holy, infinitely free, who could make creatures always holy, always happy, should rather choose to make them criminal, and eternally miserable, is a thing that shocks reason; and so much the more, because it cannot reconcile man's free will with the quality of a Being created out of nothing.'[101] But he does have at his disposal the resources at least to begin an answer to the somewhat different question just raised.

Part of the answer to the question depends on the very notion of creativity exercised by any author, divine or human. Although he is the creation of Dostoevsky, who also creates the story in which he figures, Raskolnikov kills the pawnbroker freely and with full responsibility for what he does. (This is a point, perhaps the main point, of the story.) Another part is of the answer that the character–plot relation is not in any obvious sense part–whole. The relation between the Karamazov brother Ivan and *The Brothers Karamazov* is much more complex, for characters act freely and have meaning independently of the story in which they occur. The meaning of history may be the Redemption, but this is not achieved by everyone's, or even anyone's, being saved. Nor is a dramatic and, at the individual level, non-fatalistic reading of Providence particularly eccentric or peculiar to Bayle. Rather, it seems obvious and, if anything, perfectly orthodox. Consider Bossuet's discussion of the meeting of Peter and John with the owner of the ass (Mark 11: 4–6). The meeting may be regarded as foreseen but also as foretelling that Christ would one day ride an untamed ass as a symbol of conveying the law to the gentile nations.[102] Here is an event with dramatic and symbolic significance that none the less occurs by chance, which Bossuet

100 See Lennon, 'Mechanism As a Silly Mouse.'
101 Art. Spinoza, rem. O.
102 *Oeuvres complètes*, Paris 1862, 318–21; cited by Le Brun, 122.

clearly understands as the intersection of independent orders of causation. Each of the parties to the meeting may have been there freely, as a result of his own independent volitions, which none the less help to intend the teaching of the Gospel.

The fatalism that Bayle (like Leibniz) repeatedly dismisses as Turkish lacks the significance of such encounters. Not only does it lead to outrageous behaviour (a favourite example is of foolhardy military attacks by Turks convinced of their fate), it also robs human life of dramatic context. (One person says something and then, regardless of what another responds, again says something). In fact, Bayle rejects this form of fatalist historicism on precisely Popperian grounds. Historically, according to Popper, historicism has been a main theoretical support of one totalitarian regime after another. Historicists are inclined, not only to view events as fated, but also to claim knowledge of that fate, which is then used to justify it. The version of this thinking closest to Bayle came from Jurieu, and by contrast to Providence, Bayle will have none of it. On Jurieu's turn to monomonarchism,[103] he mused with sharp irony as follows: 'Few people rely less on Providence than those who pride themselves in having fathomed the depths of its decrees and the enigmas of the prophets.'[104]

For Bayle, the doctrine of creation is the only basis for a true conception of Providence, indeed for any conception of it at all. It is not clear to Bayle that Epicurus's mistake of denying divine interest in the world is philosophically any worse than those pagan philosophers who see the world as ordered according to the fancy of the gods. For while the latter say what is in a sense true, namely that the world has a divine maintenance and direction, it is a truth admitted 'not by the door, but by the window.' They find themselves on the 'right path, having strayed from the wrong one.' For once the creation of matter is denied, its direction becomes, as Epicurus argued it was, an absurdity.[105] Now, the denial of creation is of course the only rationally justified position. (The Socinians, for example, ought to deny it because the principle *ex nihilo, nihil fit* is as evident as those to which they appeal in denying the Trinity or the Hypostatic union.) Only from Scripture do we learn of the creation of the world, and apart from this account the more we reason, the more we go astray, particularly in response to the problem of evil. (Bayle is at great length to show that Epicurus would have no difficulty in re-

103 See Labrousse, *Pierre Bayle* I, 207.
104 Art. Braunbom, rem. B.
105 Art. Epicurus, rem. S.

butting a Platonist's appeal to goodness as an ordering principle for an uncreated world.)

Citing Malebranche, Bayle argues that only by appeal to Scripture do we learn that as its creator God can order the world as He sees fit, needs nothing other than a simple act of the will to achieve His ends, and perforce finds that nothing happens in the world outside His plan for it.[106] Thus 'if things happen He has prohibited and that He punishes, they nevertheless do not arrive contrary to His decrees, and they serve the adorable ends that He has proposed to Himself from all eternity, and that are the greatest mysteries of the Gospel.' The role of Scripture is not just to show reason its limits by conveying the fact of creation, but by doing so to reveal the kind of creation it is and the kind of Creator God is. For it teaches that 'the true God, accommodating Himself to our capacity, reveals Himself as a Being who, having known the malice of man, repented and was sorry that He had created him [Genesis 6: 5–6] and as a Being who is angry and complains of the small success of his labour [Isaiah 5, Prophets and Psalms *passim*].'[107]

Bayle's position seems to be that the fact of the world's creation entails Providence, and also that failure to recognize this fact breeds incoherence in attempts to account for the order observed in the world. A good example of that failure is Ovid's cosmogony as set out in what Bayle takes to be his best work, the *Metamorphoses*.[108] The world is supposed to have emerged from an eternal chaos, but the very notion of chaos in unintelligible.[109] Nor can the supposed chaos have been eternal and at the same time contain the seeds or principles of the world that was to be formed, for with either the

106 Art. Epicurus, rem. J. Against philosophers who deny creation, Bayle cites Malebranche, *Méditations chrétiennes* 9, 3, that if God were not the creator of the world He could neither move anything nor know anything in it. The argument against creation is that it is inconceivable; but that God moves things is no less inconceivable yet is known to happen. And, because of His impassivity God can know only what is in Him; if He did not know things from His idea and will to create, they would be eternally unknown.

107 Art. Epicurus, rem. S.

108 Art. Ovid, rem. G. Since Ovid's account 'is only an imitation or even a paraphrase of what he had found in the books of the ancient Greeks,' Bayle's criticisms of it have more than local interest. Their application to Epicureanism is particularly obvious.

109 It cannot have been homogeneous in the way Ovid supposes, according to Bayle, if it also contained the seeds of things and the oppositions necessary to bring them into being. True homogeneity would require an equal distribution throughout of the elements and of the opposition of their qualities; but this would not be chaos, but 'the most regular, most symmetrical and most proportionate work conceivable' (ibid). The same sort of reasoning led the fifth-century Neoplatonist Hierocles to argue that Plato held the world to be created from nothing. But Bayle thinks he gets this reasoning, obviously not from Plato, but from Christian authors. Art. Hierocles, rem. A.

qualitative principles of the ancient philosophers or the mechanical principles of the modern, a finite period of time would have sufficed to produce the world. (Bayle's preference for mechanical principles is based on their greater ability to demonstrate this sufficiency – as in Descartes's fictional account of the world's formation.) Hence Ovid's inclusion of a God who intervenes in the chaotic struggle of the elements is not only a *deus ex machina*, but a useless one. 'As long as we have no idea of a creation properly speaking ... we cannot understand how God could have given, or would have needed to give, motion to matter.'[110] Finally, the cosmos is not the peaceful state Ovid depicts it to be. For 'since the world is perforce a theatre of vicissitudes, nothing would be more inappropriate than to establish peace among the four elements ... It is through their clashes that nature becomes fertile ... The production of one thing is always the destruction of another. *Generatio unius est corruptio alterius.*'[111] Bayle's citation of this 'axiom of philosophy,' which he takes from Lucretius,[112] is sometimes relatively trivial. Worrying about Molière's use of neologisms, for example, he cites the axiom and observes that 'the birth of one word is ordinarily the death of another.'[113] In response to Ovid, however, the axiom is loaded with moral significance – indeed, Bayle's text reads like the nature-red-in-tooth-and-claw romanticism of the nineteenth century. Never far from Bayle's cosmic considerations is the problem of evil.

Despite Bayle's appeals to principles of Malebranche, the conception

110 Here there may be another, unacknowledged use of Malebranche. Previously, Bayle had appealed to Malebranche's notions of divine knowledge and God as a source of motion on behalf of creation. Here the appeal is to another Malebranchean concept, laws of order, and the appeal is politically volatile. God's exercise of authority over an eternal, uncreated matter would violate the laws of order, for neither His power, nor His perfection, nor even His wisdom would entitle Him to such domination. For such a God, acting beyond laws of order, we may perhaps read Louis XIV, called *le grand*. As was intoned at the outset of his funeral oration in 1715, 'Dieu seul est grand, mes frères ...'

111 Another attraction of the mechanical philosophy for Bayle is that it better explains the 'perpetual war' in the natural world. Collision is better evidence of constant struggle than any Aristotelian opposition between cold and heat, for example (ibid, rem. G). Not incidentally, Bayle portrays the mechanical world in the same anthropomorphic, dramatic terms that Empedocles, for example, used to describe the principles of things. And his sole criticism of Empedocles is that only hate or discord rules in the material world. 'The antipathy alone of elements assembles bodies in one place and disperses them in another.'

112 *De rerum natura* I, 671.

113 Yet even this instance evidences Bayle's steady-state pessimism. The linguistic zero-sum 'is true especially in France, and thus there is no hope that our language will escape its impoverishment' (Art. Poquelin, rem. D).

of creation he sees connected with Providence is very different from the relations the Cartesians see between God and the world. The difference can be expressed in a number of connected ways. 1) For the Cartesians, evil tends to be eliminated in Augustinian fashion by construing apparent instances of evil as contributing to the good of the whole. For Bayle, evil is an ineliminable, brute fact about the world. 2) Contrary to Bayle's God, the Cartesian God cannot regret what He has created – either creation is *ipso facto* good (Descartes) or necessarily good (Malebranche). 3) People do not have freedom of spontaneity on the Cartesian account except to err, and especially not to enter an exchange with God. Nowhere in Malebranche's 'dialogue' with the Word is there room for negotiation. His dialogue is not an exchange but, in his term, an illumination.[114] Needless to say, it is a one-way illumination.

Creation *ex nihilo* is unintelligible; its occurrence is miraculous, and like all miracles it is accepted as a brute fact. So much Bayle shares with the Cartesians – with Malebranche's official view, for example, that God wills to create with a freedom of perfect indifference. However, Bayle rejects the Cartesian thesis that conservation in existence is continuous creation, or re-creation, from one moment to the next, even though it is the most reasonable position, because it may be construed as a solution to the problem of evil that is unacceptable – as all such solutions are, according to Bayle. How so?

Typically, the situation is complicated because Bayle's presentation of the thesis might be interpreted as his own view, or as precisely the thesis he rejects, or as a thesis that is merely being presented. Roughly, the story goes as follows. In his presentation of the problem of evil in the articles on the Manichees, the Marcionites, the Paulicians, and elsewhere, Bayle portrays the dualist solution of those sects as rationally invincible. As part of the case for making God, or at least a divine principle, responsible *ex hypothesi* for the evil in the world, Bayle argues in a number of ways that finite creatures cannot be responsible for it. One argument was based on the Cartesian doctrine of conservation as continuous creation. Jaquelot, whose larger concern was, as the title of his book indicates, to establish against Bayle the agreement of faith and reason, took Bayle's argument to deny human freedom and thus to be part of Bayle's general failure. In response, Bayle conceded Jaquelot's criticism with respect to the consequences of the Cartesian thesis, but yet found human freedom no more rationally defensible than the denial of dualism. As will be seen, for him

114 See Lennon, *Battle*, 176–7.

both are transcended by faith. Only in this way can the problem of evil be dealt with, he thinks, and a proper conception of Providence be reached.

In remark F of the article Paulicians, Bayle argues that 'according to the idea that we have of a created being, we cannot comprehend that the principle of its action should be that it can move itself, and that receiving its existence and that of its faculties at every moment of its duration wholly from another cause, it should create in itself modalities by a power peculiar to itself.' No created being has the power of creating substances, says Bayle, hence whether these modalities are different from the substance – that is, substances themselves, as the Peripatetics would have it, or not, as the new philosophers would have it – no created thing can cause its own modalities. The power of causing change, that is, creating from one moment to the next, seems to belong only to God.

In response[115] to Jaquelot's criticism of the Paulician remark,[116] Bayle observed that Jaquelot had attacked the same argument fifteen years earlier as he found it implicit in Jurieu.[117] Here the Cartesian difficulty is in full evidence. 'According to Jurieu's system, conservation is nothing but a continuation of creation, because with the moments of time having no necessary connection with one another, it does not follow from the fact that I exist at one moment that I will subsist at the next unless the same cause giving me existence for that moment also gives it to me for the next.'[118] God thus does all, for He must create me fully determinate, as an individual, with 'all my circumstances, with a given thought, with a given action, standing or seated.' And, of course, since God does all, people are not free to do anything. In the earlier text, against Jurieu, Jaquelot had concluded that creatures were not causes in any sense – not primary, secondary, or occasional; in the later text, against Bayle, he focuses his attack on occasionalism as that view follows from the Cartesian thesis. The attack goes as follows.

A consequence of the doctrine of continuous re-creation, according to Jaquelot, is that God is the 'unique, immediate, and complete cause of all that happens in the universe. Creatures are no more than witnesses to their own actions.'[119] 'According to Bayle's principle [which is to say,

115 *RQP*, cxii; *OD* III, 787–91.
116 *Conformité*, 252–65.
117 *Avis sur le tableau du Socinianisme*, treatise 1, 36–7.
118 Ibid, 36; cited by Bayle, 787. This of course is a paraphrase of Descartes, *Meditations* III. Not incidentally, Leibniz took Bayle himself to be the author of the anonymous *Avis* (*Theodicy*, para. 383).
119 *Conformité*, 261.

the Cartesian thesis quoted in art. Paulicians, rem. F], the universe is nothing more than a mass of vain and deceptive appearances ... we delude ourselves when we imagine we perceive, deliberate, decide, and carry out some good or evil, since God does all ... it is more reasonable to confess that we do not understand the nature of God's conservation and cooperation with creatures than to turn creatures into shadows and phantasms, to destroy law and civil society, to annihilate religion ...'[120]

Bayle is quick to observe that Jaquelot here betrays the whole thrust of his book, which is supposedly to show the conformity between faith and reason. So, in a typically Baylean twist, Jaquelot unwittingly rejects the very thesis that Bayle rejects and, no less unwittingly, arrives at Bayle's own conclusion. Happily, therefore, does Bayle take Jaquelot's attack to be 'victorious.'[121] But he does not embrace it for any of the number of reasons that one might expect, for example, that occasionalism thus interpreted leaves man incapable of dialogue. Instead, he distances himself *both* from occasionalism *and* from Jaquelot's criticism of it on behalf of freedom.[122] He insists, however, that in raising the objections that he did, he was acting 'not as a Cartesian, but in the name of Zoroaster'!

Bayle's invocation of Manicheism is no mere device to secure suspension of belief by juxtaposing a contrary view. To be sure, he compares Jaquelot to those nations that, unable to prevent the invasion of their own territory, in turn ravage that of their neighbours, and to the Romans, who to rid their own lands of Hannibal, attacked Carthage itself. And referring to the image of Penelope, he reminds us that reason is much stronger on the offence, tearing things apart, than on the defence in conserving them.[123] He goes beyond this theoretical scepticism to include 'such philosophers as there may be who today would propose difficulties against a single principle, and who would declare that before all else they should be considered as sceptics not yet decided upon some sect, but who are

---

120 Ibid, 262–3.
121 *RQP*, cxii; *OD* III, 789.
122 Or, rather, he allows both that occasionalism is prefereable to the 'common hypothesis' and yet that what Jaquelot says against it stands.
123 Bayle's reference is to one of the favourite passages among his recent readers. Arguing on behalf of faith as a stance against the difficulties that reason generates concerning the problem of evil, he says that 'if reason were in agreement with itself, then it would indeed be regrettable that we find so much difficulty in reconciling it with some articles of our religion. Reason is like a runner who does not know where to stop, or like another Penelope constantly undoing what it creates ... It is better suited to pulling things down than to building them up, and better at discovering what things are not than what they are' (*RPQ* II, cxxxvii; *OD* III, 778).

quite prepared to embrace Christianity when we obviate for them the difficulties surrounding the origin of evil.'[124] It does no good, according to Bayle, even to point out that a system of two principles is 'abominable' and 'absurd' – especially with the details in which it has so foolishly been filled out, or to point out that even the best philosophical efforts can do no more than to make the system less indefensible.

What does all this come to? The context, it will be recalled, is the nature of the Creator and reason's inability to solve the problem of evil except with dualism. And, according to Bayle, the refutation of dualism, or at least its rejection, can only be *a posteriori*. It is a truth *de fait*, as he explicitly calls it,[125] both that there is but one principle and yet that there is evil in the world. That there is but one principle is known from Scripture, which is accepted on faith. Here is Bayle's argument. 'According to Scripture there is but one good principle, and yet moral and physical evil have been introduced among mankind: it is not therefore contrary to the nature of a good principle, to permit introduction of moral evil, and to punish crimes; for it is not more evident, that four and four are eight, than it is evident that if a thing comes to pass, it is possible. *Ab actu ad potentiam valet consequentia – from fact to possibility the consequence is good*, is one of the clearest and most uncontestable axioms in metaphysics. This is an impregnable rampart, and this is sufficient to render the cause of the orthodox victorious, altho' their reasons *a priori* may be refuted.'[126]

It remains, however, that the fact driving the argument is accepted on faith. The horrible possibility thus remains that we are mistaken about God. The being whom we take to be God and thus according to reason incapable of deceit, may as an autonomous being deceive us as might any autonomous being who acts other than as expected, who acts out of what we take to be their character. In this case, Providence becomes the nightmare that Bayle himself often enough experienced it as. But the possibility of such a nightmare is the price to be paid for the ultimate exercise of Bayle's most cherished value, autonomy. If one is not autonomous, either because one is incapable of autonomy or because one refuses to exercise it, the nightmare may be no more than a pleasant, albeit deceitful, dream. But only fear and trembling can accompany us if with Moses we approach the burning bush. The conclusion that one is led to is that Providence involving autonomous beings is intrinsically a gamble.

124 Ibid.
125 Ibid.
126 Art. Paulicians, rem. E.

Epilogue

With all of the above, has the essential Bayle at last been found and the Bayle enigma solved? Bayle has certainly not been categorized in any of the terms, or sorts of terms, that made it possible to state the enigma. The Bakhtinian reading of Bayle is not itself a hidden message; rather, it is precisely the reading that there is no hidden message. In fact, the Bayle enigma has in principle been extended to all authors of a certain kind of text, who like Dostoevsky (or God Himself) are able to relate in a special way to the people they evoke. In this sense, only a confirmation, or at best, a clarification of the enigma has been achieved. Nor is this reading merely that Bayle himself is puzzled but intellectually honest enough not to conceal his puzzlement. Monophonic writing is not precluded from puzzlement and the candid expression of it any more than polyphonic writing guarantees this result. In principle, scepticism is no less compatible with the former than dogmatism is with the latter. What emerges, instead, is a principled conscientiousness – integrity, in Ciceronian language – that leaves Bayle liable at every point to revise his views (unlike the monophonic Descartes, who never revises his views or shows hesitation about anything).

If Bayle is at all worth reading, the result should be an attempt to engage his texts in just those terms that have made him seem enigmatic. A text in response to reading Bayle should itself be open-ended and allow for independence of personal voice by extending the argument, or at least showing how it might be extended. It should enter the conversation proposed at the end of the Dostoevskian chapter 2 above. A plausible point of engagement is Bayle's own principal engagement – that with his Catholic opponents on the issue of the Real Presence.

The issue of the Real Presence, for Bayle, is not the metaphysical question of whether the miracle of transubstantiation takes place. To be sure, he is at pains to argue that the age of miracles had ceased over a millennium earlier with the successful promulgation of Christianity, and he for a while supported Cartesianism because he saw it as a metaphysics incompatible with transubstantiation. But the source of Bayle's animus towards the doctrine lies on a different level, with two related considerations. One is, as we might call it, the plastic Jesus phenomenon, that is, the raft of relics, processions, medals, etc. that epitomized Catholic idolatry for Bayle. The Catholic understanding of the Eucharist was based on a sacramental economy that functioned *ex opere operato*, that is, from the mere fact that certain words were uttered or certain actions performed, a spiritual reality was automatically achieved, independent of the intentions of those involved. For Bayle, such an effect, the special presence of Christ, for example, necessarily depends on faith. Secondly, the Christ of the Catholic Eucharist could not be consubstantial with, or in any way identical to, the living God of Scripture. Such a being, lying dead upon the altar, is incapable of dialogue.

Quite apart from the status of transubstantiation, these are apparently insurmountable differences. But perhaps not really so. Likely the most prominent document to issue from the Second Vatican Council (1962–5) is *Gaudium et spes*;[1] surprisingly, important passages from it could have been written by Bayle himself. Most notably, the argument of the Council is that conscience, witness, and social justice entail one another. It is not much of a stretch to regard the Council as extending Bayle's argument that the principal and perhaps only role of conscience is to give witness to the truth, particularly religious truth as it is perceived, and that the principal and perhaps only form of social injustice is to interfere with this role of conscience, that is, to engage in religious persecution.[2]

What conclusion is to be drawn from this unlikely convergence of views between Bayle and Vatican II? Has the Church just seen the light? Not likely, and at any rate, a case can be made that the Church has always subscribed to the views of Vatican II (recall Bossuet's Cartesian account of religious truth) – this, despite such aberrations as the Revocation that the Church has been called upon to support (Bossuet himself famously preached in support of it).[3]

---

1 Certainly, it is the most frequently quoted source apart from Scripture in the most recent *Catechism of the Catholic Church*.

2 See also *Dignitatis Humanae*, which also issued from Vatican II: 'Man must not be forced to act contrary to his conscience. Nor must he he be prevented from acting according to his conscience, especially in religious matters.' Quoted in *Catechism of the Catholic Church*, 378.

3 See the texts, Scriptural and otherwise, cited by the *Catechism*, 377–80.

To push the argument in the other direction, as in fact Jurieu did push it, a case can be made for the eighteenth-century reading of Bayle's work as indifferentist, deistic, and Socinian.[4] This is a case that can be made independent of any irony or dissimulation in Bayle. How so? While Bayle may carefully respect differences between kinds of texts, never using a historical text to correct or corroborate a biblical one or conversely, for example, or a philosophical one to correct or corroborate a literary one or conversely, he has no means of distinguishing the various kinds themselves. Moreover, even if differences between kinds of texts may be respected, they cannot be evaluated. Why live according to biblical texts, but not according to literary ones? Why obey God rather than Jupiter? Bayle has no answer because he recognizes no ecclesiastical authority of the relevant sort;[5] he has no way to authorize certain texts as divinely inspired; he is at a loss to establish God as the author of Scripture.

Rome's authority, on the other hand, is based in tradition – the Apostolic succession, symbolized by the Real Presence, which according to that doctrine is literally embodied in the tradition.[6] The Eucharist is supposed to be not just an act of thanksgiving, praise, and memorial after the fact of redemption, but a continuation of that fact in the Church. This was an early view, to be found, for example, in Augustine's *City of God* – in fact, this embodiment *is* the city of God. 'This wholly redeemed city, the assembly and society of saints, is offered to God as a universal sacrifice by the great priest [i.e., Christ] who in the form of a slave went so far as to offer himself for us in his Passion, to make us the body of so great a head ... This is the sacrifice of Christians, "we who are many are one body in Christ." The Church continues to reproduce this sacrifice in the sacrament of the altar ... wherein it is evident to them that in what she offers she herself is offered.'[7]

Bayle's difficulty can be seen with respect to the Calvinist distinction between the Catholic way of authority by contrast to the Calvinists' own way of investigation. In the interpretation of Scripture, the Catholic is supposed to cede his judgment to the authority of the Church, whereas

---

4 That is, Bayle would be a Socinian in the way that Descartes is a sceptic according to Popkin – in spite of himself. The case outlined below in no way upsets the case based on the anti-Socininian texts in Bayle cited by Tinsley, who also gives a nice account of Bayle's plea for toleration of the Socinians.

5 Kenshur (38) has essentially the same worry with Bayle.

6 Consider the Congregation of Rites (1967): 'The Eucharist is the efficacious sign and sublime cause of that communion in the divine life and that unity of the People of God by which the Church is kept in being.' Cited in *Catechism*, 285.

7 Augustine, *City of God*, 380.

the Calvinist relies on his own light as inspired by the Holy Ghost. But even if that inspiration were to make the individual infallible, his conscience is still empty. When one looks for content, one is at a loss, especially in seeking the living God. In this sense, Bayle's texts are no less dead than the Eucharist as he sees it. He seems faced with the following dilemma. Either God, or the Truth of the Enlightenment, or whatever it is that is conveyed by the word (or by the Word) speaks through *all* the texts, which is to say that Scripture is superfluous, or at least without privilege. This is the deistic, indifferentist, Socinian horn of the dilemma.[8] The other horn is that there is some living community (namely, the Church) which provides the proper content for conscience. This is the doctrine of infallibility that so sticks in the craw of the Calvinist Bayle, and we can see why.

---

8 Bost has a similar worry (118). Asserting the rights of conscience may upset the claim of any church to be the true Church, but it risks a 'decline into [mere] critical individualism.'

Bibliography

Abel, Olivier. 'La suspension du jugement comme impératif catégorique,' in Abel and Moreau, 107–29.

Abel, Olivier, and P.-F. Moreau, eds. *Pierre Bayle: la foi dans le doute*. Geneva: Labor et Fides, 1995.

Aquinas, Thomas. *Philosophical Texts*. Trans. Thomas Gilbey. Oxford: Oxford University Press, 1951.

Ariew, R. 'The Infinite in Descartes' Conversation with Burman,' *Archiv für Geschichte der Philosophie* 69, 140–63.

Armogathe, J.R. *Theologia Cartesiana*. The Hague: Martinus Nijhoff, 1977.

Arnauld, A. *Oeuvres*. Paris, 1775–83. Abbreviated: *OA*.

– *On True and False Ideas*. Trans. E. Kremer. Queenston: Edwin Mellen, 1990.

– *Réflexions sur ... préservatif contre le changement de religion*. Antwerp, 1682.

Arnauld, A., and P. Nicole. *Logic, or The Art of Thinking*. Ed. & trans. Jill Vance Buroker. Cambridge: Cambridge University Press, 1996.

Ashton, John. *A History of English Lotteries*. London, 1893.

Augustine. *Concerning the City of God against the Pagans*. Trans. H. Bettenson. Harmondsworth: Penguin, 1972.

Bakhtin, M. *Problems of Dostoevsky's Poetics*. Ed. and trans. Caryl Emerson. Minneapolis: University of Minnesota Press, 1984.

Barbeyrac, Jean. *Traité du jeu, où l'on examine les principales questions de droit naturel et de morale qui ont du rapport à cette matière*. Amsterdam, 1709; 2d ed. 1737.

Basnage de Beauval, Henri. *Histoire des ouvrages des sçavans*. Rotterdam, 1687–1709.

Bayle, François. *The Cartesian Empiricism of François Bayle*. Trans. P. Easton and T. Lennon. New York: Garland, 1992.

Bayle, Pierre. See Bibliographical Note, xi.

– *De la tolérance* (parts 1 and 2 of *Commentaire philosophique*). Ed. J.-M. Gros. Pocket, 1992.

– *The Dictionary Historical and Critical of Mr Peter Bayle*. Trans. Desmaizeaux. London, 1734–7. Rpt: New York: Garland, 1984.

– *Pensées diverses sur la comète*. Ed. A. Prat. Paris: Nizet, 1984.

– *Receuil de quelques pièces curieuses concernant la philosophie de Descartes*. Amsterdam, 1684.

Bellarmine, R. *Disputationum (Opera omnia)*. Vol. 3. Cologne, 1619.

Bossuet, J.-B. *Exposition de la doctrine de l'Église catholique sur les matières de controverse*. Paris, 1671.

– *Oeuvres complètes*. Ed. F. Lachat. Paris, 1864.

Bost, H. *Pierre Bayle et la religion*. Paris: Presses Universitaires de France, 1994.

Bourne, H.R. Fox. *The Life of John Locke*. 2 vols. London, 1876.

Bracken, H.M. 'Bayle Not a Sceptic?' *Journal of the History of Ideas* 25 (1964), 169–80.

Brenner, Reuven, and Gabrielle Brenner. *Gambling and Speculation: A Theory, a History, and a Future of Some Human Decisions*. Cambridge: Cambridge University Press, 1990.

Briggs, E. 'Bayle ou Larroque: De qui est l'*Avis important aux Réfugiez* de 1690 et de 1692?' in Magdelaine et al., 509–24.

Brueys, D.-A. *Défense du culte exterieur de l'Église catholique*. 2d ed. Paris, 1686.

– *Examen des raisons qui ont donné lieu à la séparation des Protestans*. Paris, 1683.

– *Oeuvres de théatre*. Paris, 1735.

– *Réponse au livre de Mr. de Condom intitulé, Exposition ...* Geneva, 1681.

– *Traité de l'Eucharistie*. Paris, 1686.

Catechism of the Catholic Church. Ottawa: Canadian Conference of Catholic Bishops, 1994.

Cicero. *De natura deorum*. Trans. H. Rackham. Cambridge: Harvard University Press, 1933.

Daneau, Lambert. *Les jeux de sort, ou de hazard*. Np., 1591.

Davis, Natalie Zemon. *The Return of Martin Guerre*. Cambridge: Harvard University Press, 1983.

Delvolvé, Jean. *Essai sur Pierre Bayle: religion, critique et philosophie positive*. Paris: F. Alcan, 1906.

Denzinger, H. *Enchiridion Symbolorum*. Barcelona: Herder, 1963.

Descartes, R. *The Philosophical Writings of Descartes*. Trans. J. Cottingham, R. Stoothoff, D. Murdoch. Cambridge: Cambridge University Press, 1985. Abbreviated: *CSM*.

Dibon, P., ed. *Pierre Bayle: le philosophe de Rotterdam*. Amsterdam/Paris: Elsevir/ Vrin, 1959.

Doucin, L. *Histoire du Nestorianisme*. The Hague, 1698.

Dupleix, Scipion. *La physique ou science des choses naturelles* (1603). Ed. R. Ariew. Paris: Fazard, 1990.

Fatio, Olivier. 'Lambert Daneau,' in Raitt, 105–19.

Fauré, Christine. *Les déclarations des droits de l'homme de 1789*. Paris: Payot, 1992.

– *Democracy without Women*. Trans. C. Gorbman and J. Berks. Bloomington: Indiana University Press, 1991.

Fénelon, François de la Mothe. *Démonstration de l'existence de Dieu*. 2d ed. Paris, 1713.

François de Sales. *Introduction à la vie devote*. Paris, 1686.

Gale, Theophilus. *The True Idea of Jansenism, Both Historic and Dogmatic*. London, 1669.

Gataker, Thomas. *Of the Nature and Use of Lots: A Treatise Historical and Theological*. 1619; 2d ed. London, 1627.

Gaukroger, S. *Descartes: An Intellectual Biography*. Oxford: Clarendon Press, 1995.

Gayot de Pitival, F. *Causes célèbres et intéressantes*. Paris, 1734.

Gazier, A. *Histoire générale du mouvement janséniste*. Paris, H. Campion, 1922.

Gerberon, D. *Histoire générale du jansénisme*. Amsterdam, 1698.

Gigas, Emil, ed. *Bayle*. Vol. 1 of *Lettres inédites de divers savants*. Copenhagen, 1890–3.

Grimarest (J.-L. Le Gallois). *La vie de ... Molière*. Paris, 1705; rpt: 1877.

Grussi, Olivier. *La vie quotidienne des joueurs sous l'ancien régime à Paris et à la cour*. Paris: Hachette, 1985.

Gueroult, M. *Malebranche*. Paris: Aubier, 1955–9.

Haag, Eugene, and Emile Haag. *La France Protestante*. Paris, 1846–59.

Hausman, D., and A. Hausman. *Descartes's Legacy: Minds and Meaning in Early Modern Philosophy*. Toronto: University of Toronto Press, 1997.

Heyd, M. *Between Orthodoxy and the Enlightenment: Jean-Robert Chouet and the Introduction of Cartesian Science in the Academy of Geneva*. The Hague: M. Nijhoff, 1982.

– 'A Disguised Atheist or a Sincere Christian? The enigma of Pierre Bayle,' *Bibliothèque d'Humanisme et Renaissance* 39 (1977).

Huet, P.-D. *Traité de la situation du paradis terrestre*. Paris, 1691.

James, H. 'Scepticism and Fideism in Bayle's *Dictionary*,' *French Studies* 16 (1962), 307–24.

Jaquelot, Isaac. *Avis sur le tableau du socinianisme*. Np., 1690.

– *Conformité de la foi avec la raison*. Amsterdam, 1705.

Jolley, N. *Leibniz and Locke: A Study of the 'New Essays on Human Understanding.'* Oxford: Clarendon Press, 1984.

Joncourt, Pierre de. *Quatre lettres*. Np, 1714.

Jossua, Jean-Pierre. *Pierre Bayle ou l'obsession du mal*. Paris: Aubier Montaigne, 1977.

Jurieu, Pierre. *Des droits des deux souverains en matière de religion* ... Rotterdam, 1687.

– *L'esprit de M. Arnauld*. Deventer, 1684.

– *Examen d'... Avis*. The Hague, 1691.

– *Factum selon les formes, ou disposition des preuves contre l'auteur de l'Avis aux refugiez*. 1692.

– *Le janséniste convaincu de vaine sophistiquerie, ou Examen des Reflexions de M. Arnauld sur le 'Préservatif contre le changement de religion.'* Amsterdam, 1683.

– *Jugement sur les méthodes rigides et relachées d'expliquer la Providence et la Grace*. Rotterdam, 1686.

– *Nouvelles hérésie dans la morale denoncée au Pape* ... The Hague, 1689.

– *Le Philosophe de Rotterdam accusé, atteint et convaincu*. Amsterdam, 1706.

– *La politique du clergé de France*. The Hague, 1681.

– *Préservatif contre le changement de religion*. The Hague, 1681.

– *La religion des Jésuites*. The Hague, 1689.

– *Suite du Préservatif ou Reflexion sur l'adoucissement des dogmes et des cultes ... proposé par M. Brueys avocat de Montpellier*. La Haze, 1683.

– *Le tableau du socinianisme où l'on voit l'impureté et la fausseté des dogmes des sociniens et où l'on découvre les mystères de la cabale de ceux qui veulent tolérer l'hérésie socinienne*. The Hague, 1690.

– *Traité de l'unité de l'Église et des points fondamentaux, contre M. Nicole*. Rotterdam, 1688.

– *Le vray système de l'Église*. Dordrecht, 1686.

Kant, I. *Foundations of the Metaphysics of Morals*. Trans. L.W. Beck. Indianapolis: Bobbs-Merrill, 1959.

Kenshur, O. 'Sincerité oblique chez Bayle: le scepticisme et la foi dans le *Dictionnaire*,' in Abel and Moreau, 31–47.

Kilcullen, J. *Sincerity and Truth: Essays on Arnauld, Bayle and Toleration*. Oxford: Clarendon Press, 1988.

Klaits, J. *Servants of Satan: The Age of the Witch Hunts*. Bloomington: Indiana University Press, 1985.

Klajnman, A. 'Spinoza au delà du théologico-politico,' *Futur Antérieur* 39–40 (1997), 179–90.

Knetsch, F. *Pierre Jurieu: Theoloog en Politikus der Refug*. J.H. Kok: Kampen, 1967. English summary in *Acta historia neerlandica* 5 (1971), 213–42.

Kors, A.C., and E. Peters. *Witchcraft in Europe, 1100–1700: A Documentary History*. Philadelphia: University of Pennsylvania Press, 1972.

Kremer, E.J. *The Great Arnauld and Some of His Philosophical Correspondents*. Toronto: University of Toronto Press, 1994.

– *Interpreting Arnauld*. Toronto: University of Toronto Press, 1996.

Labrousse, E. *Bayle*. Oxford: Oxford University Press, 1983.

– *Conscience et conviction: Études sur le XVIIe siècle*. Oxford, Paris: Voltaire Foundation, Universitas, 1996.

– *Notes sur Bayle*. Paris: Vrin, 1987.

– *Pierre Bayle* (2 vols.). Vol. I, *Du pays de Foix à la cité d'Erasme*. The Hague: Martinus Nijhoff, 1963.

– *Pierre Bayle* (2 vols.). Vol. II, *Hétérodoxie et rigorisme*. The Hague: Martinus Nijhoff, 1964.

– 'La tolérance comme argument de controverse: Les *Nouvelles Lettres* de Pierre Bayle,' *Studies in 18th Century Culture* 4 (1975): 247–52; reprinted in Labrousse, *Notes*, 177–82.

Lacoste, Edmond. *Bayle: Nouvelliste et critique littéraire*. Paris: Picart, 1929.

La Placette, Jean. *Divers traités sur des matières de conscience*. Amsterdam, 1697.

– *Réponse à deux objections*. Amsterdam, 1707.

– *Traité de la conscience*. Amsterdam, 1695.

– *Traité des jeux-de-hazard défendu contre les objections de ... Joncourt et quelques autres*. The Hague, 1714.

Larroque, Daniel. *Le proselyte abusé*. Rotterdam, 1684.

Le Brun, Jacques. *Bossuet*. Paris: Desclée de Brouwer, 1970.

Leclerc, Jean. *Reflexions sur ce que l'on appelle bonheur et malheur en matière de lotteries et sur le bon usage qu'on en peut faire*. Amsterdam, 1696.

Leibniz, G.W. *Theodicy*. Ed. D. Allen. Indianapolis: Bobbs-Merrill, 1966.

Lelevel, Henri. *La vraye et la fausse métaphysique*. Rotterdam, 1694.

Lenfant, Jacques. *Considerations générales sur le livre de M. Brueys, intitulé, Examen*. Rotterdam, 1684.

Lennon, T. 'Arnauld and Scepticism: *Questions de fait* and *questions de droit*,' in Kremer, ed. *Interpreting Arnaud*, 51–63.

– *The Battle of the Gods and Giants: The Legacies of Descartes and Gassendi, 1655–1715*. Princeton: Princeton University Press, 1993.

– 'Bayle, Locke and the Metaphysics of Toleration,' in *Oxford Studies in the History of Philosophy*, ed. M.A. Stewart, vol. 2: *Studies in Seventeenth-Century European Philosophy*. Oxford: Clarendon Press, 1997, 177–95.

– 'Bayle's Anticipation of Popper,' *Journal of the History of Ideas* 1997, 695–704.

– 'Gassendi et Pierre Bayle: Deux acolytes de Clio,' in *Gassendi: sa posterité, 1572–92*, ed. S. Murr. Paris: Vrin, 1997, 165–74.

– 'Jansenism and the *Crise Pyrrhonienne*.' *Journal of the History of Ideas* 38 (April 1977), 297–306.

– 'Lady Oracle: Changing Conceptions of Authority and Reason in Seventeenth-Century Philosophy,' in *Women and Reason*, ed. E. Harvey and K. Okruhlik. Ann Arbor: University of Michigan Press, 1992, 39–61.

– 'La logique janséniste de la liberté,' *Revue d'Histoire et de Philosophie Religieuses*, no. 1, 1979, 37–44. (Reprinted in *Port-Royal to Bayle* (Vol. 4 of *Essays in Early Modern Philosophy*), ed. V. Chappell. New York: Garland,1992, 71–92.)

– 'Malebranche's Argument for Ideas,' in *Minds, Ideas and Objects*, ed. P. Cummins and G. Zoeller, *North American Kant Society Studies in Philosophy* 2 (1992), 57–71.

– 'Mechanism as a Silly Mouse,' in *Causation in Early Modern Philosophy*, ed. S. Nadler. University Park: Pennsylvania State University Press, 175–95.

– 'Occasionalism, Jansenism and Skepticism: Divine Providence and the Order of Grace,' *Irish Theological Quarterly* 45, no. 3 (1978), 185–90.

– 'Pandora, or Essence and Reference: Gassendi's Nominalist Objection and Descartes's Realist Reply,' in *Descartes and His Contemporaries*, ed. R. Ariew and M. Grene. Chicago: University of Chicago Press, 1995, 159–81.

– 'Taste and Sentiment: Hume, Bayle, Jurieu and Nicole,' in Abel and Moreau, 49–64.

Lennon, T., J.M. Nicholas, and J.W. Davis, eds. *The Problems of Cartesianism*. Kingston and Montreal: McGill-Queen's University Press, 1982.

Leti, Gregorio. *Critique historique, politique, morale, économique et comique sur les lotteries anciennes, et modernes, spirituelles, et temporelles des états et des églises*. Traduit de l'italien. 2 vols. Amsterdam, 1697.

Locke, J. *Epistola de tolerantia: A letter on toleration*. Ed. R. Klibansky, trans. J. Gough. Oxford: Oxford University Press, 1968.

Magdelaine, M., A. McKenna, C. Pitassi, and R. Whelan. *De l'humanisme aux lumières*. Oxford: Voltaire Foundation, 1995.

Maia Neto, J. 'Academic Scepticism in Early Modern Philosophy,' *Journal of the History of Ideas* (1997), 199–220.

Malebranche, N. *Oeuvres complètes*, ed. A. Robinet. Paris: J. Vrin 1958–69. Abbreviated: *OC*.

– *The Search after Truth*. Trans. T. Lennon and P. Olscamp. Cambridge: Cambridge University Press, 1997.

McKenna, A. 'Pierre Bayle et Port-Royal,' in Magdelaine et al.

McRae, R. 'Descartes' Definition of Thought,' in R. Butler, ed. *Cartesian Studies*. Oxford: Blackwell, 1972.

Millikan, R. *Language, Thought and Other Biological Categories*. Cambridge: MIT Press, 1991.

Molière, J.-B. P. *The Dramatic Works*. Trans. Henri Van Lauw. Edinburgh, 1876.

Mossner, E.C. *The Life of David Hume*. Austin: University of Texas Press, 1954.

Nadler, S. *Arnauld and the Cartesian Philosophy of Ideas*. Princeton: Princeton University Press, 1989.

- *Malebranche and Ideas*. Oxford: Oxford Universirty Press, 1992.
Ndiaye, A.R. *La Philosophie d'Antoine Arnauld*. Paris: Vrin, 1991.
- 'The Status of Eternal Truths in the Philosophy of Antoine Arnauld,' in Kremer, *Interpreting Arnauld*, 64–75.
Nelson, A. 'Cartesian Actualism in the Leibniz-Arnauld Correspondence.' *Canadian Journal of Philosophy* 23 (December 1993), 675–94.
Newman, J. *Foundations of Religious Tolerance*. Toronto: University of Toronto Press, 1982.
Nicole, P. *Préjugez legitimes contre les calvinistes*. Paris, 1671.
- *Les prétendus réformez convaincus de schisme*. Paris, 1684.
Norton, D.F. 'Leibniz and Bayle: Manicheism and Dialectic,' *Journal of the History of Philosophy* 2 (1964), 23–36.
O'Cathasaigh, S. 'Scepticism and Belief in Pierre Bayle's *Nouvelles Critiques*,' *Journal of the History of Ideas* 45 (1984), 421–33.
Ogonowski, Z. 'Faustus Socinus,' in Raitt, 195–209.
Olin, D. 'Newcombe's Paradox: Further Investigations,' *American Philosophical Quarterly* 13 (1976), 129–33.
Osler, M. 'Baptising Epicurean Atomism,' in M. Osler and P. Farber, eds. *Religion, Science and Worldview*. Cambridge: Cambridge University Press, 1985.
Ozment, S. *The Age of Reform: 1250–1550*. New Haven: Yale University Press, 1980.
Paganini, G. *Analisi della fede critica della ragione nella filosofia di Pierre Bayle*. Florence: La Nuova Italia Editrice, 1980.
Pascal, B. *Oeuvres*. Ed. L. Brunscvig. Paris: Hachette, 1923.
Perkins, William. *The Works*. Cambridge, 1613.
Popkin, R.H. *The High Road to Pyrrhonism*, ed. R. Watson and J. Force. San Diego: Austin Hill, 1980.
- *The History of Scepticism from Erasmus to Spinoza*. Berkeley: University of California Press, 1979.
Popkin, R.H., trans. *Pierre Bayle: Historical and Critical Dictionary, Selections*. Indianapolis: Bobbs-Merrill, 1965.
Popper, K.R. *The Poverty of Historicism*. London: Routledge, 1957.
Pritchard, H. 'Does Moral Philosophy Rest on a Mistake?' *Mind*, 1912.
Raitt, Jill, ed. *Shapers of Religious Traditions in Germany, Switzerland, and Poland, 1560–1600*. New Haven: Yale University Press, 1981.
Regis, P.-S. *Réponse ... Censura*. Paris, 1691.
- *Système de philosophie*. Paris, 1690.
Rétat, Pierre. *Le Dictionnaire de Bayle et la lutte philosophique au XVIIIe siècle*. Paris: Les Belles Lettres, 1971.
Rex, Walter. *Essays on Pierre Bayle and Religious Controversy*. The Hague: Martinus Nijhoff, 1965.

Robinet, A. 'L'aphilosophie [sic] de Bayle devant les philosophies de Malebranche et Leibniz,' in Dibon, 48–61.

Rorty, R., et al., eds. *Philosophy in History.* Cambridge: Cambridge University Press, 1984.

Ross, D. *Aristotle.* London: Methuen, 1964.

Sandberg, K.C. *At the Crossroads of Faith and Reason: An Essay on Pierre Bayle.* Tucson: University of Arizona Press, 1966.

Schmaltz, T. 'What Has Cartesianism to Do with Jansenism?' *Journal of the History of Ideas,* forthcoming.

Searle, J. 'Proper Names,' *Mind* 67 (1958).

Sedgwick, Alexander. *Jansenism in Seventeenth-Century France: Voices from the Wilderness.* Charlottesville: University Press of Virginia, 1977.

Shea, W. *The Magic of Numbers and Motion: The Scientific Career of René Descartes.* Canton, MA: Science History Publications, 1991.

Tawney, R.H. *Religion and the Rise of Capitalism.* 3rd ed. New York: Mentor, 1950.

Thiers, Jean-Baptiste. *Traité des jeux et des divertissements.* Paris, 1686.

Thomas, Keith. *Religion and the Decline of Magic.* Harmondsworth: Penguin, 1973.

Tinsley, B. Sher. 'Sozzini's Ghost: Pierre Bayle and Socianian Toleration,' *Journal of the History of Ideas* (1996), 609–24.

Voltaire, (J.B.F. Arouet). *Oeuvres complètes.* Paris, 1879.

Watson, R.A. *Representational Ideas: From Plato to Patricia Churchland.* Dordrecht: Kluwer, 1995.

Weibel, L. *Le savoir et le corps: essai sur le Dictionnaire de Pierre Bayle.* Paris: L'Age d'Hommes, 1975.

Whelan, Ruth. *The Anatomy of Superstition: A Study of the Historical Theory and Practice of Pierre Bayle.* Oxford: Voltaire Foundation, 1989.

– 'Reason and Belief: The Bayle-Jaquelot debate,' *Rivista di storia di filosofia* 48 (1993), 101–10.

White, H. *Tropics of Discourse: Essays in Cultural Criticism.* Baltimore: Johns Hopkins University Press, 1978.

Wilson, Catherine. 'Liebnizean Optimism,' *Journal of Philosophy* 80 (1963): 765–83.

Wittgenstein, L. *Tractatus Logico-philosophicus.* Trans. D. Pears and B. McGuinness. London: Routledge & Kegan Paul, 1961.

Yates, Frances. *Gordon Bruno and the Hermetic Tradition.* New York: Vintage, 1969.

– *The Rosicrucian Enlightenment.* Herts: Paladin, 1975.

– *Theatre of the World.* London: Routledge & Kegan Paul, 1969.

Index